The Armour-Plated Ostrich

The Hidden Costs of Britain's Addiction to the Arms Business

TIM WEBB

Radical Writing
Comerford & Miller

The Armour-Plated Ostrich first published in 1998 by Comerford & Miller
36 Grosvenor Road, West Wickham, Kent, BR4 9PY
under their Radical Writing Imprint.

UK Distributors. Central Books, 99 Wallis Road, London, E11 5LN

Cover design: Ad Lib Design, London N19 / (0171) 263-1531
Cover picture Graham Turner, Guardian News Service
Typeset Simon Burgess Design, 6 Cook Road, Crawley, Sussex, RH10 5DJ
Printed and bound in the EU (Finland) for MARKSPRINT 7a Arundel Terrace, Brighton Sussex BN2 1GA

A catalogue record for this book is available from the British Library.
IBSN 1 871204 08 9 hb
IBSN 1 871204 09 7 pb

THE AUTHOR

Tim Webb's radical opinions are not the outcome of student politics. His views were formed by his experience in the British Army. He was posted to Africa and the Middle East.

He spent three years in Prague with an international trade union organisation and travelled throughout Eastern Europe. His incompatibility with the Soviet forces when they occupied Czechoslovakia in 1968 led to his swift departure.

In 1969 he became an official of the Association of Scientific, Technical and Managerial Staffs and later Assistant General Secretary of its successor, Manufacturing, Science, Finance (MSF). He dealt with the main defence companies, particularly those in the aerospace and electronics sectors.

Tim Webb was one of the few trade union officials invited to Downing Street when Margaret Thatcher was Prime Minister. He was a member of the Engineering Industry Training Board and chair of the Electronics and Employment Task Force at the National Economic Development Office (NEDO).

He lives in Stoke Newington, North London and his interests include listening to jazz and watching Arsenal.

APPRECIATION

This book is written in appreciation of David Danskin and his fifteen far-sighted colleagues who decided in 1886 that there was a better future in sport than work in an armaments factory. They collected sixpence each and formed a football club at Woolwich Arsenal in South London. The Arsenal Football Club, which later moved to Highbury, North London, is popular and successful. The factory is closed.

ACKNOWLEDGEMENTS

My sincere thanks are due to all those I interviewed and who are mentioned by name in the book. Our discussions were stimulating and on the occasions when opinions differed it was always in a good-natured and tolerant manner.

I am equally indebted to the many people I met and who generously shared their time and expertise. They include: Colin Adkins, John Barnes, Anne Beech, Derek Braddon, Bronwen Brady, Andy Danford, Alastair Fraser, Adrian Kendry, Harriet Lamb, Nigel Lewis, Patricia Lewis, Rab MacWilliam, Paul Noon, Derek Perkins, Ron Ralph, Barrie Sherman, Colin Silman, Mike Walsh and Susan Willett.

For many years the members of the trade union Manufacturing, Science, Finance (MSF) were my greatest source of information. Their knowledge and skills deserve the highest recognition by employers and government.

All matters of interpretation, conclusions and, of course, any errors are my own.

Tim Webb
September 1998

ACKNOWLEDGEMENTS

STATISTICAL NOTE

The sums of money involved in the defence industry are huge. There is an understandable tendency for the average reader's eyes to glaze over when scanning the billions and millions. One billion is one thousand million (1,000,000,000). To put that into context, the overall estimated cost of the UK Eurofighter programme is over £16 billion (£16,000,000,000) at around £60 million (£60,000,000) per aircraft. The cost of providing a typical district general hospital is around £90 million. To build and equip a normal comprehensive school for 1,000 children costs £9 million.

References are made to Gross Domestic Product (GDP) and Gross National Product (GNP). GDP is the total value of goods produced and services provided in a country in one year. GNP is GDP *plus* net income from abroad. These definitions are often referred to as 'national income.' Defence expenditure is sometimes given as a percentage of GDP (occasionally GNP) and indicates the proportion of a country's income that is spent on military equipment, armed forces and support.

Some items of US expenditure have been converted into sterling. The exchange rate at the time of writing was 1.62 dollars to the pound.

Contents

INTRODUCTION

Few people in Britain, even in inner-city areas, wish to own electric shock batons, anti-aircraft missiles or a main battle tank. They do, however, buy cars, television sets, radios, video recorders, CD players, fax machines and computers in large quantities. The vast majority of these are made by foreign-owned companies. Was it by design or chance that British manufacturers attempted to satisfy the demands of the military but neglected those of the consumer? Was their devotion to one market connected with failure in the other?

The preparation for war—'defence'—is a big and expensive business. In Britain it costs the taxpayer over £22 billion a year and absorbs the skills of 400,000 of some of the most highly qualified people in our diminishing manufacturing industry. Most of its products were designed to combat the now defunct Warsaw Pact. Since the end of the Cold War home markets for weapons have decreased sharply and the defence companies have become increasingly dependent on exports, often to unsavoury regimes. If these countries are unable or unwilling to pay—like Iraq—the British public often foots the bill.

Even towards the end of the Cold War the British defence industry was confident of the future. The potential enemy was still visible, the government was allowing military spending to continue at a high level and oil-rich countries wanted the latest in high-tech weaponry. Its staff—including the best and brightest from the engineering faculties of the universities—were virtually guaranteed a secure career. Within a few years the manufacturers had become unsure, overawed by the US defence giants and worried that the crisis-ridden 'tiger' economies of the East could no longer afford their products. The industry shed 150,000 jobs soon after the collapse of the Warsaw Pact. The defence companies and their employees are people in a business that did well in very different times but who now find themselves in a world where the certainties of the past no longer exist.

Since the last world war successive British governments have attempted to square the circle by achieving a match between military aspirations and scarce financial resources. None succeeded. The men in uniform protested that they could not carry out the job required with the equipment they were given and the civilians in the Treasury complained that defence spending never seemed to be under control. The root of the problem was that while the politicians may have understood that Britain's economic power was in decline, they continued to behave as if the rest of the world would be impressed by our military might. Ministers talked about "punching above our weight" in terms of international influence. Such boxing metaphors meant little in a world dominated by economic sumo wrestlers. The result was a succession of expensive, over-ambitious plans to provide equipment and armed forces for a role that ceased to make sense long ago.

All this was overseen by the Ministry of Defence which in 1998 controlled the activities of 333,000 people—214,000 service personnel and 119,000 civilians. It has been the most wasteful and secretive government department. Serious overspending and weapons that didn't work were the norm rather than the exception. Its record on Gulf War syndrome, equal opportunities and institutional racism in the armed forces was abysmal. In a commercial organisation there would have been calls for the resignation of the board. Its mismanagement was made possible by the lack of democratic controls within Parliament. The power and resources of the Defence Select Committee, the body designated to monitor the ministry's activities, were inadequate.

Defence 'debates' in the House of Commons often consisted of ministerial anecdotes about Britain's leading role in multinational operations overseas, bellicose noises directed at enemies in the Middle East and all-party support for the latest defence project. Occasional questions about the cost or direction of defence policy were brushed aside as unpatriotic irrelevancies. Few MPs bothered to attend unless some immediate military action was being proposed.

It was a situation ripe for the attention of a new government pledged to sweep away the inefficiencies of the past, to provide fairness not favours and, not least, transform its party's traditional policies into action relevant to the modern world. In its own words, the government led by Tony Blair "hit the ground running" and quickly announced a series of initiatives on the economy, Europe, welfare and education. Defence was to await the results of a Strategic Defence Review, originally scheduled to take six months. It announced that there would be an ethical dimension to foreign policy, particularly in relation to arms sales. Hard but obvious choices were there to be made. Would New Labour's cutting edge slice through the protective armour of the bureaucracy at the Ministry of Defence? The outcome is described in the final chapter.

This book is not about the 'merchants of death.' Nor is it an academic study of UK defence policy. It shows how British governments followed policies—at home and abroad—that diverted scarce resources into an industry that now finds itself trapped in an increasingly difficult corner of the world's economy. It also suggests some actions that could secure a different path for the future.

Tim Webb 1998

CHAPTER ONE

THE MISSING ENEMY

*So long as the Communist threat was alive and well, we could expect even-
tually to be pulled out of the doldrums.*
William A Anders. Chairman and Chief Executive of General Dynamics 1991.

A man with silvery blond hair wearing a beige suit and a striped tie climbed
stiffly up the metal rungs of the aircraft ladder. Sitting uncomfortably in the cock-
pit, he gave a Biggles-style thumbs-up and smiled broadly for the cameras.
Michael Heseltine, Deputy Prime Minister, was visiting the 1996 Farnborough
Air Show to celebrate the announcement of the go-ahead for Britain's most
expensive military project. The Conservative government had decided to order
232 Eurofighter aircraft. Three years late and £1.49 billion over budget by 1997,
the Eurofighter will cost the taxpayer £16 billion, or £350 for every man, woman
and child in the country. The first plane is due to be delivered in the year 2001.

Farnborough is one of the most important military equipment exhibitions in
the world. It attracts thousands of visitors from home and overseas, mingling the
anoraks with the suits, Arabs with Israelis and ex-Communists with capitalists.
Rather like an international fashion show, people are there to see and be seen
while the supermodels of the sky flirt noisily above them. Little buying or selling goes on during the event but it demonstrates the virility of the aerospace
industry and provides an excellent public relations opportunity. New contracts,
more business opportunities and, of course, greater export successes are
announced at its press conferences. The commercial aircraft are there in force but
the macho combat planes grab the most interest.

Four years before, in 1992, I was with company executives, their guests and
customers talking loudly in the comfortable hospitality suite and giving the occasional glance at what was happening above the airfield outside. Several light
planes were twisting and diving between the clouds in the dull skies. Suddenly,
the shrieking roar of two powerful turbofan jet engines cut across our chatter, rat-
tling the plates and glasses in front of the food on the cloth-covered tables. Heads
turned to watch the aircraft swoop down above the runway, slow, then lift its nose
like a striking cobra before disappearing in a cloud of kerosene fumes. We had
just seen the 'fire and forget' manoeuvre of the Sukhoi 27 Flanker, one of the latest and most formidable products of the ex-Soviet military aerospace industry.

The MiG-29 Fulcrum went through its paces later, burning through the air in
an impressive series of turns and runs that drew enthusiastic nods of appreciation
from the spectators. The Eurofighter, which was not then flying, was designed

specifically to counter the Sukhoi and the MiG. The Cold War was over and the original purpose of the three aircraft had disappeared. In a world turned upside down, they would soon be on offer to almost anybody with enough money to spend. The magnificent flying machines that zoomed overhead had become costly albatrosses.

Changing times

The Army Equipment Exhibition at Aldershot was much more traditional and formal than Farnborough. My first impression was of a mixture of a multinational Officers Mess, the Motor Show, and a video display. The civilians were the company men and their guests, the military seemed to come mainly from Africa and Arabia. Men with epaulettes, batons, badges, leather belts, straight backs and loud voices were everywhere, welcoming, hand-shaking and occasionally saluting. Their razor-creased trousers looked as though they could prove useful in close combat. The people in uniform didn't seem particularly interested in the goods on display but were enjoying meeting their old pals. When taken to a stand they mostly stood around nodding and smiling. The bonhomie was reminiscent of a public school reunion, the authoritative tones were the same, whether from England or parts of the old Empire. It was a reminder of a military education that still reverberated in distant Third World countries.

Some of the gregarious visitors were representing military dictatorships. Twenty years earlier, Lord Carrington had congratulated foreign governments for sending their young men to Sandhurst military college rather than to the London School of Economics. He told cadets at a passing-out parade that a Sandhurst education was "more reliable" than that provided at the LSE. Britain still gives free training for about 500 military leaders from foreign countries each year. In 1995-96 nearly £700,000 was spent on 'hosting' Indonesian officers. The Ministry of Defence said: "It is regarded as an important part of our policy of defence diplomacy."[1]

Getting into the show had been a bit of a problem. I had forgotten the wad of credentials that confirmed me as a bona-fide guest of British Aerospace. The jobsworth security guard at the entrance informed me in the staccato tones and missing aitches that seemed to go with the job, that my credit cards were not proof of anything. They could have been stolen. He told me that the driving licence showing my old address was illegal. As I spread plastic and paper before him, he picked up and scrutinised a small card, looked at me, nodded twice and handed over a clip-on badge printed with my name. Lowering his voice, he said that years ago he had played trumpet in a jazz band at his local pub. He was a great fan and collector of the records of 'Hot Lips' Page. He waved me through. Membership of Ronnie Scott's jazz club had gained me access to the world of weaponry.

The men on the exhibition stands were well briefed on their products, mainly British guns, grenades, mortars, missile-launchers and communications equipment. They answered most questions readily but in a manner that somehow managed to distance real flesh and blood from the weapons' technology. They said that a new mortar bomb "was designed for maximum lethality in an all-weather situation." There were only two questions they ducked completely. When asked whether the weapons might be used by a foreign military dictator against civilians or British troops, they said that they only sold to countries approved by the government: "We don't take the decision." They were not prepared to give the names of their customers as they were "commercially confidential."

Strangely out of place, but extremely popular, was a stand displaying military footwear. A small crowd had gathered round, gazing at boots to be worn in desert or swamp, on the back of a horse, jumping from a plane or guarding a palace. Delicate patent leather dress shoes posed alongside massive boots designed to be marched around a parade ground. Alongside all the high-tech gizmos, people seemed fascinated by these mundane products made in Northampton and the other towns of the boot and shoe industry. It struck me that the psychological undertones of the British Army's fixation with polished leather could make a useful subject for academic study.

On the surface it was business as usual at the arms fair but behind the scenes serious doubts were beginning to be expressed. Orders that were thought to be firm were being cut back; the price of oil was fluctuating; Tornadoes were being cancelled for the cheaper Hawk, and above all, what was going to happen if the Soviet Union dropped out of the arms race? European governments had already started to reduce their military budgets and defence ministries were no longer confident that the hardware they wanted to buy would move past the planning stage. It was a period of growing uncertainty and large numbers of redundancies were being announced. For the first time, many of these were qualified professional and managerial staffs. The companies believed that their only option was to export more to compensate for the loss of domestic orders. The icing on the cake was becoming the main ingredient.

The purpose of the Aldershot exhibition was to demonstrate physically and publicly that Britain was a leading contender in the business of making and selling some of the most sophisticated weapons in the world. In his farewell speech as President, Eisenhower warned of what he called "the military-industrial complex." He defined it as "the conjunction of an immense military establishment and a large arms industry." The fears he expressed were based on his experience in the United States of dealing with the world's largest, richest and most powerful military-industrial complex. All the participants in the Cold War enthusiastically adopted similar systems, distorting social priorities, creating huge budget deficits and producing complex weaponry that often failed to perform. There were many ironies and contradictions, which looked at in a certain light, could be regarded as pure human folly. The preparation of the means of war, however, is a serious business.

Our ancestors first started beating each other over the head with animal jaw-bones. These were followed by clubs, spears, daggers and swords. Catapults and slings were succeeded by the bow and arrow, which was used for over five hundred years, only being discarded after the invention of the arquebus or gun. In the West, the invention of gunpowder in the 13th century was credited to an Englishman, Roger Bacon. A German monk made the first cannon, an instrument of war that threatened its users as much as the enemy. Boadicea's idea of a good drive around Colchester was on a chariot with sword blades attached to the wheels, making her even more dangerous than the other Essex girls (and boys) racing around in their personalised cars centuries later. The Belgian city of Liège can claim to have been the first arms capital of the world, defying a fifteenth century edict and subsequent razing by Charles the Bold, to establish a tradition of weapons manufacture that still continues. Hundreds of other towns and cities around the world followed its example, devoting their political, financial and industrial resources to this lucrative business.

Those who flew the spotter planes over enemy lines during the First World War soon realised that it would be relatively easy to drop a few pounds of explosives on the bogged down infantry and the newly introduced tanks they saw below. They invented the hand-dropped bomb, later improved by a mechanical release hung beneath the aircraft. The tanks, bombs, artillery and machine guns used in Belgium and France during that war combined to produce industrialised slaughter over large areas of mud. During the Second World War fighter and bomber aircraft struggled for supremacy of the skies above the industrial cities and ports of Europe. The forerunners of the cruise missile, focus of protests at Greenham Common, were the 8,000 V-1 and V-2 rocket 'doodlebugs' launched by Hitler against London.

The planning and execution of large-scale wars changed irrevocably on 6 August 1945, when the first atomic bomb—*Little Boy*—was dropped on Hiroshima. Equivalent to 12,700 pounds of TNT it killed over 100,000 civilians. The ground temperature immediately beneath the explosion was 5,000 degrees centigrade and the inferno was described as "a peep into hell" by the bomber's tail gunner. The plane that delivered the bomb was the *Enola Gay*, named after the pilot's mother. US President Truman said it was "the greatest thing in history."[2] Three days later Nagasaki was devastated by *Fat Man*, a bomb of 20,000 pounds' worth of TNT. 87,000 people died and Japan surrendered.

Since then the world has gone on to develop even bigger and better weapons, atomic became hydrogen, giving "more bangs to the buck" in military jargon.

Anti-missile systems knock out missiles which in turn are protected by anti-anti-missile devices. The day of the intercontinental bomber carrying free-fall bombs is almost over, replaced by submarines, lurking underwater with their missiles programmed and targeted on major centres of population.

Chemical and biological weapons have caused public revulsion and more progress has been made in prohibiting their use than other methods of human destruction. Despite this the Ministry of Defence has spent £3.5 million on a new complex at Porton Down that will carry out chemical warfare experiments on volunteer troops. The US stopped testing nerve gas on human beings in 1975. The last general use of gas was during the 1914-18 war, causing 82,571 deaths and 1,044,292 non-fatal casualties.[3] The US Air Force used a biological defoliant named Agent Orange in Vietnam to destroy enemy cover. It also poisoned local people and some of their own troops suffered from the effects. More recently Saddam Hussein gassed Kurdish villagers to suppress their campaign for independence.

American attempts to develop a neutron bomb that would destroy people but not buildings were scoffed at even though it would have provided the perfect weapon for a property-owning democracy. Shields against missile attack, the 'Star Wars' advocated by President Reagan, were given little credence, especially after their demonstrations were discovered to have been faked. The target missile was packed with explosives and a proximity fuse that would be detonated if the interceptor missile came reasonably close. The resulting explosion would then be claimed as a direct hit. In the first three tests the interceptor failed to get close enough to detonate the explosives; the fourth test was cancelled.[4] The principle was no different from the old Army trick of the rifleman persuading a friend in the target area to jab a hole through the bullseye. It took the Pentagon nine years to admit the deception.

The Gulf War was billed as the ultimate high-tech conflict. The Patriot missile played a leading role in boosting confidence that targets in Israel and Saudi Arabia could be protected. The US Army claimed a 96 per cent success rate of Patriots eliminating incoming Scuds. 'Scudbuster' T-shirts were sold and the share price of Raytheon, its manufacturer, rose swiftly. George Bush went to the Raytheon plant and told cheering workers: "42 Scuds engaged, 41 intercepted!" Afterwards the Army admitted that 40 per cent of Scud attacks on Israel were successful; 70 per cent of those on Saudi Arabia. The final truth that had been kept top secret by the military was revealed on the fifth anniversary of the war— the Patriot did not destroy a single Scud.[5]

The US government watchdog, the General Accounting Office (GAO), was scathing in its assessment of the 'smart' weapons used in the Gulf. It said that the claims made by the manufacturers and the military forces were "overstated, misleading, inconsistent with the best available data, or unverifiable." Undeterred by this blow to their credibility the wordsmiths of weaponry have designated the latest and improved versions of airborne armaments 'brilliant' missiles. These are smarter than 'smart.'

Invisibility to enemy radar by the use of 'stealth' technology has been heralded as a method of guaranteeing surprise attack. The GAO contradicted the claim by the US air force that 80 per cent of the missiles launched by the F-117 Stealth fighters hit their targets during the Gulf War. The real figure was nearer 40-50 per cent. Another of its investigations revealed that the B-2 Stealth bomber was far from invisible if it got caught in the rain. Water washed off its radar absorbent paint which had to be replaced after each flight.

The GAO confirmed the failure of the Patriots and went on to criticise the vast cost of missiles. Each Tomahawk cruise missile cost £643,000 and the new B-2 Stealth bomber £1.29 billion.[6] It should give pause for thought to military planners who promote the new guided weapons as a cheap and easy way to conduct warfare. Old methods of mass bombing were no more successful in the Gulf than they were in Vietnam. American B-52 bombers dropped 75,000 bombs into open desert, missing enemy emplacements completely.

These dream factory failures are not new. During the war in Vietnam a body called the Defense Communications Planning Group was set up by the US government to look at new methods of combating the Vietcong with the minimal involvement of troops. One plan was to train munitions-carrying pigeons to alight on North Vietnamese army trucks which they would blow up with a triggering device that exploded on contact with metal. This was abandoned eventually as the pigeons found difficulty in identifying a Communist from a non-Communist vehicle. A negative reaction from animal rights campaigners was also feared.[7] The main problem with the American infantry weapons in Vietnam was not so complicated—they jammed. The state of the art M-16 carbine, famed for its 'stopping power,' was notorious. Many troops preferred to use captured Chinese or Soviet-made AK-47s which were less sophisticated but more reliable in close combat.

The search for perfect weapons continues. *Defense News*, the journal of the US military industry, provides this breathless account of the modern soldier at work:

"Imagine this scene...A US infantryman, dressed in black, approaches a seemingly abandoned village in a wooded area in South America. It's pitch dark. The soldier takes cover behind a tree and, using an indirect viewing module attached to his weapon, is able to detect and kill an approaching enemy soldier without being seen. An enemy sniper fires from atop a tree several yards away. The soldier aims at the sniper and within seconds his weapon has calculated the distance to the sniper, the time it will take the bullet to get there and the wind conditions. The sniper is killed."

"...A monitor worn on the soldier's wrist gives the commander a readout of the soldier's physiological condition. All is well on the battlefront."[8] The Ministry of Defence is looking to replace the traditional British infantryman by hi-tech 'lethality man,' similar to his US counterpart, under a programme called Future Infantry Soldier Technology (FIST).

The modern images of war are vivid and detailed. Television camera crews and reporters with satellite communications can bring pictures of atrocities in Rwanda, fighting in Bosnia and riots in Palestine into almost every household. The scenes of sprawled bodies, weeping refugees in horse-drawn carts and celebrating soldiers firing their guns in triumph are not very different from any other war this century. What has changed is the size of the audience and the speed of information transmission. Armed conflict can now be viewed in close-up from a safe distance. Jets roaring over rooftops, tanks exploding and ships firing volleys of shells are watched by millions in front of their screens yet remote from the terror caused by such organised mayhem. During the first hours of the Gulf War, CNN viewers around the world knew more about the attacks on Baghdad than most people in that city.

Weapons are not surgical, painless killing instruments but often badly targeted, cruel and messy destroyers of life and limb. What the military planners call 'collateral damage' means bombed hospitals, dead children and wrecked schools for the people on the receiving end. Those who deliberately break the rules of war by committing atrocities are labelled war criminals. Few are ever found among the victors. The losers pay—at least in the short term—and the winners write history.

Making the weapons

All weapons systems, whether traditional or based in the realm of science fiction, have one thing in common—they all need a manufacturer—staffed by teams of scientists, engineers, production workers and, equally important, salespeople. A small war like the Falklands is ideal in achieving the ultimate seal of approval; all arms marketing people seek the competitive edge provided by 'combat proven.' The people who work in the industry do not have a high profile unless a major contract is on the horizon. More jobs are promised if it's won and redundancies threatened if it's lost.

The workers have not always been thanked for their efforts. The law that now allows British pubs to open during the afternoon was enacted almost eighty years after they were forced to restrict their hours. Most frustrated drinkers probably didn't realise that they were being punished for a series of blunders by British generals at the Battle of the Somme during the First World War. Thousands of troops were massacred as they floundered across the fields towards the German machine guns. The British suffered 57,470 casualties, the Germans only 591. Someone had to be held responsible for the debacle. The generals were said to be men of integrity, the government said it was not responsible for operational decisions, so the munitions workers were blamed. The politicians alleged that they had produced inferior ammunition because they spent too much time in the alehouses. Legislation was passed forcing the pubs to close in the afternoon.

It's not easy to define the boundaries of the defence industry; in loose terms it could include both Lockheed Martin, the giant US corporation with a $14.4 billion defence revenue in 1995, and a small British company making army boots. The abolition of conscription in France caused a slump in the beret manufacturing industry. The most important measure of risk is the level of dependency on defence sales as a percentage of total turnover. The higher the dependency, the greater the vulnerability. British Aerospace has 74 per cent of total revenue in defence, Rolls-Royce 27 per cent, GEC 26 per cent, GKN/Westland 25 per cent, Hunting Industries 43 per cent, Racal 34 per cent, Smiths Industries 33 per cent and Vosper Thorneycroft 75 per cent. In the United States, prior to some mergers, Lockheed Martin was 63 per cent dependent, McDonnell Douglas 70 per cent, Northrop Grumman 82 per cent, Boeing 40 per cent and Raytheon 34 per cent.

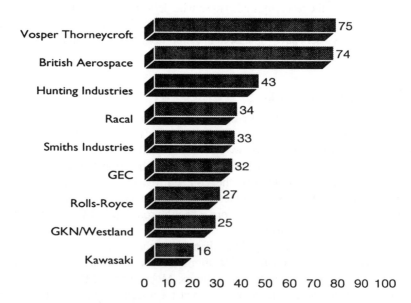

Percentage of company revenue derived from defence sales

The largest German aerospace and defence company, Daimler-Benz, has 31 per cent of its revenue tied up in military production. The highest defence dependent company in Japan is Kawasaki at only 16 per cent.[9] A rough estimate would be that firms with around 25 per cent could be defined as dependent, over that figure as highly dependent. These figures are causing a great deal of concern in many boardrooms as world-wide arms spending is slashed. The military manufacturing habit is more difficult to kick than to acquire.

It would be foolish to pretend that arms manufacture has had only negative effects. The amount of resources poured into this global industry has developed new technologies, employed hundreds of thousands of people and earned the producers vast profits. The main reason for its success was the total support from governments who intervened to finance, direct, market and buy the products, thereby minimising the risk and uncertainty found in the more competitive civil field. Overall, however, these advantages were outweighed by the handicaps, one of the most important being the need to persuade a country's citizens that they faced the perpetual threat of armed attack. This led to national paranoia, chauvinism and irrational fear at all levels of society, blocking possible solutions to the world's many problems.

The Cold War

World military spending started to spiral out of control at the onset of the Cold War. That dismal period in history can be dated from Winston Churchill's 'Iron Curtain' speech in Fulton, Missouri on 5 March 1946 when he declaimed "From Stettin in the Baltic to Trieste in the Adriatic, an Iron Curtain has descended across the continent." Despite the presence of President Truman alongside him, his comments were heavily criticised. Walter Lippmann, the leading US political correspondent, called them "an almost catastrophic blunder" and the *Wall Street Journal* also disapproved, albeit in more moderate tones.[10] It was only a year since Roosevelt, Stalin and Churchill had met at Yalta to shake hands and divide Europe into spheres of influence. Most politicians, press and public in the West were still favourably disposed towards the Soviet Union, not least because of the enormous suffering inflicted on it by the Germans. The crucial role of Stalin's armies in the defeat of Nazism was also acknowledged widely although it was played down later as Nato and the Warsaw Pact began to freeze into confrontational postures.

Churchill was not the first person to use the 'Iron Curtain' phrase. In March 1945, Joseph Goebbels, Hitler's minister of propaganda, warned that if the Soviet Union were victorious: "an Iron Curtain would come down at once behind which the mass slaughter of the people would take place."[11] The war was almost over and he was appealing to the Western powers not to sign the Yalta Agreement with the Soviet Union.

There was one enthusiastic audience for Churchill's views—the US military. Although he had been rejected by the British voters, they felt that he still spoke for a country that was traditionally a close ally and now heavily reliant on US aid. The British Empire had been terminally weakened by the war; it was time for the real Western superpower to engage in some serious muscle flexing. The Joint Chiefs of Staff at the Pentagon seized the opportunity to trumpet the Soviet threat and call for massive re-armament, knowing that it would be echoed by their counterparts in the UK who still harboured delusions about Britain's world role. Top British military men were not reluctant to lean heavily on their government to push through policies that gave priority to the armed forces.

A new word entered the language of diplomacy. 'Brinkmanship' is defined in the dictionary as: "the art or policy of pursuing a dangerous course to the brink of catastrophe before desisting." The Berlin crisis of 1948-49 pushed brinkmanship to the point where an uncontrollable outbreak of war within hours rather than weeks seemed highly likely. It was difficult to discern any "art" in the aggressive, tub-thumping speeches of the leaders but the policies of both sides certainly seemed likely to lead to catastrophe. The Soviets wanted to prevent West Germany from joining any alliance that would boost its military strength. They were fearful, to the point of paranoia, that German re-unification would again pose a threat to their security. It was their firm belief that their concern had historical justification and they moved swiftly to blockade the city. The US and British airforces responded by carrying 1.5 million tons of supplies into Berlin between July 1948 and May 1949. After 318 days the Russians lifted the embargo.[12]

Western leaders claimed that the success of the Berlin airlift was proof that their determination had triumphed over Soviet aggression. The media publicised the continuing migration of large numbers of East Germans to West Berlin as demonstrating the superiority of capitalism over communism. Vast amounts of money had been pumped into West Berlin with tax concessions for residents. Young men were exempt from national service. In contrast the Russians made it clear that they expected the Germans to pay for the crimes they had committed. While they distinguished officially between the German 'people' and the Nazis, they stripped East Germany of large amounts of machinery and other equipment. This was used to assist in re-building the wrecked Soviet industries. Their problem was that if the German Democratic Republic was to be viable it could not afford to lose large numbers of skilled workers who could obtain jobs, houses and relative freedom across the border. At one stage over one thousand people were crossing each day. The Berlin Wall went up on the night of 13 August 1961.

One month previously Khrushchev had announced that the planned 1.2 million reduction in Soviet armed forces had been cancelled and he raised the defence budget by 30 per cent. President Kennedy responded by increasing his armed forces by 15 per cent and ordered $3 billion dollars to be added to US military spending. The arms race went into over-drive.

For the next forty years Europe was divided by walls, electric fences, razor wire, ignorance and intolerance. Sometimes it reached the small points of absurdity. A loyal Czech Communist proudly showed me the most popular exhibit in their police museum—a stuffed Alsatian dog. It had won first prize and national publicity (when alive) for catching the most people trying to escape across the border into Austria. The language of politics became militarised and countries outside the continent were coerced or bribed to take sides. It was boom time for the universal soldiers of the military-industrial complex, on both sides of the divide.

Spend, spend, spend

The financial cost was enormous. US defence expenditure rose from $10.9 billion in 1948 to $77.8 billion in 1970. Between 1979 and 1988 it leapt from $122.2 billion to $289.0 billion. The Soviet Union spent $13.1 billion in 1945, rising to $72.0 billion in 1970. [13] Estimating Soviet expenditure was an exercise in creative accounting. The US Central Intelligence Agency calculated the cost of Soviet military equipment as if it were manufactured in the USA. The comparison was false as raw materials and labour were far cheaper in the Soviet Union than in the United States. It had the strange result that if a US Navy helicopter programme went above budget (they always did) this additional cost was added to Soviet helicopter spending. A pay increase for United States armed forces was deemed to have been passed into Soviet troops' wage packets. This would then bring forth more demands from the Pentagon for increased US expenditure to maintain parity. And so it went on.

The Brookings Institution, a Washington think-tank, calculated total US defence spending during the Cold War at 19 trillion dollars ($19,000,000,000,000). Of that, $5.461 trillion was spent on nuclear weapons. The overall amount was 5 times greater than US government spending on health and medicare. The 4 atomic bombs/devices developed under the Manhattan Project through to August 1945 cost $20 billion. Over 67,000 nuclear missiles were built between 1951 and 1998. The facts were hidden from the public. The chairman of the Brookings research project said: "even rudimentary standards of government policymaking and accountability were lacking."[14]

The arms burden was far too great for any one country, with the possible exception of the US. The statistical details were bent and used to suit everyone's purpose. The UK, wanting to demonstrate that it was pulling its weight within Nato, showed a 1980 defence spending level of 5.1 per cent of national income

(Gross Domestic Product) in that organisation's statistics but needing to prove financial prudence to the domestic taxpayer, the Ministry of Defence published only 4.7 per cent in its own official figures.[15] Ruth Sivard, editor of *World Military and Social Expenditures*, a publication that examines national priorities and the contrasts between military spending and that on health and education, said: "Statistics are just people with the tears wiped off...behind the numbers is the pain of millions of lives lost to neglect as well as violence." [16]

Not that violence was lacking. In Korea and Vietnam there were major confrontations involving the two superpowers, although the Soviet Union did not (officially) participate directly. Despite the nuclear stalemate, there were 149 wars, killing over 23 million people between the end of the Second World War and 1993.[17] To this grim total we can now add the deaths of those victims in Bosnia, Rwanda, Somalia, Zaire, Kosovo and other impoverished countries where slaughter is an everyday occurrence, often carried out by government police or troops.

The thaw

The advent of Mikhail Gorbachev to the Presidency of the Soviet Union in 1985 effectively ended the Cold War. The economy of his country was in a mess, industries were inefficient, producing low quality goods that no-one wanted to buy and nationalist pressures were mounting, particularly in the Baltic republics. Anti-Soviet feeling was running high in Eastern and Central Europe where Communist Parties were either trying to reform themselves or suppress political revolt. Military expenditure was absorbing 19 per cent of Soviet national income, a cost that the state could no longer bear.

Gorbachev's internal reforms were not popular and were opposed by both the members of the old Communist Party apparatus and the new breed of free marketeers, inspired by the urgings of Mrs Thatcher and right-wing Western economists towards unregulated capitalism. The long-suffering public expected instant success. Like Mrs Thatcher, Gorbachev was far more popular abroad than in his own country. He struck a chord in the West; his obvious humanity, wit and sincerity made it impossible for him to be stereotyped as yet another hardline Soviet leader. In every foreign policy speech he stressed the need for international understanding by breaking down barriers between people. His public refusal to support the Chinese and East German leaders in their harsh treatment of dissidents showed clearly that he was determined to shake up the old order.

The Western leaders had no option but to treat him with respect. Mrs Thatcher said he was: "A man you could do business with." The chemistry between the British Prime Minister and the Soviet Premier seemed to be more than just political. The former Soviet Ambassador to London, Leonid Zamyatin, wrote about the time he saw her preparing to greet Gorbachev at Brize Norton airfield. "There was Maggie in a suit of unusual cut, showing off her long legs. The suit was trimmed with sable, which is very rare in Britain. There was a strong smell of perfume. In front of me was sitting a woman with her eyes glistening in anticipation."[18]

In fact, the main business was done between the Soviet Union and the United States. Mrs Thatcher was a vocal but relatively uninfluential participant. Both countries felt that it was in their national interests to establish a form of detente. Gorbachev made deep cuts in Soviet defence spending, providing one justification for some leaders of the armed forces and party hardliners to seek his downfall. Their attempt at a take-over ended in disorganisation, drunkenness and recrimination. If they had succeeded it would have restored the old Soviet enemy, allowing Nato to call for increased vigilance, improved weaponry and, of course, more money. Gorbachev was subsequently outmanoeuvred and succeeded by Boris Yeltsin.

World arms spending reached its peak in 1987 at an estimated total of $1,000 billion. Since then it has declined by 3-4 per cent per year in both industrialised and developing countries.[19] The Stockholm International Peace Research Institute (SIPRI), the accepted world authority on arms trends, listed three major factors for this development:

- The changed political climate in Europe following the collapse of the Soviet Union and the   Warsaw Pact.
- Financial constraints. National budgets became much tighter and the end of the Cold War allowed most governments to argue for other priorities.
- Reduced possibilities for arms exports. The value of world exports of conventional weapons shrank by 30 per cent between 1990 and 1994. Past heavy buyers of arms, especially Third World countries, did not have sufficient hard currency reserves to continue to purchase expensive equipment.[20]
- The combination of those factors meant that the going was increasingly tough for the defence manufacturers and those who depended on them. The good times were over.

Nato

This created a dilemma for the main Western alliance. Robin Beard, former Nato Assistant Secretary-General for Defense Support, put it bluntly: "Nato used to be a much more comfortable environment in that you needed only one Cold War speech—more tanks, more planes, more guns."[21] Twelve countries formed the North Atlantic Treaty Organisation in 1949. Greece and Turkey joined in 1952, followed by West Germany in 1955 and Spain in 1982. Iceland is a full member but has no armed forces. The main binding principle that brought the countries together—Article 5—was that an attack on one would be treated as an attack on all.

The Warsaw Pact was created in 1955 and both blocs claimed they were operating within the spirit and provisions of the United Nations Treaty. They were not clubs that anyone could join. Their sponsors, the US and the Soviet Union, controlled the policy-making, demanding conformity to a tough confrontational posture. Yugoslavia, although led by Marshal Tito and the League of Communists, had fallen out with Stalin over national self-determination and was not part of the Eastern bloc; De Gaulle's France left Nato's integrated military structure in 1966, opting to pursue an independent nuclear *force de frappe*. He also emphasised his disapproval of the American dominance of the alliance by closing all Nato administrative centres in France and expelling its personnel.

The formation of Nato led to an immediate increase in defence expenditure. The European members doubled their spending in two years from $4.4 billion in 1949 to $8 billion in 1951. This strained national budgets to the limit but was overshadowed by US spending in 1951 of $50 billion—over six times that of the Europeans combined.[22] In the early 1980s, member states agreed to annual defence spending increases of at least 3 per cent above the rate of domestic inflation. Britain was one of the few members that adhered to the target when others found it convenient to ignore it.

In 1975 Turkey invaded Cyprus, occupying two-fifths of the island and displacing 200,000 Greek Cypriots, but Nato played no part in brokering the eventual settlement. It had not envisaged conflict between two member states. In early 1996 armed hostilities almost broke out between the two countries over a small island inhabited only by a few goats. It was only averted after frantic phone calls from the White House to the Greek and Turkish Prime Ministers. As a proportion of national income, Greece and Turkey have the highest European defence expenditures in Nato. Mutual antagonism within the alliance has proved expensive for two relatively poor members. The organisation's largest military operation was not to assist an ally but to intervene in the civil war in Bosnia where it carried out air and artillery attacks on the Bosnian Serbs.

Nato Secretary-General Willy Claes resigned in October 1995 after the Belgian Parliament removed his immunity from prosecution. He was required to answer allegations of involvement in kickback payments from Augusta, the Italian helicopter company, in return for a £250 million order for the Belgian armed forces. Those charges related to his time in office as a government minister. Commissions paid at the highest level are common in the allocation of large defence contracts. In 1966 Prince Bernhardt of the Netherlands was caught with $1 million from Lockheed in his back pocket as a reward for trying to get the Dutch government to buy the F-104 Starfighter. This plane was known as the 'widowmaker' in Germany as over 100 had crashed. It was no surprise, therefore, that even his persuasive talents and elevated position as the Queen's husband failed to convince his country's airforce.

Former Warsaw Pact countries, some of whom have little love for each other, are attempting to become Nato members. Those who knocked loudest on the door were the Czech Republic, Hungary and Poland and they were invited to join in 1999. Russia was extremely nervous and hostile to any Nato expansion, particularly if German armed forces were to be allowed to exercise on its borders with the new member countries. An agreement between Nato and Russia was reached in mid-1997 with both sides claiming satisfaction but with the Russian leadership having an extremely difficult task to convince its public that it had not been forced into concessions. The admission to Nato of former states of the Soviet Union such as the Ukraine and the Baltic states—where there was a fair amount of collaboration with the German invaders during the war—would be a gift to rabble-rousing Russian nationalists.

One Nato study stated unequivocally that new member countries will have to allow the troops of other (Western) nations on their territory. That was perceived as a direct threat by Moscow whose own military study responded by advocating the movement of Russian forces and weapons into Lithuania, Latvia and Estonia if Nato carried out its proposals. *The Times* described this as "the first concrete sign that a new Cold War fault line could be established through the heart of Eastern Europe."[23]

The price of entry to the alliance is not cheap. A US Congressional study warned that membership could increase the defence expenditure of an East European country by as much as 60 per cent.[24] Nato estimates the total cost of expansion as £3 billion, the US Defense Department between £17-£22 billion. If the lower costs forecast in the Nato study were distributed in the same way as the 1997 budget, it would cost Britain £400 million.[25] The running costs of Nato HQ alone were £637 million a year in 1996; about £531,000 per employee.[26]

A 1997 Nato military assessment of the Czech Republic and Hungary condemned their armed forces as "thoroughly incompetent." It found that in the Czech army there were more colonels than all other ranks and lack of money meant that pilots managed as little as 15 hours flying time a year.[27] An internal Polish report found that only 22 MiG 29 fighters were suitable for service and ammunition stocks would last only 2 weeks in combat. It would take 15 years to integrate into Nato. Javier Solana, Nato Secretary-General, told the Polish parliament that combat readiness was not essential as the country faced no serious territorial threats.[28] He said that Poland would not be expected to pay for the modernisation of its armed services. This meant that Britain and other Nato allies would be required to add the cost of the re-armament of former enemies to their own budgets.

It was not surprising therefore that Western defence companies hovered in eager anticipation. Saab, the Swedish manufacturer of the Grippen fighter plane, is part of the same financial group as Electrolux, one of the biggest private investors in Hungary. It offered to create 16,000 jobs in its Electrolux factories if Hungary bought the aircraft.[29]

There are serious doubts about Nato's future role. George Kennan, the most eminent expert on US-Russian relations has written that expansion "would be the most fateful error of American policy in the whole post-Cold War era."[30] Rather like an exclusive gentlemen's club, the rules need to be re-written to come to terms with a world that has changed dramatically. But do the old members really want change? The present evidence is that they prefer to see Russia continue to be paraded as a potential enemy, in order to provide a reason for the larger Nato alliance, while ensuring that it is economically dependent on Western investment.

Some European members, particularly France but not Britain, have taken the opportunity to try to loosen the American grip on Nato policy. The US has reluctantly agreed that the alliance can supply military equipment and forces to the West European Union, the body that is formally the defence arm of the EU. The French have indicated that they will return to play a full role in Nato. All this begs the question: what is the purpose of Nato? In the interests of stability, it might be thought sensible to lower its profile rather than boost its size by taking in Russia's neighbours. Old enmities and conflicts could easily flare up again if a new member felt that they had the guaranteed backing of a powerful military bloc. Would public opinion in Britain or the US allow their troops' lives to be risked in a conflict on the Polish-Russian border?

Coming soon

While Nato tries to work out a role for the future and even before current projects are delivered, the order books are open for the supply of the next generation of military equipment. Learning nothing from past mistakes of cost overruns and weapons designed for a world that no longer exists, the planners press ahead and the multinational manufacturers start jumping into bed with each other to create 'consortia' to promote their bids. A few dogs may bark but the armoured caravan moves on. There is no time to pause, think or question, the momentum has to appear to be unstoppable. Money must be spent quickly so that the promoters can claim that it will be lost if a project is cancelled.

A pre-election period always brings good news for the defence manufacturers. The Conservative government dispensed public money with a largesse not seen in other areas of expenditure. July 1996 was no exception. Orders for equipment worth £4 billion were announced. One of the first was the Replacement Maritime

Patrol Aircraft for the RAF at a cost of £1.8 billion. This re-furbished Nimrod from British Aerospace and Boeing will succeed the old version and is designed to track Russian submarines. The planners still believe that this activity is essential for the defence of Britain. Lockheed Martin, the unsuccessful bidder, promised more than 50 per cent UK content in their Orion aircraft. That offer was intended to be a heavy selling point in creating British jobs but was meaningless as the MoD makes no checks to see whether such pledges are honoured. Previous similar promises, including the one at the time of the purchase of the early warning (Awacs) aircraft from Boeing in 1989, were never monitored by the MoD, in breach of a promise they made to the House of Commons Defence Committee. The ministry admitted that it had not collected the evidence and, in any case, it was confidential.

Other orders included Storm Shadow, an air-to-ground missile with an explosive warhead planned to destroy hardened targets at a range of 185 miles. It had been delayed many times since its requirement was announced ten years previously. It was ordered from the joint venture between British Aerospace and Matra of France at a cost of at least £800 million. Kenneth Clarke, a jazz and beer lover, was not believer in hellfire and brimstone. Conscious of the cost, the former Chancellor opposed the purchase of the aircraft-launched Brimstone anti-tank missile. This will complement another anti-tank missile called the Hellfire which is launched from a helicopter. He argued that two such similar weapons were expensive and unnecessary. The cabinet ruled in favour of the Defence Secretary, Michael Portillo, who needed such a 'victory,' according to some commentators, to repair his image as a contender to succeed John Major. Brimstone missiles cost over £650 million.

Much excitement was generated within the industry over the new £100 billion US-sponsored Joint Strike Fighter (JSF) programme. The MoD paid £132 million to allow Britain to participate in the project without any reference to Parliament. This aircraft is intended to replace the Harrier and, in America, the F-16 Eagle and AV-8B seaborne Harrier. The technology is a generation beyond that of Eurofighter and will involve the pilot in being able to "absorb a dazzling whirl of information on a vast range of targets and threats."[31] Britain is also buying US Tomahawk cruise missiles at a cost of £180 million for up to five new nuclear powered hunter-killer submarines.[32] The total cost of the submarines will be between £2.5 billion and £3 billion.[33] An £8 billion Horizon frigate project for 20 ships faced "endless delays" following a row between the Royal Navy and the navies of France and Italy over design details.[34]

Virtual weapons, real money

Unlike the underwater Russians, whose submarines pose a threat and have to be monitored constantly, the airborne Russians are the West's friends. The Yakolev Design Bureau which developed the Soviet version of the Harrier assisted Lockheed Martin in its JSF bid. BAe teamed up with the US manufacturers McDonnell-Douglas and Northrop Grumman to promote a supersonic jump-jet fighter without a tail fin. This partnership received short shrift from William Perry, US Defence Secretary, who announced in November 1996 that the competition would be reduced an all-American final, Boeing against Lockheed. Boeing has since absorbed McDonnell-Douglas and British Aerospace switched its allegiance to Lockheed. The project is only at the early planning stage but as more money is spent and people employed, the lobbyists will swing into action. The old boy networks between the defence ministries and the manufacturers will be activated and the competition will intensify. Few questions will be asked publicly whether the aircraft is really needed.

Two consortia—US and European—launched bids in mid-1998 for the multi-billion-pound contract for the Meteor 'beyond-visual-range-air-to-air missile' (BVRAAM) to be fitted to the Eurofighter. The initial contract will cost the Ministry of Defence £900 million with more to be spent later. The European consortium included, for the first time, the old arch-rivals British Aerospace and GEC. The American bid was led by Raytheon which said that its "lower cost, lower risk" missile would bring assembly work to Shorts of Belfast.

A top secret stealth bomber called Halo (High Agility Low Observable) is under development in Hampshire according to *The Sunday Times*.[35] It will be invisible to enemy radar. The MoD refused to comment. The cost is unknown. If the report is accurate, it means that the world's military industries are developing fighter aircraft that can detect anything and bombers that are undetectable.

In *Closing Time,* Joseph Heller's sequel to *Catch-22,* Milo Minderbinder tries to sell the concept of the Shhhhh! noiseless, supersonic, faster than light bomber to the US military. The generals are sceptical until he delivers the clinching point: "The plane is so fast that you can bomb someone even before you decide to do it. Decide today—it's done yesterday!"[36]

Some of these projects may be necessary and even cost effective. Planning computerised wars seems harmless and even technologically attractive. The problem is, however, that the projects have never been independently scrutinised before they move towards manufacture. Their acronyms and strange titles are unknown to anyone outside military specialists and defence journalists. Most of the latter make holiday correspondents seem like savage critics. The defence establishment can quite easily exclude the unreliable. The convention that the government's Defence Estimates are not challenged in Parliament is a continuing relic from the past when the perceived enemy was identifiable and unity of purpose between the parties was supposed to be necessary. The Defence Estimates mention few future projects and the MPs—at least those who bother to turn up—

nod through over £21 billion of public money after an annual two day debate which is largely unreported in the media. Virtual wars cost real money.

Two cities—Dnepropetrovsk and Bristol

Away from the grand strategies of the military planners, the economies of many towns and cities throughout Europe have been badly affected by the end of the Cold War. Dnepropetrovsk and Bristol are two cities in very different countries but they have one important connection—both acquired a high degree of defence dependency during the long period of East-West confrontation—and both have been hit badly by the rundown in military production.

Dnepropetrovsk, a city in the Ukraine with 1.3 million people, straddles the river Dnieper. Its population was increased by many thousands of people displaced from the Chernobyl region after the nuclear catastrophe. The Ukraine was the powerhouse of Soviet weapons manufacture with over 2 million people working in 1,800 factories, constituting 70 per cent of Ukrainian industrial production. It was also a main launching pad for Soviet inter-continental nuclear missiles.

Dnepropetrovsk was a 'closed' city until 1989, which meant that no foreigners were allowed in and Soviet citizens from outside needed a permit to visit. The reason for this was simple. It was a major centre of advanced electronic missile technology with its economy rooted in the Soviet arms drive. The largest and most important factory was the Yuzmash plant that designed and manufactured the SS-9 and SS-18 inter-continental ballistic missiles and the intermediate range SS-4 and SS-5. Its best-known product was the Scud missile. Previously reliant on supplies from Russia, the management decided to diversify to civil products and achieved a level of 70 per cent of previous total output. These included tractors, wind power units and trolley buses. The city's football team was probably unique in world soccer by being sponsored by a guided weapons factory.

Our group of three were the first Western trade unionists to visit the city in 1993 after it was opened to outsiders. We were the guests of one of the groups of entrepreneurs who had invited us in the mistaken belief that our trade union, Manufacturing, Science, Finance (MSF) was an organisation of small businesses. After a sleepless overnight train journey from Kiev, we were met and interviewed by the local television station who asked us what proposals we had brought with us to help regenerate the region's economy.

Even the proudest citizen of Dnepropetrovsk, and we met quite a few, would not describe the city as beautiful. It still had all the hallmarks of a rundown outpost of the Soviet Union—shabby hotels with ferocious *babushkas* guarding each floor, pitted streets, long queues, waitresses offering sex for ten dollars, and total shutdown after eight o'clock. We were driven around in an old Mercedes by a sinister young man wearing shades, a purple track suit and Adidas trainers. The car was full of Marlborough tobacco fumes and the suicidal sounds of a Leonard Cohen tape that he played endlessly.

At the House of Political Initiatives, headquarters of the Society of Entrepreneurs, Gennady, a young man in a double-breasted suit and white shoes, told us of his ambition to be the next mayor of the city. In his newly furnished offices, framed pictures of various Playmates of the Month smiled down on Japanese and Korean office equipment. Recalling his humble origins, he enthused about the vision of the future that had struck him suddenly in the duty-free shop at Dubai airport three years earlier. The galaxy of consumer goods in that traveller's oasis had made him realise that his mission in life was to go out and sell, for the benefit of all. It had already brought him the ownership of a shopping mall and other property in Dnepropetrovsk from which he generated enough capital to import and sell second-hand Mercedes and Volvos. His ambition was to become a dollar millionaire within five years.

Lady Thatcher's memoirs had just been published and we had bought a copy at Heathrow. It seemed appropriate that we should give the book to someone who wished to apply her principles to transform Dnepropetrovsk, if not quite into duty-free Dubai, but perhaps into the Basingstoke of the Ukraine. Gennady was delighted. After a great deal of back-slapping, he grabbed the phone. Television and newspaper reporters were summoned and a presentation ceremony was arranged. One of our colleagues—Ian Gibson, who later was to become a Labour MP—made a short speech and held the book aloft to show the photographers the Prime Minister's steely smile on the cover. The following day we saw ourselves featured in the Ukrainian media as a group of British entrepreneurs lending our support (and that of the Iron Lady) to Gennady's political initiatives.

Mr Gusev, director of the Production Union Machine Building Plant, was not so upbeat. Since 1948 his factory complex had been devoted to designing and producing military products: latterly radar, space tracking equipment, missile warning systems and radio communications. Business had slumped during the past five years. Ukraine was now independent, there was no longer a demand for the equipment and, even if there had been, nobody could pay for it. He and his colleagues were making every effort to diversify into the commercial field. What they had found, however, was that the high levels of skills and technology that were appropriate in the defence industry did not transfer immediately to civil production. They had attempted to produce refrigerators, microwave ovens, coffee grinders, watches, cassette recorders and other consumer goods. The problem was that these were heavy, complex, expensive and unattractive as they had been manufactured on the same principles as military equipment. The Ukrainian consumer, who was increasingly aware of Japanese and other imported goods, was reluctant to buy anything without a foreign logo, regardless of reliability. Image was important. The management realised that their only chance of making any progress was in joint ventures with more experienced overseas partners. So far they had not had much success.

In the meantime, they had started to produce electronic equipment for the Ukrainian telephone system which until then had incorporated most of the features usually found in Third World countries. It would not have been tactful to ask why it was more difficult to make a phone call from Dnepropetrovsk to London than to track the speed, trajectory and precise point of impact of an intercontinental missile. There was, however, one area of diversification that had proved successful. A meat processing plant, producing excellent salami and pork sausages had been installed.

Although the number of employees had fallen from 20,000 to 15,000, nobody had been laid off compulsorily as it would have been unlawful. The good news was that everybody was about to receive a 300 per cent wage increase. The bad news was that this was just below the annual rate of inflation. Mr Gusev's pessimism seemed justified. It was clear that he and his colleagues were highly intelligent, dedicated and well qualified but the type of work for which they had been educated and trained was no longer needed. The world had changed; the demands of the consumer were replacing those of the military. Our farewell dinner for seven people cost two and a half million Ukrainian coupons, about seventy pounds.

Like Dnepropetrovsk, Bristol is situated on a river. The Avon flows down from Bath, site of the invading civilisation of Rome whose disciplined warriors seem unlikely forebears of modern Italians. Bristol is an attractive place; it has a mixture of town and country, the city centre shops and offices are modern, the railway station, port and Clifton Bridge reflect the pioneering achievements of Isambard Kingdom Brunel, the nineteenth century British engineer. Visiting the waterfront, with its cafes, bars and art gallery, it is difficult to imagine that Bristol is the centre of a region that has been more dependent on defence than any other area of Britain.

The recent history of three companies illustrates clearly the changing fortunes of the local defence industry. Rolls-Royce Military Engines, previously Bristol Siddeley, was formed in 1968 during a period of rapid consolidation in the aerospace industry. It and its predecessors have a record of producing excellent engines for world-renowned British aircraft: the Merlin for the Spitfire, the Pegasus for the Harrier jump jet and the Olympus for the Vulcan and Concorde. It now manufactures the EJ 200 for the Eurofighter. 13,500 people were employed in 1979, dropping to about 8,500 in 1992. Following government defence spending cuts, it provided work for only 5,000 by 1996. Reduced Ministry of Defence purchasing, some contracting out of work and less flying time by military aircraft to save fuel and engine costs were the main causes. Any reduction in the number of Eurofighter aircraft would be a severe blow; the cancellation of the programme a disaster.

British Aerospace in Bristol comprises two main parts; BAe Aircaft and BAe Dynamics. The former became mainly a civil aircraft manufacturer after the war, it now produces the wings of the highly successful European Airbus. Its most recent military connection was a contract to re-furbish the US F-111 bomber which flew from Upper Heyford and bombed Libya in 1986. Redundancies were caused when the contract ended a few years later.

BAe Dynamics is the development and production unit for guided weapons systems. Created in 1948 as a small design office by Hawker Siddeley Dynamics, it grew rapidly as demand soared for new weapons during the Cold War. Later it became part of the British Aircraft Corporation which was merged into the then nationalised British Aerospace. It produced the Bloodhound ground-to-air missile during the 1950s, Swingfire and Striker anti-tank weapons in the 1960s and the Rapier missile in the late 1970s. The order book for the latter was reduced sharply after the fall of the Shah of Iran who was a major arms customer of Britain.

Work continued on the Sea Wolf and Sea Dart with a new order for the ASRAAM air-to-air missile awarded by the government just before the 1992 election. Conservative MPs in marginal seats had lobbied extremely hard because if the Americans had won the contract many of their constituents would have been redundant. This would not have produced votes for the party in power that advocated a free market and open competition.

British Aerospace Dynamics in Bristol is now a small organisation. Savage cuts in the workforce from a total of 4,700 in 1986, to about 400 in 1996, included the dismissal of 1,500 people (including 800 graduates) in 1991. These included specialists in avionics, stress, design, planning and electronics. The company blamed the MoD for cancelling or postponing previously firm orders. The workforce and their trade unions were not passive. Apart from demonstrations and publicity, they also produced a detailed analysis and proposals for civil production together with Bristol City Council and the University of Bristol. They were given short shrift by the local management whose thinking was narrowly focused on military production and unable to deal with alternatives. They eventually managed to meet Admiral Sir Raymond Lygo, then BAe Chief Executive. He was no more helpful than his local managers and dismissed the idea that civil products could use defence technology.

Westland Helicopters is not far from Bristol and employs 36 per cent of the total workforce of Yeovil. A relatively small company, it hit the headlines over a dispute about whether United Technologies/Sikorsky of the United States should be allowed to buy a substantial shareholding or whether there should be a European stake in the company. Mrs Thatcher believed that market forces should decide the issue. This would allow the Americans a free run. Michael Heseltine, her Defence Secretary, did not. She over-ruled him and he stormed out of a cabinet meeting to face the media who—perhaps coincidentally—were waiting in Downing Street to hear the news of his resignation. Leon Brittan also resigned from the government over the Westland episode and departed to Brussels. For a week or so it looked as though the Prime Minister was on the brink of defeat but she survived, albeit with a dented reputation.

Westland, which was later taken over by GKN, has made a number of famous helicopters: the Lysander during the last war, the Sea King, Lynx and, under agreement with Sikorsky, the Apache. Michael Portillo, the Defence Secretary, ordered the updated version for the Army, thereby enraging the French and Germans who together with British Aerospace were promoting the Eurocopter. The EH 101, produced jointly with state-owned Augusta of Italy, can be converted from military to civil use and it is in the latter role that it probably has greatest potential. The military programme received a blow when Canada cancelled a large order after the defeat of its Conservative government. Employment has fallen from around 14,000 in 1979 to about 3,800 in 1998. The company announced a merger with Augusta in April 1998.

The world of defence manufacturing has been severely shaken. Dnepropetrovsk struggles to come to terms with shortages, the market economy and the collapse of the Soviet system that provided massive orders for its weapons factories. Relatively prosperous Bristol is becoming used to the idea that not even its previously expanding insurance and finance industry, which later experienced substantial cuts under the impact of new technology and mergers, can be a substitute for the loss of thousands of qualified engineers and production workers. Weapons once provided a degree of local affluence and large numbers of jobs. Both cities paid the price of military dependency and have to find difficult alternative paths to provide good quality jobs and economic well-being.

References

1   *Sunday Telegraph* 15 March 1998
2   *The World at Arms*. Reader's Digest 1989.
3   *Weapons*. Russell Warren Howe. Abacus 1981.
4   *The Sorcerer's Challenge*. David Shukman. Hodder & Stoughton 1995.
5   *The Gulf War*. BBC TV January 9 1996.
6   *The Guardian* 10 July 1996.
7   *The Electronic Battlefield*. Paul Dickson. Marion Boyars Ltd 1977.

8   *Defense News* 11 September 1995.
9   *Defense News—Top 100 Worldwide Defense Firms*. 1996.
10 *The Cold War*. Martin Walker. Vintage 1994.
11 *Armed Truce*. Hugh Thomas. Hamish Hamilton Ltd. 1986.
12 *World Politics Since 1945*. Peter Calvocoressi. Longmans 1991.
13 *The Rise and Fall of the Great Powers*. Paul Kennedy. Fontana Press 1989.
14 *The Guardian* 2 July 1998. Full details are available on the Brooking Institution's website:
    http://www.brook.edu/fp/projects/nucwcost/weapons.htm
15 *Nato Facts and Figures* 1984. *UK Defence Statistics 1995*. HMSO.
16 *The Gaia Peace Atlas*. Pan Books 1988.
17 *World Military and Social Expenditures (WMSE)*. Ruth Leger Sivard. World Priorities Inc. 1993.
18 *Daily Telegraph* 14 October 1995. Quoted from Moscow News.
19 *Arms Industry Limited*. Edited by Herbert Wulf. SIPRI 1993. OUP.
20 *Ibid.*
21 *Defense News* 25 September 1995.
22 *The Cold War*. Martin Walker.
23 *The Times* 30 September 1995.
24 *The Guardian* 3 June 1996.
25 *Ibid.* 29 October 1997.
26 *Ibid.* 11 November 1995 quoting Hansard Vol. 264 No. 143.
27 *Ibid.* 7 July 1997.
28 *Ibid.* 24 January 1998.
29 *The Observer* 16 November 1997.
30 *International Herald Tribune* 16 May 1997.
31 *Sunday Times* 18 February 1996.
32 *Defense News* 23 November 1995.
33 *The Times* 19 April 1996.
34 *Ibid.* 20 May 1996.
35 *Sunday Times* 12 November 1995.
36 *Closing Time*. Joseph Heller. Simon & Schuster 1994.

CHAPTER TWO

ECHOES OF EMPIRE

We don't want to fight, but by jingo if we do,
We've got the ships, we've got the men, we've got the money too.
We've fought the Bear before, and while Britons shall be true,
The Russians shall not have Constantinople.
George William Hunt 1878.

In mid-1995 John Major decided to apply for his own job. Faced with open revolt within his Parliamentary Party on Europe, the lowest poll ratings ever for a Prime Minister and a new leader of the Labour Party, he called for a vote of confidence from his colleagues. He was challenged by John Redwood, nicknamed 'the Vulcan' for his extra-terrestrial appearance and opinions. Michael Portillo, a more credible rival who had wider backing from the hard right of the party, remained on the sidelines loudly professing loyalty. This was undermined when it was discovered that phone lines had been installed for him in a potential campaign headquarters. After his re-appointment the Prime Minister re-shuffled his cabinet and awarded government posts to those who had not jumped ship.

Portillo's dazed expression as he left Downing Street after being moved into the top job at the Ministry of Defence didn't reveal whether he thought he'd been promoted or knifed. It probably didn't take him long to realise that in the best British Army tradition, Major's bayonet was highly polished and stuck in with precision. Any dreams he may have had about waving from tank turrets with top brass standing to attention and the Union Flag fluttering would have been dispelled swiftly as he faced a number of extremely difficult and unpopular decisions. He had inherited fifty years of government self-deception about Britain's post-war role.

Michael Xavier Portillo, whose father was a minister in the pre-war Spanish Republican government, wasted no time in self-promotion by making one of the most bizarre speeches ever delivered on Britain's military role, even at a party conference. He launched a salvo of hot air missiles against the real enemies of Britain—Brussels and Johnny Foreigner. "The European Court would probably want to stop our men fighting for more than forty hours a week—they would send half of them home on paternity leave!" "Britain will not be told when to fight and when not to." "Around the world three letters send a chill down the spine of the enemy—SAS—and those letters spell out one clear message—don't mess with Britain!" He singled out the subversive forces of metrication as a threat to British cap badges and uniforms. One commentator said: "grown newspapermen were slack jawed and white faced at the sheer gung-ho relish with which he took on the factual world and defeated it with overwhelming verbal force."[1] 'Brussels' reacted with weary indignation, quite used to hearing yet another British politician creating and attacking Euro-myths, in this case for a conference audience whose main characteristics seemed to be a mixture of deference and ignorance. All his efforts were wasted, however, when his immediate political ambitions were snapped by a man called Twigg, his Labour opponent in Enfield—the birthplace of the Bren gun—in the 1997 general election.

The post-war Labour government

Ernest Bevin was appointed Foreign Secretary in the Labour government of 1945 and was not the sort of person you would normally expect to find in the same political category as Mr Portillo. They were men of very different times, politics and stature. They did, however, have two important things in common—they shared an exaggerated view of Britain's influence in the world and a suspicion of European institutions. Previously General Secretary of the Transport and General Workers' Union, Bevin was a shrewd and capable negotiator who embodied many of the characteristics of the ruthless fixer. He was quite accustomed to riding roughshod over any opposition, whether in the trade union movement or in government. Wary of foreigners and a master of the mixed metaphor, he once observed of the Council of Europe: "If you open that Pandora's box, you never know what Trojan 'orses will jump out."

As a trade unionist he was cautious, conservative and, by his definition, realistic. As Foreign Secretary he rapidly became what one historian has termed "a world power fantasist."[2] Clement Attlee, the Prime Minister, was trying to develop policies that would allow the country to come to terms with its greatly reduced circumstances following an exhausting and economically debilitating war. The Bretton Woods Agreement had already provided for the dollar to elbow sterling aside as the major international currency. This allowed the US, which was providing this country with aid, to move into Britain's previously protected colonial trade areas. Robert Boothby, Conservative MP, called it "selling the British Empire for a packet of cigarettes."[3]

The Chiefs of Staff, seeking to maintain their influence, were determined that Britain should play a military role well outside the borders of the UK, arguing that: "The position of the United Kingdom is peculiar in that it contains 63 per cent of the white man-power (sic) of the British Commonwealth and an even greater proportion of its industrial potential... Eventually it may be possible to build up the war potential of the Dominions to such an extent that the relative importance of the United Kingdom will be diminished, but short of mass immigration, which at present appears impracticable, the United Kingdom's potential in war-making will remain high."[4]

The indigenous peoples of the colonies were regarded from London mainly as a source of cheap labour, armed forces in time of war or a political problem. Hugh Dalton, Labour Chancellor of the Exchequer, described the Empire as being composed of "pullulating, poverty-stricken, diseased nigger communities."[5] His terminology, particularly from someone who was supposed to support colonial independence might (charitably) be explained by the traditional disdain of Whitehall for faraway places and the frustrations of office. The white residents of the colonies who enjoyed a far higher standard of living than the average British citizen were happy for Britain to assume the military burden. In 1950 Britain was spending 7.7 per cent of Gross National Product (GNP) on defence, Australia only 3.3 per cent, New Zealand 2.5 per cent, South Africa 1.2 per cent and Canada 3.3 per cent.[6] West Germany and Japan had already started to rebuild their civil economies and were spending nothing on armaments. Dalton complained in 1949 that if the £810 million expenditure proposed by the Ministry of Defence, again supported by Bevin, were to be spent that year, it would gravely endanger economic recovery and force a £70 million cut in the social services budget. He also explained that the economy was short of 650,000 workers and yet the MoD and the Foreign Office were demanding military forces of 1,200,000 with a further 323,000 for the munitions industries. Bevin replied brusquely, saying that he "did not feel that he should be called upon to choose between foreign policy and defence on the one hand and social services on the other."[7]

Britain builds the bomb

In October 1946 Attlee summoned a secret inner cabinet committee which took the momentous decision that Britain should develop its own atomic weapons. He did not inform other cabinet colleagues and there was no Parliamentary or public debate. The decision was not revealed until the early 1950s, buried in miscellaneous expenditure accounts. Bevin, one of the few in the know, said about the bomb: "We've got to have the bloody Union Jack on top of it."[8] Covert decision making on major defence issues, particularly those that involve substantial increases in the expenditure of taxpayers' money, has been followed by a number of other Prime Ministers.

If the wrangling over finances, men and the deployment of troops overseas was a hangover from the past, the decision to go ahead with the production of atomic weapons mortgaged Britain's economic future for the next fifty years. The nuclear technology was relatively cheap but the delivery and support systems proved way beyond our means. Margaret Gowing, the official historian, reported that "although the meeting was being held when Britain was almost at her darkest economic hour with factories closing down for lack of coal, neither the

Chancellor of the Exchequer nor the President of the Board of Trade was present."9 It was strange decision for a government that had had promised a nation fed up with wartime shortages that it would give priority to homes, health, education and employment.

Britain and the US had collaborated during the war on the development of the atom bomb. British scientists crossed the Atlantic to work on the Manhattan Project under General Leslie Groves. An extremely forceful character, he proved to be no friend of the British government in its attempt to retain the trappings of a world power. He persuaded President Truman to distance himself from the Anglo-US wartime co-operation built up between Churchill and Roosevelt by arguing that the dissemination of knowledge about atomic energy—military or civil—would be a breach of Article 102 of the recently signed United Nations Charter. This forbade secret executive agreements between member states. The McMahon Act, passed in 1946, enshrined his view in US legislation and effectively slammed the door on the official transmission of nuclear information to the country that still believed it had a 'special relationship' with its former colony. Dean Acheson, the US Under-Secretary of State, said: "the honeymoon of Anglo-American relations existing during the war was coming to an end, and some of the commitments of the marriage seemed to be causing pain to one of the spouses." 10 It was far from what Churchill had envisaged in his Fulton speech when he proposed "a fraternal association of the English-speaking peoples."

Attlee and his five cabinet confidants had taken the decision to develop the atom bomb not only to emphasise Britain's position as a world power but also "to show them (the US) they don't know everything."11 Those who knew least were the British Parliament and public. Even Stalin was better informed, thanks to the activities of Klaus Fuchs, a scientist at the Aldermaston Atomic Weapons Research Establishment, who was convicted of spying for the Soviet Union in 1949. This confirmed the Americans in their view that Britain was not a safe haven for nuclear secrets. They underlined their technological superiority when they exploded the much more powerful hydrogen bomb before the first British atomic test at Monte Bello in October 1952. It took the British scientists a further four years to produce the H-bomb.

Clement Attlee made a hurried trip to the US in 1951 to try to persuade President Truman not to use the atom bomb in Korea. Conventional British wisdom has it that his sleeve tugging influenced Truman's decision but there is no doubt that his request for a British veto was "perfunctorily refused."12 Although Truman promised to inform the British Prime Minister before a bomb was dropped, he refused to consult on the decision itself. The bomb was not used in Korea because the US military were overwhelmingly of the opinion that it was not suitable for that type of war. They were also worried that if targets were not hit accurately it would lessen the deterrent effect of their nuclear arsenal.

The Soviet Union exploded an atom bomb in 1949, spurring the United States to continue the development of the hydrogen bomb. Caught in the never ending race of chasing the superpowers, Britain continued with research on its own bomb. The Korean War broke out in 1950 just after the US had decided to undertake a massive rearmament programme. Britain, living far beyond its means, but wanting to prove a loyal ally, tagged along by raising arms expenditure by £1 billion—from £3.7 billion to £4.7 billion. Hugh Gaitskell, Labour Chancellor of the Exchequer, abandoning his office's role of keeping tight purse strings, stated that the economy could bear the extra burden as the Americans had promised further financial aid. Aneurin Bevan and two junior ministers, Harold Wilson and John Freeman, resigned over the effects they said the decision would have on social spending. They were proved right.

Defence manufacturers competed with civil companies for skilled labour, machine tools and raw materials, all of which were in short supply. Inflation and the balance of payments deficit worsened considerably. The Americans sent less money than originally envisaged and the revived economies of West Germany and Japan, unburdened by excessive defence expenditure, started to make major inroads into the European markets for manufactured goods. Rationing for food and clothing continued in Britain until 1952, guaranteeing queues, the black market and the man who could always find goods that were in short supply (at a price). He was known as the 'spiv' and was a prominent figure in every local community. There was a sharp contrast between austerity at home and the government's grandiose ambitions overseas. Sir Henry Tizard, Chief Scientific Adviser to the Ministry of Defence, summed up the post-war situation: "We persist in regarding ourselves as a Great Power, capable of everything and only handicapped by economic difficulties. We are not a great power and never will be again. We are a great nation, but if we continue to behave like a Great Power we shall soon cease to be a great nation."[13] Tizard's statement of the obvious was met "with the kind of horror one would expect if one made a disrespectful remark about the King."[14]

The Foreign Office gave a birthday celebration for Ernest Bevin on the occasion of his 70th birthday. He was presented with a desk, a dinner service and a huge birthday cake. His trade union biographer described it as "a unique event," as previously only a reigning monarch had been so acclaimed. Every member of the Foreign Service, throughout the world, had donated a sixpenny piece. This was in recognition of the 1889 strike for the 'dockers tanner' that led to the formation of the TGWU. It was "a fitting symbol of all that Bevin held most dear."[15] It must also have been the first and last time that a gathering of the sovereign's ambassadors had raised a glass to commemorate workers taking industrial action. Perhaps they felt it was worth it if they had successfully absorbed a Labour minister into the conventions and beliefs of the Foreign Office.

Industrial neglect

Britain's pre-war industry was inefficient, uncompetitive and in many areas inhuman. The coal owners showed little compassion or thought for the dangers that miners faced, the privately-owned rail companies were loss making and suffering from under-investment and the engineering industry relied heavily on captive markets within the old British Empire. The unique British class system allowed greed and indifference to flourish among those wealthy enough to enjoy it on a scale not seen again until the 1980s. The post-war Labour government faced enormous difficulties in grappling with the physical damage caused by the war and the lack of financial resources needed to create the welfare state. The tragedy was that ministers allowed themselves to be pressurised by the defence establishment, in some cases willingly, away from the priorities that had won them the election.

The historian Correlli Barnett examined the government's priorities in his book. While not sympathetic to the social reforms made by the government, he is even more scathing about the successful lobbying carried out by the military. He points out that in 1947 they were complaining that the export drive was diverting Research and Development (R&D) away from the needs of the Royal Navy. The pressure paid off and the cabinet Production Committee recommended that there should be "every effort" to speed up plant and equipment for "high priority" military R&D. Defence R&D in 1947 amounted to £66.1 million and he says that had that sum "been directly invested in civilian R&D it would have unquestionably have bettered Britain's pitiful post-war performance in developing modern business systems and machine tools as well as all forms of civil electronics production."

He illustrates graphically the situation in 1950: "Despite the patching and piecemeal improvement of the last five years, the broad industrial scene remained much the same as in 1945, with most of the country's energy derived from out of date coal mines; with the majority of British export goods still Victorian staples manufactured on time-expired machinery in cramped old 'works'; with these goods being conveyed to Victorian ports via Victorian goods-yards in primitively braked steam trains chuffing along poorly maintained track, equipped for the most part by mechanical semaphore signalling... But what else could be expected if the government chose to allot only 9 per cent of GNP to investment in the entire British industrial system?"[16]

He who pays the piper

The unequal relationship between the US and Britain was again highlighted in 1956 when President Eisenhower forced Sir Anthony Eden to withdraw from

Suez. On 16 October, the Foreign Ministers of Britain, France and Israel met secretly to plan an attack on Egypt. Its stated purpose was to recover the Suez Canal—which had been nationalised by President Nasser—and to return it to the Universal Maritime Suez Canal Company, a private organisation whose share-holders included the British government and some French companies. However, the operating rights were due to be returned to Egypt in twelve years time; Nasser had offered compensation and had complied with the other provision in the orig-inal agreement that the Canal should be kept open. It was not possible to prove that he was acting illegally. After Britain had provided £5 million for the inva-sion—one historian called it "imperialism on a pittance"[17]—the government was shocked to learn that they could not launch it within one week, as planned, because the armed forces were completely unprepared. On Guy Fawkes Day, weeks later, British paratroopers dropped into the Canal Zone, followed by a seaborne landing force. The adventure was abandoned the next day.

Large numbers of army reservists had been hauled away from their jobs, wages and families to be paid a few pounds and shillings a week to participate in an unsuccessful attempt to regain a strip of water a long way from home. They were in a state of highly vocal discontent; to an extent that worried their officers. If the Americans had not pulled the rug out from under the whole episode, the British Army might have found itself faced with the same situation as the RAF ten years earlier. In 1946 more than 50,000 servicemen, angry at not being demo-bilised and sent home from Asia after the war was over, took strike action, marched and demonstrated. They refused to accept that once Germany and Japan had been beaten, their release should be delayed in order to prop up parts of the Empire against people demanding national independence. The RAF tried to pun-ish the leaders through rigged trials but the Attlee government conceded to pop-ular pressure and released them.[18]

Britain had lost about $400 million during the last quarter of 1956 and des-perately needed borrowing guarantees from the United States and the International Monetary Fund. Both refused unless the invasion was terminated. The loose change rattling around in Britain's reserves could not fund the expedi-tion and a humiliating retreat took place, accompanied by much huffing and puff-ing about American betrayal. Apart from the government's red face and the demise of Eden, the main outcome was the elevation to hero status of President Nasser and the rise of Arab nationalism throughout the Middle East. Few lessons were learnt in Whitehall, however, as foreign policy continued to be based on the belief that Washington would bail us out in time of crisis.

From bombs to missiles

The country's nuclear deterrent was based on the V-Bombers (Vulcan, Valiant and Victor) which delivered free-fall bombs. Faith in the effectiveness of the aircraft was shaken in 1962 when an American U2 spy plane was shot down by a Soviet missile with a range that could reach easily any incoming V-Bomber. For the first time a British government had to acknowledge that if the deterrent was to have any apparent credibility, it would have to include the US Thor missile. The only problem was, however, that it could only be used with the permission of the United States. It was no more independent than a company car.

President Eisenhower took a more benign view of the reliability of the British than Truman. He believed that as Britain possessed nuclear weapons it must share some of the problems of responsibility. In 1958, after considerable opposition from within Congress, he allowed US scientists to help their British counterparts develop new nuclear warheads. When they arrived at Aldermaston they discovered the equivalent of a "cottage industry," technically far behind their own efforts.[19] This was not the image our government had been promoting. Newspapers and newsreels had loudly praised the efforts of Britain's nuclear scientists; boffins beating the world to the leading edge of technology. It was now painfully clear, although not publicised, that not only had we bought US missiles but also had been forced to seek their assistance in producing the warheads. Further humiliations were to come.

The Americans had decided to develop the air-launched Skybolt missile as part of their overall nuclear strike force, complementing the Polaris submarine. Britain's Blue Streak solid fuel ground-to-ground missile had already been written-off after some catastrophic test failures. Now Britain had to go again to the US to ask for help. The RAF chiefs lobbied hard for Skybolt and persuaded the government that they, rather than the Navy, had the most effective means of deterrence. The Americans agreed readily, seeing an opportunity to lock Britain into their overall Nato command and, not least, make a lucrative sale. To the embarrassment of all concerned, Skybolt developed massive technical problems and President Kennedy cancelled it in 1962. Prime Minister Harold Macmillan rushed to meet him at Nassau in December of that year to plead for its re-instatement. Kennedy was unmoved on Skybolt but did offer to sell Polaris to Britain. This angered General De Gaulle, the French President, who saw this as yet another example of Britain acting as the United States' agent in Europe. He subsequently vetoed Britain's application to join the increasingly prosperous Common Market.

Britain continued to decline in relative world economic terms in the sixties but despite a series of Defence White Papers expressing concern, military expenditure continued at a high level. Labour Defence Secretary Denis Healey described it as a "runaway train."[20] After much haggling and disagreement, West Germany did agree to make a small increase in payment for British troops stationed in their country. In contrast, in the world of pop music and fashion Britain was the international leader; groups like the Beatles and the Rolling Stones, together with clothes designers, were major foreign currency earners. Official recognition of this came when the Beatles were awarded the MBE by Harold Wilson. John Lennon eventually returned his medal in protest against the government's support for the war in Vietnam.

Lennon was certainly more in touch with public opinion than the government on that issue. Harold Wilson wanted to placate the House of Commons by demonstrating that the Americans would listen to the concerns of a friendly government under pressure from anti-war protests. Previously secret cabinet papers revealed that he telephoned Lyndon Johnson, then US President, pleading for talks and pledging that "we shall support and stand by whatever action you take." [21]

The response was as brutal as any received by a British Prime Minister from the White House. Johnson was known for his blunt language and he said: "You have your hands full in Malaysia. I won't tell you how to run Malaysia and you don't tell us how to run Vietnam. If you want to help us some in Vietnam, send us some men and send us some folks to deal with these guerrillas. And announce to the press that you are going to help us. Now, if you don't feel like doing that, get on with your Malaysia problem. When you have trouble in Malaysia, I do not ring up my ambassador and come rushing over to see you." [22] Johnson was referring to the fact that in yet another overseas military venture Britain had 50,000 troops involved in border clashes in Malaysia. The only result of the episode was to further underline the fact that the views of a deferential British government would be ignored if it dared question any aspect of US policy.

Facing reality

1968 should have been designated 'European Year of Upheaval.' Throughout the Continent stone-throwing (and often stoned) students behind barricades faced police armed with tear gas and batons. Soviet tanks smashed their way through the baroque streets of Prague to enforce the 'Brezhnev Doctrine' of politically subservient neighbours. It was also the year that an element of common sense entered British defence planning.

Defence Secretary Denis Healey had recommended cutting the number of aircraft carriers based in the Far East and suggested they be replaced by 50 American FB-111A bombers. He had already cancelled the British TSR-2 bomber to save £300 million. The new American aircraft would have been dependent on countries in the region supplying bases and re-fuelling facilities. Despite the obvious drawbacks, Healey declared in terms that echoed Bevin: "We have no intention of ratting on our commitments... We do intend to remain, in a military sense, a world power." [23] The F-111, an expensive and difficult to maintain aircraft, later became known for its heavy losses in Vietnam and the inaccurate US bombing of Libya from bases in Britain. The disparity between the latest military dream and Britain's shaky economy became a cabinet issue. A group led by the Chancellor Roy Jenkins defeated Healey, James Callaghan, George Brown and Michael Stewart. It was a close thing; Prime Minister Harold Wilson had to use his casting vote. The F-111 order was cancelled. Denis Healey said that he almost resigned but feared that Richard Crossman would replace him.

That effectively ended Britain's role East of Suez and defence spending fell from 5.5 per cent of national income (GDP) in 1967 to 4.6 per cent in 1969.[24] The respite was short-lived as the Cold War was warming up with Nato military spending in Europe rising sharply. More prosperous allies were reluctant to pay as much as Britain on defence; in 1970 France spent 4.2 per cent of GDP and West Germany 3 per cent, compared with Britain's 4.8 per cent.

Labour lost the general election of 1970 and Edward Heath formed a Conservative government. He was more pro-European than his predecessors and ignored calls from his back-benchers for a return to Britain's imperial role. The Navy had lost one-seventh of its surface fleet and the Conservative gunboat tendency had been enraged when Royal Navy fishery protection vessels had been unable to prevent Icelandic craft cutting the nets of British trawlers. The Americans, however, were insisting that the Europeans should share a greater part of the defence burden through Nato. This had considerable financial costs and the savings made by the retreat from East of Suez were eaten up by expenditure closer to home, particularly in Germany. The governments of Heath and Lord Home kept to the well trodden path of high military spending.

Paying for Polaris

The Polaris submarine warheads that had been developed at Aldermaston were essentially copies of the US version. It would have taken far too long for the British scientists to have designed an alternative type. The weapon was obsolescent and the Americans had decided to proceed with Poseidon, a much more sophisticated and expensive missile that incorporated a MIRV (multiple independently targeted re-entry vehicle) system. In plain English it meant that each missile carried eight warheads directed at different targets. This was well beyond Britain's strained resources so Heath commissioned a feasibility study on updating the Polaris warhead. The Chief Scientific Advisor to the MoD said that: "the people who knew about it could be counted on the fingers of two hands."[25] It was codenamed Chevaline. The project went ahead under conditions of the utmost secrecy until the decision to manufacture or abandon it landed on the desk of James Callaghan who had succeeded Harold Wilson as Prime Minister.

In the by now well established tradition, he kept it hidden from the majority of his cabinet, Parliament and the public. By authorising its go-ahead he ignored the policy of his party which was that the existing Polaris should not be replaced. The Americans granted permission for the warheads to be secretly tested underground in the Nevada desert. The project was a financial debacle, eventually costing £1 billion at 1970 prices, four times the original estimate. Denis Healey later wrote in his memoirs: "I regard it as one of my mistakes as Chancellor not to get Chevaline cancelled after 1974 when the following Labour government found that its costs had escalated beyond control..."[26]

The disparity between Britain's economic performance and military expenditure in the period 1960-80 was clear. In the league tables of industrialised countries Britain was second lowest in productivity growth in the manufacturing industries, second lowest in investment as a share of national income (GDP) and second lowest in manufacturing capital growth. It was, however, second highest in military spending (as a share of GDP) and third highest in the rate of unemployment (1973-81).[27]

America in Britain

Most people believed that the US forces stationed in Britain would return home after the war. Many did not. Successive British governments were dragged behind US strategic military planning and allowed the Americans to establish a growing and secret network of air bases, nuclear dumps, coastguard stations, communications posts and submarine bases. In reply to a question in the House of Commons, Conservative Defence Secretary Francis Pym said that there were about a dozen establishments—11 air bases and the Holy Loch submarine base in Scotland—plus some support facilities. Later, under further questioning he admitted to 53 and later again to 56, including one of the most important, an underwater surveillance base in Wales. The investigative journalist Duncan Campbell discovered 103 sites by researching Soviet and US publications and records.[28] Americans were able to know much more than British citizens about what the US military was doing over here. Their law, based on the US Constitution, allowed them greater access to such information. British officialdom took the opposite view with the Official Secrets Act and media 'D notices' used by governments against journalists to suppress the publication of awkward facts.

The bases were established here through Nato agreements yet the US military had a separate chain of command that did not require it to tell its allies what actions it was planning. President Nixon ordered the alert and use of US forces at British bases during the 1973 Middle East crisis but did not inform the British government. In the atmosphere of the Cold War there may well have been a case for a US military presence in the UK. That case, however, was never discussed in

Parliament before any decision to transfer control of chunks of British territory to Washington. Rear Admiral Gene LaRocque, a former strategist in the Pentagon, said: "We fought World War I in Europe, we fought World War II in Europe and if you dummies let us, we'll fight World War III in Europe..."[29] The British could claim to have been under occupation without representation. There were a large number of public protests outside many of the air and submarine bases.

In 1958 a United States Air Force bomber loaded with nuclear weapons and based at Greenham Common was involved in a serious fire that could have caused a catastrophe. The MoD, true to form, denied any such incident. Following the leaking of secret documents in 1996, the ministry first continued the denials than later said it would have to ask the Americans for more information. Either the ministry knew the facts and had lied, or the United States Air Force had not told the government that a potentially life-threatening incident had occurred on British soil. If the first is true, the MoD treated the public with contempt, if the second is the case, the Americans obviously felt they could ignore a subservient government without any fear of recrimination. A journalist who visited the base on the day after the accident recalled being ushered in—under armed guard—to meet the American commanding officer. He was told: "This is not England, this is American soil. What happens here is the responsibility of myself and Washington. It is nothing to do with you."[30]

Peace protesters around the bases were ridiculed in the media as "woolly minds in woolly hats." Some thirty years after the Greenham Common nuclear incident, a man in a flak jacket watched approvingly as women demonstrators were dragged around by police at the American cruise missile site at Molesworth in Cambridgeshire. Michael Heseltine, Her Majesty's Secretary of State for Defence, was on duty. Much earlier in his life he had shown less enthusiasm for dressing up in military attire when he cut short his two years' national service in the Welsh Guards by standing for Parliament in a seat he was highly unlikely to win. The law at the time allowed prospective MPs to be released from compulsory national service. The idea caught on; over 600 men applied for application papers in two bye-elections.

The four minute warning

The Ballistic Missile Early Warning System (BMEWS) at RAF Fylingdales in North Yorkshire was operated by RCA, the American electronics company. The technical staff, management and station chief were British although overall command was held jointly with a senior American officer who reported directly to the military network HQ inside Cheyenne Mountain near Colorado Springs in the US. The purpose of Fylingdales was to provide a four minute warning of incoming Soviet missiles. There were a lot of jokes about what people would do with the last four minutes of their lives. Later its main task switched to Space Track which recorded the position of military satellites. At the time the Soviet Union was believed to lead the West in this field. As often happens in isolated or high security sites, small problems assumed an importance that they would not have had in a normal working environment.

The staff were members of the union ASTMS (the Association of Scientific, Technical and Managerial Staffs) and early one morning in the mid-1970s I received a phone call from a very agitated RCA personnel director. He told me that during the previous night there had been a disagreement about flexible working. Union members had not complied with some shift duties, there had been a technical glitch and Space Track had been down for a short time. I replied that as we were both still alive I presumed that the Soviets had not attacked during the blank period. He agreed but said that if the news leaked out, the public might lose confidence in Fylingdales. If they knew that the Soviets hadn't pressed the button when the base wasn't fully operational, they would ask why the place existed. Jobs would be at stake, including his. It was difficult to disagree.

Safe as houses

Fylingdales was not designed to provide a warning for the civilian population of Britain to allow them to take shelter; it operated as a link in the North American Air Defense Command (NORAD) based at Colorado Springs. The theory was that it would provide enough warning time for US aircraft to take off and retaliate if the Soviets launched a first strike. Part of the story that had to be sold to their citizens by governments with nuclear weapons on their territory was that these safeguards were part of the ultimate deterrent. If the enemy was foolish enough to attack, not only would retaliation be swift and devastating but also large numbers of the population could survive the enemy attack. Nobody believed this cheerful scenario except, perhaps, those civil defence volunteers who stoically faced the fact that they would have to clear up the radioactive remains of a nuclear holocaust.

Civil defence promotional films assured people that despite the destructive effects of "these new weapons," community effort, courage and a wartime spirit could save many lives. The Home Office booklet *Protect and Survive*[31] advised people to whitewash their windows (against the nuclear flash), go down to the cellar, make a cubby hole covered with sandbags, books and heavy furniture then creep into the holes with food and water and wait for fourteen days. Other items should include a portable latrine, radio (and batteries) and the essential tin-opener. That comforting publication managed to convince anyone who read or heard of it that their chances of surviving nuclear war were approximately zero.

The Warsaw Pact countries propagated the same myth. Communist Party functionaries told their grumbling comrades that even though Western imperialism was poised to attack, the shelters of socialism were strong enough for workers' protection. Regular civil defence exercises were compulsory. About twice a year the inhabitants of the block of flats in Prague where I lived during the late sixties were herded into its basement. The paint on the outside of the building was peeling and there were cracks in the masonry. It had not had much success in resisting the weather but the authorities had designated it as nuclear safe. We used to spend about half an hour underground, drinking Pilsener beer from the nearby restaurant, complaining about the central heating and joking with the local Sparta Prague football star who lived in the luxury block down the road.

The reality was that the only shelters that provided any form of protection were those built specifically for the secretly selected members of the ruling establishments of the countries concerned. Some nuclear bunkers in Britain were called Regional Seats of Government (RSGs) that were designated as the headquarters of the chosen few who would govern what remained after the blast. A group called 'Spies for Peace' traced a large number of these establishments and picketed them. It became popular as a kind of political train-spotting.

In 1965 the BBC commissioned then banned a film by Peter Watkins called *The War Game,* which accurately depicted the horror of a nuclear attack. Hugh Carleton-Greene, the BBC Director General said in a reply to an MP who had asked for it to be shown late at night: "The problem of a late night showing accompanied by a warning of the type you suggest is that, after all the publicity the film has had, people with neurotic tendencies might be encouraged to watch rather than discouraged." [32] The government knew the facts. Viscount Watkinson, a member of the Conservative cabinet from 1957-62, said that the government authorised a study of simulated nuclear attacks on Carlisle and Birmingham.[33] A one kiloton bomb was to be dropped on Carlisle, a two megaton bomb on Birmingham. The study found conclusively that if these attacks had occurred they would have wiped out both cities—leaving no people, no roads, no communications and nothing for Regional Seats of Government to govern. A 1955 official report came to the same conclusions but it has never been published. Watkins' film proved to be based on fact; the civil defence publications were works of deliberate fiction.

Keeping quiet

The passivity of Parliament during the post-war years was remarkable. Weapons that could kill millions of human beings within hours had been invented and deployed but there was no debate whatsoever on the uses of atomic energy—military or civil—under the Labour government of 1945-51. When the purchase of

Trident was raised in the House of Commons in January 1980, it was the first time in fifteen years that MPs had officially debated the issue of nuclear weapons.[34] This suited the leaders of successive governments very well as not only were their decisions closed to public scrutiny but also the errors and costs were covered up until much later.

The historian, Margaret Gowing, wrote: "when Mr Churchill returned to Number 10 Downing Street, he was surprised and impressed by the size of the atomic energy project built up by the Labour government. He found with a mixture of admiration, envy and the shock of a good Parliamentarian that his predecessors had spent nearly £100 million on it without informing Parliament."[35] The newspaper proprietors ensured that there was little investigative journalism in the field of defence or nuclear matters. A number of individual Labour MPs did question the whole basis of Britain's nuclear policy but they were either ostracised or disciplined by their leadership. It was regarded as particularly bad form to vote against the Defence Estimates.

During the 1945-79 period, Britain had a defence policy that was overstretched, politically bipartisan and financially crippling. Although we had lost a substantial share of the world markets, particularly in manufacturing, governments of both main parties continued to believe that the size of our armed forces and nuclear arsenal determined our status and well-being. As we became increasingly dependent on the United States for expensive weaponry, our European allies, who were also our commercial competitors, were much more successful in producing goods that people wanted to buy. Winning the World Cup in 1966 was small consolation.

References

1 *Independent.* Andrew Marr. 11 October 1995.
2 *The Lost Victory.* Correlli Barnett. Macmillan 1995.
3 *The Cold War.* Martin Walker. Vintage 1994.
4 *The Lost Victory.* Correlli Barnett.
5 *Ibid.* Quoted from Labour in Power 1945-51. Kenneth O Morgan. Clarendon Press 1984.
6 *The Lost Victory.* Correlli Barnett.
7 *Ibid.*
8 *The Times* 30 September 1982. Article by Peter Hennessey. Quoted in *Whitehall* by the same author. Fontana 1990.
9 *Independence and Deterrence Volume 1.* Margaret Gowing. Macmillan 1974.
10 *The Winning Weapon—The Atomic Bomb in the Cold War 1945-50.* Greg

Herken. Alfred A Knopf 1980.

11 *The Moscow Criterion*. BBC 2 TV programme 1995.

12 *The Winning Weapon*. Greg Herken.

13 *Independence and Deterrence Volume 1*. Margaret Gowing.

14 *Ibid*.

15 *Ernest Bevin—Unskilled Labourer and World Statesman*. Mark Stephens. TGWU 1981.

16 *The Lost Victory.* Correlli Barnett.

17 *World Politics Since 1945*. Peter Calvocoressi. Longmans 1991.

18 *Secret History. Mutiny in the RAF*. Channel 4 TV programme 8 August 1996.

19 *The Moscow Criterion*.

20 Quoted in *British Defence Since 1945*. Michael Dockrill.

21 *The Guardian* quoting cabinet papers released under the 40 year rule on 1 January 1996.

22 *Ibid*.

23 *Paying for Defence*. Malcolm Chalmers. Pluto Press 1985.

24 *Ibid*.

25 *The Moscow Criterion*.

26 *The Time of My Life*. Denis Healey. Penguin Books 1990.

27 *Military Expansion Economic Decline*. Robert W. DeGrasse Jr. Council On Economic Priorities (US) 1983. Countries included Austria, Australia, Belgium, Canada, Denmark, Finland, France, Germany, Italy, Japan, Netherlands, New Zealand, Norway, Sweden, Switzerland, UK and US.

28 *Britain and the Bomb*. Duncan Campbell. New Statesman 1981.

29 *Ibid*.

30 *The Shadow of the Bomb. World in Action*. 9 September 1996. Interview with Brian Vine.

31 *Protect and Survive*. HMSO 1980.

32 *Nukespeak: the Media and the Bomb*. Chapter by Michael Tracey quoting a letter to Charles Mapp MP. Comedia 1982.

33 *The Moscow Criterion*.

34 *How To Make Your Mind Up About The Bomb*. Robert Neild. Andre Deutsch 1981.

35 *Independence and Deterrence Volume 1*. Margaret Gowing.

CHAPTER THREE

BATTING FOR BRITAIN

In politics if you want anything said, ask a man. If you want anything done,
ask a woman.
Margaret Thatcher 1975.

The silence seemed to last for a very long time. The Prime Minister stared straight at me with laser precision and a thin smile. Then her body relaxed, she opened her mouth and gave a low chuckle. The men sitting alongside her at the top table took their cue, shuffled their feet and emitted muffled ho-ho noises, relieved that they had not laughed first. Those of us in the audience—mostly company directors, PR people and technologists—were perched on gilt chairs at Number 10 Downing Street in front of Mrs Thatcher, Denis and half a dozen ministers. It was our reward for helping to organise the awareness campaign called 'Information Technology Year 1982.'

I had just been introduced by IT Minister Kenneth Baker and she had asked why a "trade unionist" was involved in the project. I said that I had been equally surprised to receive her invitation and wondered if it had been sent to the wrong person. Little used to humour, however weak, and certainly not to any form of insubordination, it had taken her a few seconds to decide whether this was some kind of Scargillite disrespect on my part. Later Denis and I talked about football and he asked me if I had ever heard of a team called Queens Park Rangers.

Information Technology Year culminated in a barnstorming rally at the Barbican with the cheerleading Prime Minister urging embarrassed company executives to come on down to receive her personal acclamation. As they grinned sheepishly and half-heartedly waved their arms, they might well have been reflecting on the real rather than the hyped performance of their industry.

Failing the challenge of the chip

Electronics is the single most important enabling technology in modern society. It has overtaken the internal combustion engine as the driving force behind change in industrial and social life. Cars, aircraft, railway signalling systems, home appliances, telephones, recorded music, design, health care equipment, financial transactions and factory machine tools all depend on microelectronics. Electronic consumer goods are unique in that they are cheaper to buy today than ten years ago. The price of videos, televisions and the phenomenally popular personal computer has fallen sharply. There is hardly any aspect of life left untouched by the ubiquitous chip.

The military also are heavy users of the technology. More than half the development costs of a new fighter aircraft are spent on avionics, the airborne version of electronics. Politicians, most of whom have a weak grasp of detail, but who need to sound knowledgeable about anything modern, started making speeches about the "microchip" in the late seventies. Today, every declaration about life in the future has to have a reference to the "information super-highway" or "infobahn" depending on whether Californian or German technobabble is preferred. Despite all the publicity, Mrs Thatcher presided over a sharp decline in this key industry. In some areas it reached near extinction. ICL, the last large UK computer company, is now majority-owned by Fujitsu of Japan. The country of John Logie Baird no longer has a British-owned television manufacturer.

In the year of IT '82 the National Economic Development Office (NEDO) spelt it out diplomatically: "The United Kingdom's electronics industry has a number of technological and product strengths, but it is relatively weak in most of the businesses where world markets are growing fastest and amongst which are the best opportunities for growth in the future. This is reflected in an annual trade deficits, in a declining share of world markets and in deteriorating company performance as measured by the real growth of firms, which is very slow in comparison with firms in the UK's major international competitor countries."[1]

Senior industrialists and trade unions had become so worried about the performance of their industry that they asked NEDO to undertake a study to investigate how more resources could be transferred from defence electronics, which was then flourishing, to commercial applications. Sir Ieuan Maddock, former Chief Scientist at the Department of Industry, conducted a survey and reached some disturbing conclusions. He found that there was a widening "culture gap" between civil and defence-orientated companies, even where they existed within the same group ownership. There was little movement of scientists and engineers between the two areas because employers regarded them as "so different."

Defence manufacturing was tied to unclear MoD requirements and the civil products had to struggle to compete with overseas competition, particularly Japanese. He said that one of the reasons why Britain had responded so well to the technological challenges of the Second World War was that the military needs were met from a strong civil industrial base. That base was disappearing.

Maddock's conclusions included the firm recommendation that the MoD: "should be urged, or indeed compelled in certain cases, to purchase standard commercially available products and services, rather than highly specialised items tuned to their own needs." The government should scrutinise every one of its defence orders and projects to see whether they provided for existing or emerging high technology to thrive. He rejected completely the idea that the free market would advance the interests of British electronics because the US defence industry, with massive support from its government, was so dominant. Unlike Britain, its new technology was being transferred into the civil sector. Other countries could not compete on equal terms without government assistance. If it was not forthcoming then electronics in Britain: "would surely go the way of typewriters, sewing machines, motorcycles, shipbuilding and textiles." As a prescient final warning he commented: "there may be some who are content to see the UK become a technological colony of large offshore companies who will determine what products are made where and when, and how high the national standard of living should be."[2]

The MoD's response was complacent. It said that the main form of successful exploitation of defence electronics was through further military sales overseas; it would not be possible to divert significant MoD resources to facilitate civil exploitation of defence-orientated technology. If any new forms of organisation were created to liaise between the MoD establishments and industry, they would have to be funded and staffed from somewhere else. In its reluctance to provide new resources, the MoD, understandably, did not mention that its budgets (£14 billion in 1982/83) were expanding faster than those of other government departments, including Health and Education.

Sir Ieuan Maddock's analysis and blunt warnings, written at the height of the Thatcherite changes, have been proved accurate. Britain now has a massive annual trade deficit in electronics with its large companies being taken over or forced into junior partnerships with foreign companies who provide the technology. They also make the decisions on the location of new investment. Control of the research, design, software development and finance remains firmly back in the company's country of origin.

Paying the price

The government publicity machine goes into over-drive whenever a foreign multinational company decides to establish a base in Britain. Credit-grabbing ministers, local politicians, development agencies and the media trumpet the good news for jobs and the economy. The Japanese, German, Dutch, or latterly, Korean or Taiwanese management sometimes manage to squeeze in a word to say something complimentary about the locality and workforce. Golf courses for company executives, especially the Japanese, are heavily promoted to enhance the pulling power of a location. In areas of high unemployment all jobs are welcome and applications always exceed the number available. However, the harsh truth is that the jobs are usually the repetitive, less skilled type with low pay a common feature. They are an integral part of our 'flexible' workforce. The better jobs at the new plants are drawn from the limited pool of local skilled labour, most of whom are already employed.

In July 1996 the Korean company Lucky Gold Star (LG) announced that it would build a £1.7 billion silicon chip and TV monitor factories at Newport, employing 6,100 people. The Wales TUC General Secretary called it a "magnificent catch for Wales." It was an even bigger catch for Korean employers who paid a typical wage of £173 a week in the UK compared with the British national male average of £374. In Korea, electronics workers received an average of £211 a week.[3] Although the Conservative government pleaded confidentiality, it was later discovered that it had given a £247 million grant to the company, at a cost to the UK taxpayer of £41,000 for each job created. Most regional grants to foreign investors vary between £12,000-£20,000 per job.

The scramble between the various UK regional development agencies to hand over large sums of taxpayers' money became farcical. We were giving handouts to foreign companies to produce goods and pay low wages to create jobs in an industry that our governments had abandoned. The beggar offered money to the passing trader. Such generosity may not be reciprocated. In 1997 South Korea's banking industry and national currency collapsed. Its government had to go cap in hand to the International Monetary Fund for assistance. This meant that the development of Korean factories overseas was put at risk. Its exports to the UK and the rest of Europe also became much cheaper. Ominously, in March 1998 Lucky Gold Star announced that the building of its research laboratory at Newport would be delayed by six months.[4]

The German electronics giant Siemens (and the Queen) opened a semi-conductor plant on Tyneside in mid-1997. The company had received £50 million in development aid. In July 1998 Siemens announced the factory closure. Over 1,100 employees faced unemployment. Its French and German plants stayed open. The shutdown was cheaper and easier in Britain.

The collapse of manufacturing

The Department of Trade and Industry (DTI) was created to oversee and help British industry. Sir Keith Joseph was the first Industry Secretary in Mrs Thatcher's 1979 government. A radical right-wing intellectual, nicknamed the 'Mad Monk,' he had no experience of industrial life and was so sceptical of the role of government that on his first day at the DTI he is reported to have asked: "What is this place for?" It was a good question. In the Bible of the free market, government should not intervene but allow the private sector to put on their go-faster stripes and become world-beaters, unhindered by bureaucratic controls such as basic employment rights. Although all the other successful manufacturing economies, including Japan, Germany and other European countries, involved government in planning the right framework, providing finance and export assistance, the British monetarists did not feel the need to be over-burdened with the evidence. This theoretical approach was underlined when Sir Keith suggested a reading list for his staff that comprised twenty-nine books, twelve of which came from his Centre for Policy Studies and seven from the right-wing Institute of Economic Affairs. He was author or co-author of eight of the publications.[5] Sir Keith was followed by a further eight Secretaries of State for Industry during Mrs Thatcher's period in office, about the same rate of managerial turnover at an unsuccessful football club.

The results speak for themselves. The balance of payments in manufactured goods fell by over £23 billion between 1978 and 1989. Output was lower in 1987 than in 1973 although it rose to become slightly higher in 1992.[6] The share of manufacturing in the economy declined from 28.4 per cent in 1979 to 22.2 per cent in 1989. Employment in the sector fell by over two million, or 29 per cent, during the 1980-89 period.[7]

For some, particularly the Chancellor, Nigel Lawson, a sharp rise in manufacturing productivity provided more than enough compensation. He claimed that a "miracle" 5.5 per cent per annum increase during the 1980s was proof that the British economy had been "transformed." Official statistics measure productivity as output per person employed. It does not need a mathematician to calculate that if employment falls sharply, as it did, and output rises only slightly, then output per employee must rise significantly. In any case, this apparent transformation of a slump into a boom did not take account of the fact that employees in UK manufacturing work more hours per year than their European counterparts. If his statistics had been calculated as output per employee *per hour* worked, the figure would have been reduced to 4.2 per cent.[8] In a league table of twenty OECD (Organisation of Economic Co-operation and Development) countries, the UK came eighteenth—only above France and Greece—in the increase in manufacturing output during the Thatcher period of 1979-88.[9] Our defence spending, as a proportion of national income (GDP), was the highest except for the US, Turkey and Greece.

The overall figures disguise the massive impact of the loss of manufacturing in specific areas of the country. The 'North' of Britain (including the Midlands) has traditionally provided much more industrial output than the 'South.' In 1979 West Midlands manufacturing employment comprised 44 per cent of total employment in the region; East Midlands 39 per cent; North-West 36.3 per cent; Yorkshire and Humberside 35.2 per cent and North 32.9 per cent. Scotland had 28.7 per cent and Wales 30.5 per cent. The southern regions were lower with the South-East at 25 per cent; South-West 27.5 per cent and East Anglia 29.3 per cent. By 1986 the 'North' had lost an average of 31.1 per cent of its manufacturing jobs; the 'South' 14.2 per cent. Over 20 per cent of the nation's manufacturing equipment and capacity was written off. The industry suffered more during Mrs Thatcher's reign than during the Great Depression of the 1930s.

The small compensatory growth in non-manufacturing employment was 7.5 per cent in the 'South' while it actually fell by 4.8 per cent in the 'North'- thus adding to the misery created by the collapse of the productive sector.[10] These figures would have been even worse if it had not been for heavy government protection and purchasing in defence manufacturing. The unfavoured civil sector was left to cope with crippling market forces and a government that rejected intervention as a matter of principle. Hundreds of manufacturing companies, large and small, went out of business. The survivors enthusiastically adopted the spirit of the times by raking in as much in profits and dividends as they could while refusing to invest in new machinery or their employees. During the ten years from 1979 to 1989 real profits (after inflation) increased by 43.9 per cent; dividends by 73.2 per cent and share prices by 124.8 per cent. Real wages per head rose only 27.8 per cent and investment by 12.8 per cent.[11]

Those who had to deal directly with the effects of government policy (usually redundancies), including trade unions, frequently met bewildered employers with shrinking order books but who were reluctant to blame the person for whom most of them had voted. They seemed to believe that their problems were non-political. Recessions came and went, rather like bad weather. The industrial estates on the outskirts of Britain's large towns were never pretty places but they were even less attractive with the rain-sodden factories closed and roofs ripped off in order to avoid the payment of rates.

Chancellor Nigel Lawson believed that the de-industrialisation of Britain was unimportant as it could be replaced by earnings generated by services such as banking, insurance and finance. It is true that during the Thatcher period the service sector grew rapidly while manufacturing declined. The demand, however, for manufactured goods and services was the same—it rose by 26 per cent for both from 1979 to 1988. While the increase in UK services was about 27 per cent, the production of British goods was up by only 7.8 per cent.

In other words, the people of this country wanted to buy manufactured products as much as services but as insufficient were being produced here they had no option but to buy foreign goods. Imports almost doubled between 1979 and 1988. This led to a balance of trade deficit in manufacturing of nearly £15 billion in 1988.[12] During the whole of the Thatcher period, from 1979 to 1990, government expenditure to assist trade and industry fell by 47 per cent in science and technology and 57 per cent in aerospace, shipbuilding, steel and vehicles.[13] The publicity-conscious Prime Minister was fond of visiting laboratories and factories, often making a pointed reference to her chemistry degree. She took a great deal of interest in promoting exports, declaring that she was ready to "bat for Britain." Unfortunately many of the goods that were in demand in the commercial markets overseas were no longer made in Britain. We did, however, have a steady trade in weapons exports.

Turbulence in aerospace

Aerospace is a sector in which Britain played a leading world role. This role came under threat during Mrs Thatcher's premiership. British people have a romantic attachment to aircraft. This has been deeply embedded in popular culture through the generations, from comic book heroes such as Biggles, Rockfist Rogan (fighter pilot and world boxing champion), pipe-smoking, square-jawed space hero Dan Dare to today's computer games with young players zapping the inter-galactic enemy.

Spitfires, Hurricanes, Lancasters and Wellingtons became household names as they protected Britain during the Second World War. The British engineer Sir Frank Whittle invented the jet engine despite government indifference. In the commercial field the De Havilland Comet was a symbol of national pride and we hailed the Anglo-French Concorde as a triumph of British design skills. The viewing areas at British airports are crowded with plane spotters. Despite this popularity and the past success in being one of the few sectors of manufacturing to have a positive balance of trade, the UK aerospace industry came under severe pressure.

Its growth rate during the Thatcher period was only 1.5 per cent a year compared with 3.3 per cent in the US; 4 per cent in France; 8 per cent in Germany and 8.5 per cent in Japan.[14] France has now overtaken the UK as the largest European aerospace manufacturer with Germany catching up rapidly. If the future lies in the 'final frontier' of space travel and observation, then Britain is rooted firmly in the past. It is an area with considerable commercial potential. Apart from the military space effort, Britain spends, as a proportion of national income (GDP), less than half than that of India, one-tenth of China, one-fifth of France and one-third of Germany on civil space programmes.[15]

The HOTOL (Horizontal Take Off and Landing) space vehicle was invented in Britain in the early 1980s. It was designed to have a unique combination of air-breathing (jet) and rocket propulsion allowing it to take off from an airport like a jet plane and then turn into a sub-orbital space carrier. It would be invaluable, not only for travel, but also for surveillance and early warning of environmental dangers. Lack of government and private sector support still delay its progress. Other countries are making strenuous efforts to develop their own versions. Even the manufacturers' organisation, the Society of British Aerospace Companies, describes Britain's space effort as "small and undynamic." Growth from 1980-90 was only 4.3 per cent compared with 30.3 per cent in France and 25.6 per cent in Germany. [16]

The Thatcher government's obsession with defence required heavy Ministry of Defence spending on military aircraft and engines throughout the 1980s. This created a complacency amongst UK aerospace manufacturers that led them to believe that they could rely on military sales without regard for the dramatic political changes that were taking place in Eastern and Central Europe. If these were mentioned at meetings between senior directors and union officials the response was either a blank look or a remark about never quite knowing the whereabouts of the of the next enemy. They assumed, maybe hoped, that the same level of threat to national security would always be present. Their companies had highly professional marketing and communications departments but they seemed to understand little about world politics and its implications for business. They would repeat continually that they were confident that export markets would make up any shortfall in MoD spending.

Reality dawns

The aerospace companies understood eventually that the MoD was not going to be as generous with its contracts as it had been in the past. Mrs Thatcher, who had sold the publicly owned properties of the Royal Ordnance armaments factories (ROFs) to British Aerospace at prices well below their market value, had gone and the new government of John Major was in economic difficulties. The Defence Secretary, Tom King, was cutting numbers in the armed forces and the future looked less than rosy. In 1991 Professor Sir Roland Smith, part-time Chairman of British Aerospace, Manchester United and director of eight other companies, was concerned enough to write to Neil Kinnock, then Leader of the Opposition, to complain that defence companies needed government support but were not getting any. The government had told the bemused manufacturers to look for other (unspecified) markets. Despite this, and evidence of future growth in the commercial aircraft market, British Aerospace, the largest company, has continued to sell off its civil ventures, including its executive jet and space businesses, to concentrate on military sales.

Aerospace employment in Britain plunged by over 125,000 jobs between 1981-94, far more than in other European competitor countries.[17] In June 1996 the industry's trade association, the Society of British Aerospace Companies, announced that 30,000 of the remaining 130,000 jobs would have to be lost. They admitted that UK labour costs were only 58 per cent of those in the US and 52 per cent of those in Germany. They blamed lack of government support for the decline in world market share from 13 per cent in 1980 to 9 per cent in 1996.[18] All unemployment is painful for those directly affected, their families and the local communities who rely on their spending power but aerospace and electronics jobs have an extra dimension in that they have high value-added skill and technological content. They are also in industries with tremendous world potential. Every skilled and qualified engineering job that is lost reduces Britain's chances of success.

Lord Weinstock, then Managing Director of GEC and employer of a number of Conservative ex-ministers, was quite frank and one of the few industrialists willing to criticise the government openly. At a meeting of a House of Commons Select Committee on Trade and Industry in 1993 he challenged the Thatcher ethic by saying that there were some projects where the risk for commercial organisations was too high. Government should back these. Referring to the recent decline in defence spending he commented that in certain circumstances it would be helpful for government to assist technology to move from the military to the civil field. He accused the government of lacking understanding of industry's needs and compared the integrated public and private initiatives taken by the French, in particular their railways, with the British hands-off approach. In answer to a question about what would happen if there was not a change of attitude by government, he replied that we would continue to suffer continuing industrial decline.[19] Neither Mrs Thatcher nor John Major understood that simple point.

"Rejoice, Rejoice!"

Mrs Thatcher's view of what made Britain great was much different from that of John Major who said that he dreamed of warm beer, old ladies cycling to church and cricket on the village green. The Press photo of her standing in a tank turret, goggles on her forehead, a silk scarf tied around her head and the Union Flag fluttering summed up the image. It was no surprise, therefore, that she reacted with fury when a group of scrap metal merchants from Argentina, who had refused to leave the British colony of South Georgia, were followed on to the island by Argentine troops. This was followed by the occupation of the Falkland Islands. A heated debate took place in the House of Commons on 3 April 1982 when the government was accused of negligence in not anticipating the invasion. The mildest of politicians, including Michael Foot, Leader of the Opposition, demanded immediate military action. General Galtieri, head of the military junta that ruled Argentina, had stated in December 1981 that he intended to seize the Malvinas but British intelligence had given no warning of the landings. The Foreign Secretary, Lord Carrington, accepted the blame, resigned and was replaced by Frances Pym.

Argentina had laid claim to the islands since 1965 and Britain had offered to transfer sovereignty but to lease it back for a number of years. The islanders opposed this as they did any other form of compromise. Despite the high levels of defence spending, deep cuts had been made in the number of Navy vessels that were able to operate 'out of area' in places such as the South Atlantic. The Minister for the Navy had resigned in protest. The aircraft carriers *Hermes* and *Invincible* were due to go; the former to be scrapped, the latter to be sold to

Australia. Luckily they were still available and together with two assault ships *Fearless* and *Intrepid*, also reprieved from the scrapyard, they formed the core of the task force that set out from Portsmouth. They arrived in the vicinity of the Falkland Islands on 1 May. On 14 June 1982, the Commander of the Argentine Forces on the Falkland Islands surrendered, together with 11,313 of his troops.

The last of Britain's colonial wars had cost the country 225 men killed and 777 wounded, six ships sunk, ten damaged and nine Harrier jets lost. Argentina lost 652 men killed in action. The government estimated the cost of the expedition at £700 million with a further £800 million to cover losses.[20] The Prime Minister told us to "Rejoice, Rejoice!" All military observers agree that the victory was a close run thing. If the Argentines had possessed more Exocet missiles and had fused their bombs correctly, the outcome could have been very different. The 2,200 islanders and their sheep remain a small part of Britain, unlike the people of Hong Kong who were handed back to the People's Republic of China in 1997.

The Navy lobby seized their opportunity, arguing that the Falklands episode had proved that Britain needed a large surface fleet to police Britain's remaining outposts. £1 billion was found to fund naval equipment programmes and a new £215 million military airport was planned for the Falklands. Such demands were not confined to the Conservative Party. Labour's James Callaghan and John Silkin, both former naval officers, believed that somehow Britain could play a 'special' world role, different from that of its richer allies or potential enemies. Silkin said "We need a surface fleet to fulfil our obligations to Third World countries who look to Britain, rather than the USA or the Soviet Union, for protection."[21]

The Thatcher government had already decided to spend £5 billion over ten years on buying the Trident submarine C4 nuclear missile from the Americans. In 1981 the US government decided to phase out the C4 and replace it with the D5, a more expensive and powerful version. This was way beyond Britain's needs but the government had no choice but to order it or cancel the project entirely. Once again Britain had to adjust its defence policy to suit the requirements of the US military. If the government had not gone ahead with Trident there would have been scope for considerable defence savings. Defence expenditure rose by 18 per cent in real terms (after accounting for inflation) between 1979 and 1985, higher than any other European Nato country.[22] Spending then levelled out from 1985 to 1990.

Thatcher and the peace movement

Mrs Thatcher relished a battle of ideas. Her own were based on a set of firm beliefs rather than a coherent philosophy. Rather like a deck of cards these were dealt as she felt the occasion demanded. One of her ideological targets was the peace movement, particularly the Campaign for Nuclear Disarmament (CND). She displayed considerably more respect for its influence and arguments than she did for the Labour leadership. Her worries were revealed in her autobiography: "I began to be more concerned about the presentation of our nuclear strategy. I was anxious that the unilateral disarmers were still making the running on nuclear issues... although CND had begun to lose support from the high point it had reached in 1981, it remained dangerously strong."[23] As a populist herself, she appreciated fully that a radical movement with public support could do her more political damage than any Opposition front-bench.

CND was formed in 1957 by a group of writers, clerics and left-wing politicians. Its best known figures were the philosopher Bertrand Russell, Canon John Collins and Michael Foot. J.B. Priestley wrote the first policy statement in a high moral tone: "The Campaign for Nuclear Disarmament seeks to persuade people that the atomic and similar armaments are totally wrong and should be abolished, and it has no other aim. But its members believe that mere vague condemnation of atomic weapons is not enough, and that some definite action must be taken. The British government should announce its intention to abolish these armaments, and should proceed to do so, at a given date, whatever other nuclear powers may decide. One nation able to produce these weapons should set other nations an example by deliberately challenging the hysterical fear that is behind the arms race... And Britain cannot be adequately defended by atomic armaments. To retain them, at a cost that menaces our whole economy, is merely to play an idiotic game of bluff."[24]

CND was launched publicly three months later when much to the surprise of the organisers, 5,000 people turned up at Central Hall, London and four overflow meetings had to be arranged. Canon Collins spoke, over-optimistically, of "a short, sharp campaign" to ban nuclear weapons from Britain. The first Aldermaston march took place at Easter 1958, starting with only about 300 people but finishing with a respectable 4,000. Few of the people living on the route had heard of the campaign but most were friendly. One man rushed out of his house to tell the march leaders: "You might like to know that Cambridge won by three lengths!"[25] Even the thought of nuclear war couldn't diminish Middle England's interest in the Boat Race.

The largest demonstration of support was in 1961 when 150,000 people came to the rally in Hyde Park. The marches took place each year in the three days over Easter and were amazingly high spirited in spite of the grim theme and the British weather. Despite the large number of vicars, priests and Buddhist monks tramping along, word did not seem to have reached any deity that occasional sunshine would have been welcome. The local pubs did a good trade and even the most surly landlord greeted the duffel-coated, guitar playing customers with something approaching politeness. The faces of the tweed-jacketed regulars and their ladies sitting in the snug were pictures of repressed distaste as they watched the marchers take off their shoes and socks to examine their blisters. In the marquees that provided overnight shelter, shared sleeping bags heaved and rolled with young unilateralists temporarily forgetting the bomb. Quite a few of today's apolitical entrepreneurs could well have been conceived in a cold field somewhere along the A4.

The main political battle took place within the Labour Party. Trade unions, notably the largest, the Transport and General Workers' Union, had started to pass resolutions supporting CND, sometimes against the advice of their leaders, and in 1960 the Labour Party conference adopted a motion that called for the removal of nuclear weapons from Britain. This was reversed the following year after Hugh Gaitskell, the party leader, made his "Fight, fight and fight again to save the party we love" speech. The media praised his courage before reverting quickly to their normal rubbishing of Labour's policies.

In those days the party leadership had to accept that conference decisions determined policy, even though when in government, their defence strategy was mainly a continuation of that pursued by the Conservatives. The unilateralist success and its reversal created a tremendous debate but it was largely an artificial affair. Decisions at Labour conferences were swung one way or the other through the trade union block vote. This involved a considerable amount of wheeling and dealing amongst union General Secretaries and party leaders. On one famous occasion, the Amalgamated Engineering Union, whose President was Lord Carron, voted both for and against unilateralism. There were two separate motions. On the first he was instructed by his national executive to vote to get rid of the bomb; on the second, left to his own devices, he voted to retain it. Ordinary members were hardly involved.

The campaign was well aware of its mainly middle-class appeal and did try to attract the support of those preoccupied with everyday matters such as housing and jobs. It was not always successful. One CND pamphlet, aimed at trade unionists on the factory shop-floor began: "The case for CND is transcendentally simple..." There were splits, particularly between those who believed in non-violent 'direct action' by sitting down and blocking streets around government offices and military bases and those who advocated the more political route. The direct action group, the Committee of 100, was led by Bertrand Russell who dramatically tore up his Labour Party card and whose apocalyptic tactics and prophesies were opposed by Canon Collins and the majority of CND.

There were other diversions such as the decision to oppose nuclear power, which was a much wider issue, and the attempt to shift the focal point of the campaign to Europe through the formation of European Nuclear Disarmament (END). These provided plenty of scope for disagreement and some none too comradely confrontations. The Militant Tendency and other far-left groups were everywhere, often heckling at other people's peace meetings. One of their banners held aloft in Trafalgar Square carried the not very pacific message: "Fight for Peace! Defeat the Labour leadership! Smash the Ruling Class!" On later anti-racist demonstrations their placards shouted the ultimate contradiction: "Smash Intolerance!"

The Labour Party fought the 1983 General Election with a commitment to remove all nuclear bases from Britain: "within the lifetime of a Parliament." Few members of the shadow cabinet attempted to press the case and there were open disagreements during what was generally considered a disorganised campaign. Following that election defeat, the issue was quietly dropped by the leadership and annual conference decisions calling for a reduction in defence spending were ignored.

There is no doubt however that the peace movement produced some extremely coherent and intellectually powerful arguments on why it was a dangerous nonsense for a middle-ranking, economically struggling country to pretend that it could only protect itself through the threat of nuclear force. Articulate and media-friendly leaders such as Joan Ruddock (later a junior minister in Tony Blair's government) and the Roman Catholic Monsignor Bruce Kent provided an effective antidote to the Press depiction of CND supporters as subversives or over-emotional softies. People were generally pessimistic about the prospects of nuclear war. A BBC radio survey in 1980 showed that 40 per cent of those questioned thought that it would occur within the next ten years.

The support of large numbers of scientists and medical experts did ensure that the peace movement won one important political battle. They proved without doubt that nuclear war would reduce Britain to a radioactive wasteland. The government was unable to counter the scientific evidence. It shelved civil defence plans and propaganda and replaced them with the 'mutually assured destruction' (MAD) theory. This was based on the assertion that mutual terror would prevent either side from starting an all-out war. In fact, British governments have always refused to rule out the possibility of launching a nuclear strike before that of the enemy.

When Mrs Thatcher came to power in 1979, the peace movement was at a low ebb. Its numbers had fluctuated since its formation but the Prime Minister's nuclear certainties, the Vietnam war and the stationing of intermediate range missiles in Europe, by both sides, had boosted support. During quieter times, membership fell. In 1979 CND membership was 4,287 with 102 groups; three years later it had risen to 50,000 with 1,000 groups.[26] During that period the Falklands war was fought, the Iran-Iraq conflict broke out, the Soviet Union moved armed forces into Afghanistan and Ronald Reagan was elected US President. He denounced the Soviet Union as "the Evil Empire."

Mrs Thatcher's strident defence of the government's decision to buy the more expensive Trident II and her agreement to the American proposal that their cruise missiles should be stationed in Britain, disguised her real worries. The missile argument bordered on the surreal. There were two options: 1. The Americans would base the weapons here, run the sites and decide unilaterally when and to where the missiles would be fired. 2. A 'dual key' option which would ensure (in theory) that the US could not launch them without British permission. The catch in the second option was that Britain would have to buy the missiles, at a price our weak economy could not sustain. Mrs Thatcher, who always knew how to make a forced concession look as though it were her own choice, had to allow total control to be exercised by the US military.

Acknowledging this country's traditional subordination to US policy, she said: "The UK had never exercised *physical* control over systems owned and manned by the US. It was in my view neither fair nor reasonable to ask the US to break with that precedent now."[27] The dual key option was quietly dropped and Mrs Thatcher agreed a form of words with President Reagan that would gloss over the fact that neither she nor any other member of the British government would have any say in an American decision to launch the UK-based missiles.

Unlike the secret agreements of the 1960s that allowed Washington sovereignty over their British bases, this debate was very much in the public arena. It was also one of the few that she knew she couldn't win. Although most of the public when asked: "should Britain unilaterally disarm?" ("nuclear" was often deliberately omitted so that it appeared Britain might be defenceless), replied in the negative, people did not like the idea of this country becoming a target as a result of decisions taken in the US. This worried the Prime Minister as she felt it could damage her re-election chances. She admitted: "The timing of deployment (of cruise missiles) was bound to be a sensitive matter, especially with an election campaign ahead. We were anxious to avoid very visible signs of deployment in the run-up to or during the 1983 election campaign, with demonstrations stretching police resources."[28] She brought forward the election to June 1983, five months before the launchers and warheads arrived in Britain.

When the Cold War ended, the disputing parties understandably claimed the credit. The government said that it was firmness in the face of aggression that had deterred the Soviets, the peace movement retorted that its efforts had ensured that public opinion was opposed to the continuation of the balance of terror. In reality, it was the fact that Mr Gorbachev had come to power and understood clearly that his country could no longer stand the crippling cost of the arms race. He also realised that the world would be a safer place if the grip of the military-industrial complex was removed from the levers of decision-making.

Lady Thatcher continued to sing the old songs, albeit from a distance. After devoting much of her political life to a crusade against the Soviet Union, she used the 50th anniversary of Churchill's Fulton speech in 1996 to warn: "The Soviet collapse has also aggravated the single most awesome threat of modern times: the proliferation of weapons of mass destruction."[29] She seemed to believe that the demise of the enemy had made the world a less safe place. One week later, she pursued the theme: "I'm not critical of Britain, but looking at the dangers that we have now, we need to step up our defence expenditure."[30]

The silence of the lambs

Mrs Thatcher was a politician of extremes and people responded accordingly. As far as she was concerned, what you saw (and heard) was what you got, and if you didn't like it, too bad. She was extremely popular in America. The senator who presented her with the 1996 Nation's Honor Award said: "We honour Lady Thatcher for her competence, her graciousness, her eloquence, her humour." Perhaps feeling that he had understated her majestic qualities, he added: "I thank her for humbling us with her presence." A blue-collar worker in a Boston bar told me that he sure admired: "your Queen, Mrs Thatcher." Her determination contrasted sharply with the grey male doubters around her. Pushing her way to the front of photo opportunities with European politicians, the glinting hair and electric blue suits made her look like the star of a 1940s Hollywood musical surrounded by a supporting cast of wine waiters. Whatever criticisms were levelled at her, she had the perfect riposte. The electorate voted her into office on three successive occasions.

Until the final days, it was quite obvious that she hardly ever listened to any dissenting views. Those of her colleagues who proved to be: "not one of us" were sacked or, if really in her bad books, sent to the Northern Ireland Office. That was not surprising given her certainties and her narrowly focused view of life. What was remarkable, however, was that those who eventually got rid of her did not summon up the courage sooner to try change some of her policies during the disastrous collapse of Britain's manufacturing base. The real powerbrokers were not the back-bench critics, Conservative 'grandees' or even disloyal ministers but the industrialists and financiers who supported, funded and influenced heavily the party she led.

Rarely seen or heard in the media, these people allowed their interests to be damaged by a Prime Minister whose grocer shop economics were completely inappropriate to the running of successful companies. They could not understand why she never seemed to comprehend that there was an umbilical link between public expenditure and private sector contracts. Her view was simple; public spending bad, private spending good. On one occasion some directors of Thorn/EMI were complaining bitterly because one of her spending cuts had slashed orders for motorway lighting. This had resulted in reduced production and, finally, redundancies. To her it was prudent housekeeping, for them it was lost business. When we asked why they did not protest directly to the Prime Minister, or at least register their concern publicly, they made some muted comments about raising it at the next Confederation of British Industry (CBI) meeting.

The CBI was an ineffective lobbying organisation during Mrs Thatcher's premiership. Her attitude towards it was either patronising or dismissive, hardly much better than her view of the TUC which she believed she had blown away to the outer limits of space. In 1980, the then CBI leader, Sir Terence Beckett, a former Ford chairman, declared that the Conservative Party was only a narrow alliance and asked how many of its Parliamentary party had run a business. He said industrialists should be ready for: "a bare knuckle-fight." The following day he emerged from Downing Street clutching his jaw (metaphorically) after coming off worst in a short encounter with the reigning champion. He said his meeting with Mrs Thatcher had been "very encouraging" and he now supported her policies.

Even though the CBI had started to hold annual conferences, with speeches that sounded like extracts from the minutes of the last board meeting, most employers' criticisms of the government over the next decade were muffled or coded. One of Mrs Thatcher's greatest delusions was that the top people in Britain's largest and most profitable companies were firm believers in her free, non-interventionist market. Many of the big organisations, particularly the defence manufacturers, relied heavily on government contracts and money for research and development.

Despite Mrs Thatcher's indulgence in military spending, she realised that the MoD could never be satisfied. It drove her to the point of exasperation and she complained frequently: "As so often, it seemed that the Ministry of Defence had been the main villain... Having predicted a substantial underspend, they turned out to be overspending with a vengeance. Geoffrey (Howe) and I were appalled and decided to give the MoD a much-needed rebuke. But the damage had been done." "The defence budget was a special problem... the MoD had little incentive to get value for money in the hugely expensive equipment it purchased..."[31] Her radical policies had cut a swathe through traditional institutions but left the MoD culture largely untouched. It was outside pressures, notably the end of the Cold War, that restricted its previously boundless spending horizons.

If her natural allies had spoken out, the Prime Minister would at least have had to debate her attitude towards manufacturing and the gross imbalance between military and civil resources. In the demonology of the far-left, all bosses, large and small, were in a conspiracy with "Maggie" to boost profits and screw the working class. In fact, the people who did best were those such as estate agents, companies selling (and 'mis-selling') insurance policies, property developers, banks, consultants privatising public utilities, builders, bodgers, and quick buy and sell shareholders like "Sid" of British Gas. The defence companies prospered for the first seven years of her reign but were left adrift as the Cold War came to an end.

The real loser was the productive civil sector with many companies disappearing or being taken over without protest. It is easy to blame a Prime Minister for everything that goes wrong; in the case of the manufacturers they supported her politically while her theories destroyed their businesses. They went without a whimper let alone a bang. Mrs Thatcher deserves credit for realising quickly that Mr Gorbachev intended to melt the permafrost of the Cold War. Whether or not her motive was a genuine conversion to the idea of a more peaceful world or the chance to play a starring role on a stage usually occupied only by the Americans and the Russians is irrelevant. Her credentials made it extremely difficult for the British military establishment to openly oppose the new developments.

It would have been quite outside her comprehension to try to introduce any policies to mitigate the effects of the end of the international confrontation on industry and employment. The mythical gods of market forces could never be questioned. She left Britain to suffer the consequences as she toured the world reputedly charging foreign audiences £50,000 an hour to advocate the same policies that so comprehensively wrecked large parts of our industry.

References

1 *Policy for the UK Electronics Industry.* NEDO 1982.
2 *Civil Exploitation of Defence Technology.* Sir Ieuan Maddock. NEDO 1983.
3 *The Observer* 12 May 1996.
4 *Sunday Times* 15 March 1998.
5 *Britain's Economic Performance.* Edited by Tony Buxton, Paul Chapman and Paul Temple. Chapter by Sir Geoffrey Chandler. Routledge 1994.
6 *Ibid.* Chapter by David Mayes.
7 *The Economy Under Mrs Thatcher 1979-1990.* Christopher Johnson. Penguin Books 1991.
8 *Britain's Economic Miracle. Myth or Reality?* Edited by Nigel M Healey. Routledge 1993. Chapter by David H Blackaby and Leslie C Hunt.
9 *Ibid.* Chapter by John Wells.
10 *Ibid.* Chapter by Nigel M Healey.
11 *Britain's Economic Performance.* Chapter by Margaret Sharp and William Walker.
12 *Britain's Economic Miracle. Myth or Reality?* Chapter by John Wells.

13 *The Economy Under Mrs Thatcher 1979-1990.* Christopher Johnson.
14 *British Aerospace Industry.* House of Commons Trade and Industry Committee. July 1993.
15 *Setting the New Agenda.* Lecture given by C.M. Hempsell, MSc, ARCS, FBIS at MSF seminar, January 1993.
16 *UK Aerospace Statistics.* SBAC 1995.
17 *Ibid.*
18 *Financial Times* 4 June 1996.
19 *British Aerospace Industry. Minutes of Evidence.* House of Commons Trade
    and Industry Committee. 21 April 1993.
20 *British Defence since 1945.* Michael Dockrill.
21 *Hansard* 1 July 1982. Quoted in Paying for Defence. Malcolm Chalmers. Pluto Press 1985.
22 *British Defence Since 1945.* Michael Dockrill.
23 *The Downing Street Years.* Margaret Thatcher. HarperCollins 1993.
24 *The CND Story.* Alison & Busby 1983.
25 *Ibid.* Chapter by Mervyn Jones.
26 *The CND Story.*
27 *The Downing Street Years.*
28 *Ibid.*
29 *The Times* 11 March 1996. Speech at Fulton, Missouri on the 50th anniversary of Winston Churchill's speech.
30 *The Times* 14 March 1996. Speech at a conference on Kuwaitis held as prisoners of war in Iraq.
31 *The Downing Street Years.* Margaret Thatcher.

CHAPTER FOUR

COSTING A BOMB

Never ask of money spent
Where the spender thinks it went.
Robert Frost 1874-1963

The statue of Field Marshal the Viscount Alanbrooke stands outside the Ministry of Defence staring determinedly past the Whitehall Theatre towards Trafalgar Square and Nelson's Column. Alanbrooke was Chief of Staff during the Second World War and his inscription reads: "Master of Strategy." Inside the MoD lesser mortals work in a building that looks as though it has been carved from a single block of stone. Long corridors, thick walls and closed office doors emphasise its separate elements; there is no hint of a modern office environment. It is not a popular institution. Margaret Thatcher said: "The place that bothers me more than anywhere else is the Ministry of Defence. It's like a concrete bunker. If you give me a bomb, I'll put it in there."[1] The lady who believed in absolute financial prudence in the public sector was not pleased with the department responsible for the greatest waste of government money.

The structures of the MoD are based on a bureaucracy over 300 years old. The Navy (the 'Senior Service') was the traditional gunboat enforcer of British foreign policy and the Admiralty Board was created in the seventeenth century as a combined naval and civil administration. In comparison, the War Office, which co-ordinated other civil service departments that supported the Army effort, was weak and ineffectual. The Army Council with a General Staff was formed in 1904. An Air Ministry was established in 1917, reflecting a new dimension of war.

The outbreak of the Second World War brought the realisation that the administration of the three services should be co-ordinated and brought under one roof. Despite the appointment in 1955 of a Chief of Defence Staff to chair meetings that brought the separate service chiefs together, it was not until 1964 that the government formed the integrated Ministry of Defence. Inter-service rivalry has always been a major factor in the ordering of new weapons and equipment. Denis Healey recalled that: "Each of the three services tended to believe that it could win a war on its own, and spent much of the time fighting the others. But each service had its own internal divisions too. The submariners believed they could sink any carrier afloat...In the army the gunners and the sappers considered themselves superior to the infantry, the Royal Tank Corps despised the cavalry, while all tended to be suspicious of special forces like the paratroopers, the Gurkhas and the SAS. In the RAF there were similar rivalries between bomber and fighter pilots, and both were hostile to the missile forces which looked like threatening their existence."[2]

The Procurement Executive within the MoD has the task of spending public money on buying military equipment. It is divided into five divisions:

1. Central; responsible for overall management and contracts.
2. Sea Systems; responsible for sea equipment for all three services.
3. Land Systems; for land equipment for the three services, headed by the Master General of the Ordnance.
4. Air Systems; also for the three services and nuclear establishments.
5. Defence Export Services Organisation (DESO); to promote sales of British defence equipment.

Each division has four or five separate departments and within DESO there are special offices devoted solely to selling to Saudi Arabia and Malaysia. The stated aim of the Procurement Executive is: "to meet the operational requirements of the armed forces, *in the timescale in which the equipment is needed, and at minimum overall cost to the defence budget."* (Author's italics).[3] If that was intended as a mission statement, the mission failed.

In 1997 the National Audit Office (NAO) found that of the 25 largest UK defence projects, 22 would fail to meet their planned delivery dates. Of these, 6 would be over 5 years late. Only 3 were anticipated to be delivered on time. The overall cost of the projects rose by £3.084 billion (9.1 per cent) during the year 1996-7.[4]

There has clearly been something wrong with the methods of project management in the MoD. According to the NAO about 40 per cent of all delivery delays are caused by "unforeseen technical difficulties." That phrase can cover a multitude of problems, some of which are the responsibility of the supplier, including the lack of qualified staff or faulty design. Others can be caused by the MoD making last minute changes to specifications or demanding a higher performance. Artificially low cost estimates at the time of approval are frequent and serve only to highlight the inaccuracies as successive sets of figures disprove the original assumptions.

After technical problems, the next most serious factor causing delays is "budgetary constraints." This can be interpreted in two ways: either the Treasury has cut the overall amount of money available, or payments to the contractors cannot be made because the project costs have increased to the point where they cannot be covered by the current year's budget. The main stated government priority, through the MoD, has always been to fully meet the operational requirements of the country's armed forces. If we accept that at face value, the delays have meant that the services have had to continue to operate with old and inadequate equipment. By their own standards, and in purely military terms, successive governments failed to deliver what they promised.

Murphy's Law

The Eurofighter is a classic case of Murphy's Law applied to the defence industries of four countries. Things could go wrong, and they certainly did—on a
grand scale. Originally conceived in the mid-1980s as a joint project between the
aerospace industries of Britain, France, West Germany and Italy, the French
withdrew to develop their own Dassault Rafale. Spain opted in and was included
in the final agreement signed in November 1988. British Aerospace was the UK
lead company with Rolls-Royce supplying the EJ200 engines. The single-seater,
twin-engined aircraft was intended to have a primary air-to-air combat role with
a secondary air-to-surface capacity.

Ignoring the political changes in the Warsaw Pact countries, the military planners managed to persuade the politicians that the plane was still a necessity. The
RAF and the Ministry of Defence were vocal supporters. The Eurofighter was
given the development phase go-ahead just one year before the breach of the
Berlin Wall. The German Social Democrats were the only major opposition party
in the four countries to oppose the scheme. Money, jobs and technical resources
were committed, together with some of the most optimistic cost forecasts ever
made on a single military project.

The first major row between Britain and Germany broke out very quickly. The
Germans wanted to buy an updated version of a US radar system that they used
in their existing fighter aircraft. Ferranti had developed a more advanced but
untried system that had the backing of the British government. After a flurry of
diplomatic activity and lobbying, the Ferranti product was chosen. The company
was subsequently acquired by GEC-Marconi. The German Defence Minister was
then General Stoltenberg who was much more pro-Eurofighter and willing to
compromise than his successor Volker Rühe, a populist politician who showed no
reluctance to thump the negotiating table and play to the gallery of public opinion. He had well-publicised rows, not only with British ministers, but also with
Daimler-Benz, the German manufacturer in the project.

Eurofighter is extremely unpopular in Germany where its cost and the removal
of the threat from the East have made it seem more like an expensive toy for the
military than a defensive necessity. The German government found great difficulty in obtaining Parliamentary permission to allocate the huge chunks of extra
funding for the cost overruns. In 1995 its Defence Ministry avoided a debate by
a technical manoeuvre to allocate a further 375 million marks (over £168 million)
to pay the manufacturers. A reluctant Finance Ministry described it as an
"unplanned additional obligation."

In 1988 the manufacturers and government claimed that 20,000 people in

Britain would be employed on Eurofighter (directly or indirectly) when it went into full production. During the period of intensive lobbying in the early 1990s they revised the number upwards to 40,000 but when the UK production stage was announced in 1996, the figure had fallen to 14,000. Although Germany has a land area one-third greater than the UK and borders nine other countries, it plans to take only 180 aircraft compared with 232 for Britain. Italy has signed up for 121 and Spain 87. The allocation of work to each country is divided into the same proportions.

Understandably, the trade unions argued and lobbied for the continuation of the project. IG Metall, the German engineering union, was officially opposed to it but allowed its members in Bavaria—where the manufacturing plant is situated—to campaign to retain the work. The unions' dilemma was clear. There may have been no military or political justification for continuation but the problem was whether it was preferable to spend more to keep a project alive to save skills and technology or to stop throwing good money after bad. Unlike the civil sector, where there may be alternative customers, a cancelled military order means that jobs are lost immediately. In this case thousands of engineers and other skilled employees would have been thrown out of work with little chance of finding suitable employment. For them, sitting behind the wheel of a mini-cab instead of in front of a computer screen was not a welcome option.

The Eurofighter has been a financial disaster. The cost to Britain of just the development phase has risen from a planned £2.988 billion in 1988, when the project was approved, to £4.382 billion in 1997/8, an increase of £1.394 billion.[5] Total expenditure by this country will reach at least £16 billion. Each of the 232 aircraft will have cost over £60 million. It is already three years behind its scheduled delivery date. The government financial watchdog, the National Audit Office, has condemned the lack of financial controls and uncoordinated management. It is difficult to imagine a government committed to tight public expenditure allowing such generosity in any area except defence.

The four-country agreement to proceed to full production was signed in December 1997. While all those involved, particularly those whose jobs were at risk, breathed a sigh of relief, future cost and technical problems can reasonably be predicted. Sales needed to generate some profits may prove difficult to achieve.

The real lesson of Eurofighter is that before allocating such huge sums of money, government should undertake an objective assessment, politically as well as militarily driven, as to whether such a project is necessary. If the right questions had been asked at the right time, specifically when the Cold War was thawing, the answer might have been different. All resources are finite and those devoted to Eurofighter could have been spent profitably in support for civil aerospace, ultimately providing more jobs and better commercial prospects. That would have required a commitment by the defence manufacturers to shift their business emphasis to non-military products, a policy move they have so far declined to undertake.

Trident

The Thatcher government took the decision to buy the submarine-launched Trident missile system in July 1980. Even at the height of the Cold War it caused considerable controversy, protests and demonstrations. Fourteen years later and four years after the end of the Warsaw Pact, the first British Trident submarine *HMS Vanguard* began its inaugural patrol. Its companion *HMS Victorious* left Clydeside in 1995. Two more were scheduled for later delivery. Their range is 4,000 nautical miles and their underwater routes and cruising areas are secret. Only a direct order from the Prime Minister can launch their missiles at targets that are designated by code numbers. Russia is not one of these as Boris Yeltsin and John Major agreed that nuclear missiles would not be aimed at the other's country.

Trident's alternative targets are secret. The submarines can each carry 16 missiles with up to 12 warheads per missile. The Conservative government said that it would limit the total to a maximum of 96 warheads. Each of these could deliver 100 kilotons of nuclear explosive power—nearly eight times as much as the Hiroshima bomb. Even with the limit of 96 warheads a Trident submarine could hit six times more targets than Polaris.[6] John Major argued that President Clinton should end the moratorium on nuclear explosions in the US to allow the testing of British Trident warheads in Nevada. Clinton refused but it did clarify one of the reasons behind Major's vocal support for the widely-condemned French nuclear tests in 1996.

The move from Polaris to Trident in 1980 took British scientists by surprise and attempts to copy the American design of the warheads, to the extent of replicating the Los Alamos buildings in Berkshire, led to confusion, a delay of two years and an extra cost of £400 million.[7] Once again US assistance was requested. The missiles also have to be sent to Kings Bay, Georgia for servicing. In 1987 the National Audit Office revealed that most of the expenditure on the warhead's development and production would be spent in the US not Britain.[8] Our nuclear strike force would not exist without American permission.

The cost of the production of Trident was £12.153 billion by 1997. Unlike Eurofighter, there have been no major cost overruns on the submarine or missiles. The production costs, however, are only one part of the bill. Twice that amount may be needed to operate and refit the submarines over the next 25 years. This had always been denied by government. But in late 1997 Labour Defence Minister Lord John Gilbert was forced to admit to the House of Lords that £940 million was spent on non-production costs in that year, not the £200 million annual amount as claimed by previous ministers. Asked about the discrepancy, he said "Ministers always attempt to answer the question in the terms in which it has been phrased."[9] In other words, unless the question was drafted precisely, the answer was likely to be misleading.

There were also the costs of building the docks where Trident will be refitted. A contest for the contract had taken place in 1993 between the dockyards at Devonport in Plymouth and Rosyth in Fife. Accusations of electoral bribery in the South-West where the Conservatives were under pressure and anti-Scottish prejudice were levelled against the government after Devonport won the order. The Devonport bid was £237 million; £13 million lower than that of Rosyth. The Ministry of Defence had already spent £120 million of public money to start building a new dock at Rosyth in anticipation of the contract. Two years later, DML, the private consortium that runs Devonport, told the MoD that the actual costs would be about £100 million higher than its original bid. These then rose to £120 million—50 per cent above budget.[10]

The then Defence Secretary, cost conscious Mr Portillo, faced a problem. The dockyards had not yet been fully privatised. Should he allow MoD to do the work—the ministry had the capability—or should he carry on with the private contractor? The much lauded competitive element that was supposed to deliver a good deal for the taxpayer had disappeared. He took the decision to order the re-arrangement of the shareholdings of DML. That made Brown and Root, a subsidiary of a US company, the majority partner.

In June 1998 the National Audit Office reported that the final estimated cost would be £417 million.[11] The cost of the docks where Britain's 'independent' deterrent would be repaired had risen by 176 per cent (£180 million) and the money would be paid to a mainly American business.

Another strange episode had previously come to light in 1995 when the House of Commons Public Accounts Committee found that the two Trident operational bases at Faslane and Coulport on the Clyde had overrun their construction budget by £800 million, an unforeseen increase of 72 per cent. Sixty-seven companies employing 1,000 consultants were paid £240 million. Dr Malcolm McIntosh, head of defence procurement at the MoD, told the committee that, "We often hired our consultants on a pretty open-ended cost plus basis...we would say now that it is not a particularly clever way to hire consultants. A consultant...wants to maximise his return and that means he keeps going longer than he otherwise might."[12] Anyone who has ever had dealings with consultants could have told him that before the money was spent.

It was revealed in October 1997 that spare parts for Trident delivered in boxes from the US worth £2 million had gone missing. The MoD was stumped for an explanation but said the parts had been "mislaid." They decided to introduce a radical new working practice: "in future, boxes will be opened, checked and recorded."[13]

Tony Blair called the Labour Party's 1995 conference decision to support Trident a sign of "new maturity." That may be true in the narrow sense that the submarines and missiles cannot be "scrapped" instantly as some would wish. However, if he really wanted to deal with this costly reminder of a past political era, some original thinking would be needed. If his government continues to ignore the problem, new maturity may not seem too different from old dogma.

A wing and a prayer

The Phoenix was a mythical Egyptian bird that burned itself to death on a pyre every five hundred years and rose rejuvenated from the ashes. In Britain the Phoenix is a battlefield spy plane known as the "bugger-off" due to its habit of not returning after launch. Manufactured by GEC-Marconi Avionics, the Unmanned Air Vehicle (UAV), had cost £170 million out of a projected total of £230 million and was over six years late by 1995. It specifications were written in the early 1980s and its original purpose was to photograph Soviet artillery advancing across Europe. It was designed to fly over a battlefield guided by remote control, relay information, descend by parachute and land on its back to avoid damaging its surveillance equipment.

Unfortunately the propeller had a tendency to wear out, the descent was quicker than foreseen and the landing harder than the plane could withstand. The pieces then had to be collected. A car-style airbag, intended to cushion the impact, was fitted. The manufacturer, with a touch of understatement, told the House of Commons Defence Select Committee that the plane "has to be improved if we are going to take it into service."[14] The Committee also learned that the MoD had paid a further £16 million to the company above what should have been a fixed price contract. If this Phoenix does not rise from the ashes, the money already spent will have been wasted. If it does, it will cost even more, for an unknown military benefit.

Britain continued to develop weapons even when there was no demand for them. Trigat is an anti-tank missile with a long-range version designed to be launched from a helicopter or vehicle. This collaborative project between the UK, France and Germany cost Britain £128 million by 1996 with a further £66 million to be paid. There was one small problem—nobody wanted to buy it. In any other area of manufacturing it would thought prudent to discover whether there might be a demand for a product before committing large sums of money to its development. That, however, is not the way things work in the defence sector: the military decides something is necessary, the MoD commissions the manufacturers and the public pay for it. The Catch-22 for Trigat is that if Britain pulls out, we have to pay the cost of transferring the work to France or Germany. This is estimated at between £90-£170 million, making at least a total of £218 million, including the money already spent. That would be more expensive than the £194 million planned total cost of the project.[15] In the Alice in Wonderland economics of defence procurement, it is sometimes cheaper to continue than to cancel, even if there is no customer.

Mines do not distinguish between soldiers and civilians. Anti-personnel mines, some costing as little as three dollars each, still cover large areas of countries where wars have been fought. It is estimated that there are 120 million mines laid in 62 countries that continue to kill or maim 2,000 people each month. One of the legacies of the war in Afghanistan is 10 million unexploded mines. At the present rate of progress, these will take 4,000 years to clear. In Cambodia there are 30,000 amputees, the most recent victims of the killing fields.[16]

In 1996 the Conservative government refused to support a total ban on the export of anti-personnel mines despite pleas from the Red Cross and other humanitarian organisations. The blaze of publicity that surrounded Princess Diana's visit to victims in Angola put the government on the defensive and it leaked stories that she could not understand the "complexities" of the issue. In July 1998 Labour banned the use and export of mines.

The MoD was very keen on two other types of mines. The first was the anti-tank mine (ACEATM) whose development costs were forecast at £63 million. It was intended to be an 'intelligent' sideways-firing mine that could be hidden behind a bush and recognise an enemy tank. The intelligence of the MoD was questioned by former Defence Minister Alan Clark when he revealed in his memoirs that he thought it was a "complete waste of money, conceived at the height of the Cold War and now totally unnecessary." The logic of the civil servants who described its usefulness in slowing up the advance of the no-longer existing Warsaw Pact was such that he concluded: "I want to fire the whole lot. Instantly. Out, out. No 'District' commands, no golden bowlers, nothing. Out."[17]

The MoD officials hadn't improved their presentational skills by the time they met the House of Commons Defence Committee in 1994. They admitted that the mine could not distinguish between a civilian vehicle such as a Caterpillar Crawler and a tank. The Committee chairman asked: "You do not want to be a farmer with agricultural machinery going by?" Mr Julian Walker, MoD Director-General, Policy and Special Projects replied "No, a tractor especially." Surprisingly, the committee reported that they were disappointed that the programme had been delayed as the mine might have come in useful in Bosnia.[18] Bosnian tractor drivers might not have agreed.

The other mine was the Vehicle Launched Scatterable Mine System (VLSMS) which was designed to disperse mines from vehicles. After a set period of time the mines should destroy themselves. The problem was that no-one knew how many would be needed or at what cost. The MoD moved the target three times, contradicting themselves and confusing the Defence Committee. The original order was reduced in 1992. This made a saving of £6 million which then disappeared due to "costs elsewhere in the programme." The quantity was then increased in 1993 to make it more "cost effective." In April 1994 the MoD again reduced the number "as a result of the need to balance the VLSMS requirement with others within the Defence programme."[19]

Having misinformed the committee, the MoD was asked why it had changed its explanation. In the classic gobbledegook of a senior military civil servant under pressure, Mr Walker replied: "The number of mines....has gone up and down two or three times in the course of the programme, one of the more recent steps having been an up one, and that was the aspect which was seized upon in leading us to the statement that it was the increase in mines. In reality, the number of mines we have ended up with is more or less the same as we started with but having gone up and down in the meantime, but the difference in price arises from the fact that the original costs for the programme were based upon the company's very much preliminary estimates...so it is contractual prices which account for the new price, although as we go out for this final invitation to tender they have the opportunity to quote at a lower price if they wish."[20] It was not recorded whether or not a squadron of pigs flew overhead when Mr Walker made his point about lower prices. The committee noted that the MoD seemed to be "in some confusion" as to why the costs of the programme had jumped significantly over the £37 million originally forecast. The MoD said that the Treasury, usually so keen-eyed, had not questioned the increase.

When a car driver brakes too hard on a slippery surface, the vehicle often skids. The RB44 light truck, designed for towing artillery and Rapier missiles didn't skid, it went into a "controllable deviation," according to the manufacturer Reynolds Boughton/Renault. In fact it did this so often that all 800 delivered to the army were withdrawn from service on safety grounds. The RB44 was parked on military sites awaiting its fate. It was due to be withdrawn in 1999 at the end of its planned 'service' period.[21]

There are many other examples of MoD waste, delays and weapons that don't work. These include the European collaborative mobile radar system Cobra (8 years late due to "protracted negotiations between the three nations and four companies"); the GEC-Marconi Spearfish heavyweight torpedo (6 years late and £197 million over budget, "unforeseen technical difficulties"); the Westland/Augusta EH 101 Merlin helicopter (5 years overdue and a £760 cost overrun, "over optimism in the collaborative development programme") and Bowman, the ITT, Racal, Siemens Plessey combat radio system (6 years late, "budgetary restraints").[22]

Those MPs who sit on the House of Commons Defence Committee are chosen carefully for their caution and reliability; there are no wild-eyed radicals determined to undermine national security. The criticisms the committee have made of the MoD are pointed and accurate. Its main weakness is that it can only make recommendations *after* the mistakes have been discovered. However, if it were not for the committee, the public would be even less informed. It is not surprising, therefore, that MoD employs 160 public relations staff, far more than any other government department. Many national newspapers employ fewer journalists. The ministry does not promote its activities, the PR staff are there to divert or respond to criticism and enquiry.

Those who determine MoD policy obviously believe that the scope for public concern is sufficient to justify the employment of such a large number of experts in the art of swatting aside awkward questions. They are right; if such a waste of public money had taken place on a local council, on a much smaller scale, those responsible would have been jumped on by the district auditor and barred from holding office.

The good life

Class distinction continues to thrive in the services. The senior officers in their large residences and the troops in barracks or crumbling married quarters reflect a divide typical of the last century. Field Marshal Sir Richard Vincent was appointed to advise Nato on strategy in war-torn Bosnia. To assist him in carrying out his work, the MoD authorised (above his tax-free salary) the purchase of a £2 million Belgian mansion with £563,000 maintenance costs and £140,000 spent on furniture.

The ministry provided Admiral Sir Michael Layard, Chief of Naval Home Command, with a £500,000 home and expenditure of £63,000 in 1993 plus a further £2,500 on furniture. The Flag Officer of the Navy for the South-West, Admiral Sir Roy Newman, had a £500,000 house in Plymouth re-furbished at a cost of £80,700 plus furniture worth £24,000. The bill for his domestic staff was £142,200 a year. The Commander of Dartmouth Naval College got £50,000 for five dog kennels for the college and £25,000 for a 'his and hers' double garage for the two cars used by himself and his wife.

Air Chief Marshal Sir Sandy Wilson took early retirement when it was discovered, despite an MoD cover-up, that he had spent £380,000 of public money on his residence including £33,000 on carpets and curtains. Other examples of the good life include £424,000 spent on the former home of the Chief of Air Staff and a £494,000 conversion for the Commander-in Chief, Allied Forces North-West Europe.[23] The homes of the 77 most senior serving officers are worth an average of half a million pounds each. The MoD's amazing generosity with public money provides perks that match those of a director of a privatised gas, water or electricity company.

The ministry believes that the houses are part of our national heritage and need expensive maintenance. It says that hosting regimental dinners and entertaining foreign guests are onerous responsibilities. The hard-working staff running the Navy's re-settlement programme at Portsmouth are trying to find civilian work for the "surplus to requirements" lower ranks. They understand only too well the personal problems caused by the uncertainties of the labour and housing markets. The families of redundant Service people are forced to leave their less than luxurious married quarters while the Admirals, Generals and Air Marshals continue to live in a style befitting an officer and a gentleman.

The grand houses of the senior officers were not included in the scheme in 1994 to sell off 60,000 service homes through a £5.5 million quango set up by the MoD. The idea was that City bankers should take over the privatised estates with a guaranteed rate of return from the Treasury. The plan failed when, according to the MoD, the Treasury refused to provide the guarantee due to the collapse of the housing market and the problem of moving Service personnel around. The MoD seemed unaware that the housing market had been flat on its back for years. Two of the quango's directors received golden handshakes of a total of £375,000. Michael Portillo revived the scheme two years later by asking NatWest Markets, the investment bank, to find developers for the sites. Non-profit housing associations were barred from bidding.

The Treasury threatened that if the £1.6 million sale was not completed, it would cut the amount from new weapons programmes. A furore was caused when it was revealed that the houses would be sold to a Japanese-led consortium that included a bank whose chairman was the honorary treasurer of the Conservative Party. The government admitted that they paid £4 million to consultants for advice, including Sir Tim Bell, PR advisor to the party. Service families, supported by many Conservative MPs, were outraged that in future they would be dependent on a private landlord. Ten thousand of the service homes were empty. A short walk would take an MoD official from Whitehall to the Strand where dozens of homeless people sleep without hope of accommodation.

Jobs for the boys

The MoD is not only good at protecting its senior staff when they are in post, it also provides a velvet lined entry into the private sector when they decide to move on. This is known as the 'revolving door,' meaning that those leaving the MoD move seamlessly into employment with their chums in the main defence contractors and, increasingly, the lobbyists. If it was, literally, a revolving door it would be visible only as a blur, due to the speed at which it is turning. The term is a misnomer, as it implies that the door allows people through a wall or barrier.

There is no real barrier between the MoD procurement (purchasing) staff and those selling the manufacturer's products. They have the same background, military knowledge and may have worked together previously when the contractor's poacher was an MoD gamekeeper. The business is all about contacts, the vast majority informal—a word here—a phone call there. The military-industrial complex does not publicise its activities.

According to official guidelines, civil servants should no longer accept lunch, tickets to Wimbledon or similar events from suppliers. The head of the MoD fraud squad said: "Some companies target people. They can spot high-flyers quicker than the MoD and start working on them. Once such people have been promoted, the company already has them in its pocket."[24] There have been cases of blackmail over gifts but it is not the lunch or the time spent watching Steffi Graf that is the real issue. Whether Company A or Company B receives the contract is important to those companies but if neither is checked or supervised effectively on costs, after they have won the order, then whoever wins, the public loses.

The gamekeepers are turning poachers at an extremely rapid rate. British Aerospace is the largest British defence company. In two years, from 1992-94, the MoD granted approval for them to acquire 1 Air Vice-Marshal, 2 Vice-Admirals, 1 Rear Admiral, 5 Commanders RN, 1 Captain RN, 1 Lieutenant Commander, 3 Group Captains, 3 Wing Commanders, 1 Squadron Leader and 1 Lieutenant Colonel plus a number of other assorted officers.[25]

In the ten years 1984-94 approval was granted for 1,838 senior officers to take up defence industry employment. They included:
- Royal Navy: 30 Admirals, 5 Vice Admirals, 54 Rear Admirals, 88 Captains, 258 Commanders, 287 Lieutenant Commanders.
- Army: 16 Generals, 65 Major Generals, 77 Brigadiers, 71 Colonels, 125 Lieutenant Colonels.
- RAF: 13 Air Chief Marshals, 19 Air Marshals, 49 Air Vice Marshals, 51 Air Commodores, 92 Group Captains, 187 Wing Commanders, 174 Squadron Leaders.[26]

Unlike many redundant service personnel and defence employees, unemployment is not a problem frequently faced by top ex-MoD and Service staff.

Sir Peter Harding, Chief of the Defence Staff, resigned after his relationship with Lady Bienvenida Buck was revealed in the newspapers, together with some very unmilitary letters that he had written to her. Only nine months after his resignation he received a very warm *bienvenida* from GEC, whose head office is a short distance away from the Dorchester Hotel where he liaised with Lady Buck. He was appointed deputy chairman of GEC-Marconi and in an excellent position to promote the company when dealing with former subordinates.

Two years later the company acquired another well-known 'adviser' with an inside knowledge of defence matters. Jonathan Aitken, former Conservative Minister for Defence Procurement vanished from public life for a time after his failed libel case against *The Guardian* and Granada TV. He had lied when he said that he, not the Saudis, had paid for his stay at the Paris Ritz hotel. Said Ayas, the man who arranged for payment of the bill, alleged that Aitken was instrumental in saving the £5 billion second phase of the Al Yamamah arms contract with Saudi Arabia. He had persuaded King Fahd not to go ahead with the planned cancellation proposed by his brother Prince Sultan.[27] Aitken stated that the fact that he had lied for his country should be a "mitigating factor." GEC-Marconi gave him a fixed term contract in order to promote their sales in the Middle East. After some prevarication the company terminated Aitken's employment when he was arrested on suspicion of perjury and conspiring to pervert the course of justice.

The rules on a possible conflict of interest between the public interest and obtaining work after leaving government employment are extremely loose. All that is required is that if the appointment is within two years, approval has to be sought from the Advisory Committee on Business Appointments which under the Conservatives was chaired by their former minister Lord Carlisle. The government guidelines state that the application should be scrutinised if he or she "could be, or could be thought to be, significantly helpful to the employer where policy is developing."[28] That, of course, is precisely the reason they are recruited by the defence suppliers. They have few obvious civilian managerial or administrative skills that could make them valued employees. If the defence chiefs did not have the contacts, they would be of no use to their new employers. As they do, there can be no question that they influence MoD decisions. Some travel back and forth. Sir Colin Chandler, Chief Executive at Vickers, the tankmakers, moved from a company that is now part of British Aerospace (BAe) to become head of the government's Defence Export Services Organisation (DESO), the body originally set up by Denis Healey within the MoD to sell British military equipment overseas. He then transferred back to BAe as marketing director, in regular contact with DESO ex-colleagues, and then on to Vickers.

Ministers were hardly likely to question the motives of top military civil servants moving into the private sector as many of them have also been on the lookout for lucrative positions for themselves. In 1995 Richard Needham, a former trade minister, was appointed to the main board of GEC with a six-figure salary. He had close contacts with the company during his ministerial visits to Indonesia in 1993 and subsequently approved the export of Hawk aircraft to that country despite considerable controversy over Indonesian policy towards the population of East Timor. GEC supplies the electronic equipment for the Hawk and won an order to re-equip Indonesia's F-5 aircraft in 1995. Mr Needham also worked closely with the company in dealing with the run-down of its plant in Northern Ireland and in 1992 accompanied Lord Prior, GEC chairman, to China on a trade mission. He was vetted by Lord Carlisle's committee and given the all-clear. In 1997 he was paid a £247,000 salary by GEC, considerably more than his earnings as a minister.[29]

Winning friends and influencing people

As the big contracts become fewer, the companies are employing more lobbyists to press their case. They do not deal directly with the MoD, their role is to contact those who may be able to influence the decision. These include MPs whose constituency may be affected, local councils, chambers of commerce, trade unions and just about anybody who can open a door or pull a helpful lever. They spend a great deal of time and money and are extremely well rewarded by the companies, particularly if they are successful in winning the contract. A few companies, such as British Aerospace, prefer to have in-house lobbyists, sometimes known as public communications units. Journalists often complain that these departments don't respond to questions about take-over rumours, the sudden departure of a director or similar news items. They are misled by the title of the department; the purpose of the communications people is not to provide insights into what is happening in the company. Their primary aim is to promote and lobby, not to shed light on difficult issues.

Whether the companies get value for money from the lobbyists is open to question. An extremely polite, youngish man working for one of the larger organisations situated near the House of Commons invited me to lunch at the Royal Horseguards Hotel in Whitehall. This is a favourite rendezvous—just around the corner from the MoD—for those who wish to exchange quiet words. At some point between the melon and the trout, he revealed that his firm had been hired by one side in the competition for the replacement RAF transport aircraft. A European consortium, including British Aerospace, was promoting the 'Future Large Aircraft,' while the American company Lockheed and a group of other British manufacturers were pushing for an updated version of the old Hercules C-130. Both bids were being sold on the basis that large numbers of British employees would be involved and there was no doubt in his mind, he said, that jobs were the priority. His consortium would provide more of them than the other group, and in his briefcase he had the charts to prove it. He wanted to seek my advice on how his client's management could get their workforce motivated and organised to help win the bid. It was definitely all about jobs.

I suggested that company managers should explain the issue to their employees and then consult the union representatives on whether they wished to mount a campaign within their unions nationally and in the locality. They could also pay a visit to Westminster to see their local MPs. Such obvious advice appeared to him to be entirely original thinking. His gold pen squiggled in his notebook. He said he was extremely grateful for such "expert" guidance and signed the bill happily. Ten days later I was phoned by a lobbyist from the opposing consortium and I gave him the same helpful hints.

The gratitude expressed by the military suppliers to their friends in the MoD sometimes slides into illegality. Gordon Foxley was the ministry director in charge of buying ammunition for the armed forces until he was caught and convicted on twelve charges of receiving corrupt payments of a total of £1.3 million. The real amount is thought to be nearer £3.5 million. He was jailed for four years in May 1994, which seemed fairly lenient in view of the amount of money involved. Nobody knows the real figure as the MoD failed to gain access to the Swiss bank account where Foxley kept the payments he received from three foreign companies. The House of Commons Public Accounts Committee urged the ministry to redouble its efforts to obtain the information. From the MoD's point of view this was unfortunate as the more facts that come to light, the greater the ministry's potential embarrassment. It is not in its interests to uncover the results of its own ineptitude. Two of the three companies that bribed Foxley are still on the list of MoD suppliers.

Many millions of pounds were lost between 1985 and 1994 in the 191 cases of defence fraud that were discovered. The amount under investigation for 1993-94 when Foxley was convicted was £22 million. Welfare and warfare receive very different treatment from politicians and the media. In January 1996 a report revealed a £636 million loss of taxpayers' money paid in income support to fraudulent claimants.[30] The following day this became a major news item on national TV, radio and the press with politicians and pressure groups interviewed at length. The £645 million over-spent on military projects that were not completed on time received a few paragraphs in the broadsheet press. Both reports came from the National Audit Office.

The Labour government announced that it would prosecute individuals who wrongly attempt to obtain medicines without paying prescription charges. Telephone hotlines have been provided for people to inform on their neighbours who are working while claiming unemployment benefit. Fraud must be eliminated and public money saved. The US Department of Defense has a phone number available to allow confidential calls by defence employees and other insiders to provide information about price-fixing and over-charging. The British Ministry of Defence has no such facility.

The MoD is the country's second largest landowner with about 600,00 acres under its control—one per cent of Britain's total land area. Training areas and firing ranges account for 66 per cent of this space. Only the Forestry Commission is larger. Old shells and ammunition which may take decades to surface are buried across the firing areas. The best known of these is Salisbury Plain, more popular with New Age travellers communing with mystic forces at Stonehenge, than with squaddies charging around in mock battles. Opening up safe MoD land for recreational purposes and conservation would serve a far more useful purpose than having it fenced off from the British public, its nominal owners. Even some reasonably priced golf courses would be a tangible benefit. After all, the RAF is a keen supporter of the sport, it owns 25 courses around the country. In early 1998, the government told private landowners to open up blocked rights of way to the public within two years or it would introduce legislation to allow access. No such 'right to roam' was envisaged for Ministry of Defence land.

Dr Malcolm McIntosh, then head of MoD procurement, moved into his new headquarters in December 1995. Abbey Wood, the £254 million complex near Bristol, should have housed 7,800 staff but only 4,300 are employed there. They enjoy a pleasant environment with lakes, landscaped gardens, a miniature suspension bridge, a gymnasium, shops, 230 bathrooms for the most senior staff and a car park for 3,500.[31] The business of weapons purchase now takes place in a civilised environment rather than in poky little offices in Whitehall. At Abbey Wood the civil servants go about their work in the Northumbrian slate avenues of the buildings or chat in the cafes and restaurant. The banana skin that frequently ends up under the feet of the MoD also materialised at Abbey Wood. A furious controversy broke out between the ministry and John Mowlem, the builders. The MoD claimed £20 million compensation for delays and alleged poor performance by the contractor. The ministry's Permanent Secretary instructed lawyers not to pay Mowlem.

The MoD is not only responsible for the nation's defences but is also the possessor of an estimated £5 million art collection. Or rather *was*, as about one-fifth has disappeared. The National Audit Office found that the ministry had lost 161 paintings and prints, 23 of which were stolen. One painting worth £400,000 was put up for auction by a 'trust' of officers after their regiment was disbanded. The sale was stopped by the regiment's solicitors. Others went missing in transit, some were damaged by being hung over fireplaces, and in one case, a hot servery.[32] The NAO did not say whether they believed burglars were responsible for the disappearances or whether the paintings had just fallen off the back of an army lorry.

Waking up to the present

If the MoD's management of weaponry costs and property has not been total, it's understanding of social trends has been virtually zero. Its insistence that women should leave the armed forces if they became pregnant cost public funds £55 million in compensation, even though the ministry admitted that it knew that it had breached European law. Over 5,000 claims were conceded.[33] Servicewomen who may be considering having children can now be confident that the MoD has their best interests at heart as it has bought 4,000 maternity outfits in blue for the RAF and Royal Navy, and in green for the army.[34]

Long-term women partners of servicemen are treated as 'wives' for social and housing purposes even though they may not be married. If, however, their 'husband' has the misfortune to be killed in action or accidentally, they do not become 'widows.' The Ministry of Defence refuses to provide the normal pension that goes to the widow of a deceased serviceman. If they have children they are treated as single mothers and have to rely on state benefits.[35]

Gays and lesbians have also had a tough time. Although four homosexuals who had been dismissed from the armed forces lost a High Court case against the MoD, the judge commented that he thought the ban was unlikely to survive much longer. The Chiefs of Staff were adamantly opposed to any change. Sir Hugo White, Commander-in Chief of the Fleet, wrote in a memo that a "discreet survey" in the Fleet had revealed that some people thought that he and his colleagues had accepted a change of policy. That was not true, he said. They were "vigorously defending the status quo." Churchill made his view of such matters clear when he said: "Don't talk to me of naval tradition. It's nothing but rum, sodomy and the lash."

Sir Hugo did not say why he thought the ability to put on a uniform and be prepared to kill people were purely heterosexual qualities. The private lives of many past and present military heroes, particularly the Greeks, would certainly not have met with his approval. Tony Banks, then a Labour back-bencher, later Minister of Sport, asked during a Parliamentary debate whether there was not an inconsistency if a Defence Minister was gay while it was unlawful for homosexuals to be in the armed forces? The questions that day were being answered by Nicholas Soames, the rotund Minister for the Armed Forces who confirmed the government's ban. He said he had: "rarely found the government to be inconsistent."

The insensitivity of the MoD to individual problems is a matter of record. It took three years of complaints and, eventually, pressure from Parliament and the media, to force it to agree to open an inquiry into Gulf War syndrome. Its meanminded attitude in refusing to release medical records of those who served in the Gulf was an attempt to avoid a public admission that troops may have been exposed to toxic substances. It consistently denied, then admitted, that organophosphate pesticides were used by British forces. Depleted uranium tipped shells were used against Iraqi tanks. Troops who were sent to clean up after the fighting in areas where the shells were used claimed exposure to cancer-causing radioactive substances. The dosimeters that measured the levels of radiation and were issued to individual troops have disappeared. The Armed Forces Minister wrote to an afflicted ex-soldier who had worn the device denying that they were ever issued.[36]

Immunisation against chemical or biological agents was compulsory for British and American forces in the Gulf and some believe this caused their problems. Early evidence from the US indicated that this may be the case. The House of Commons Defence Committee, which was critical of the "torpor" of the MoD, noted that French troops in the Gulf did not receive injections and that there have been no complaints from them about Gulf War Syndrome.[37] The US government agreed, albeit reluctantly, to pay £100 million for research and treatment of sufferers. The Freedom of Information Act enabled US veterans to obtain the facts they needed to press their government to take action. It is easier to obtain information from American sources about what happened to British troops in the Gulf than it is from the files of the MoD.

After a barrage of public criticism the MoD executed a U-turn and agreed to initiate a research programme into possible causes. The minister, Nicholas Soames, after two years of bluffing, apologised to the House of Commons, but shifted the blame to civil servants for having "misled" him. The Labour Armed Forces Minister John Reid ordered new and wider research into the causes. If the existence of illnesses caused by service in the Gulf and MoD negligence in not taking sufficient precautions can be proved, the way will be open for families to sue for financial compensation. That is what the ministry fears most.

Many thousands of black people fought and risked their lives for Britain in the last world war. A great number came from parts of the Empire where British rule allowed them little of the democracy that was being defended in the war against Hitler and fascism. Today racism has deep roots in service life and the MoD has done little to eradicate it. Despite a shortfall of 2,500 in the infantry alone, only 1 per cent of those recruited in 1995 came from ethnic minorities. It took an investigation by the Commission for Racial Equality to stir the ministry into action. In 1992, Corporal James Malcolm was due to transfer from the Royal Electrical and Mechanical Engineers to the Life Guards, now part of the Household Cavalry. The transfer was cancelled when it was discovered he was black. No black or Asian soldier was recruited to the regiment between 1989 and 1994. The Guards Regiments are virtually all white. The CRE found evidence of "institutional racism."

The Office for Public Management, a private consultancy commissioned by the MoD, said that the RAF had an unwritten rule: "no blacks, Pakis, spots or specs on VIP parades."[38] If the people in the MoD had been more in touch with real life and understood something about civil liberties, they would have been be able to avoid many of their embarrassing and expensive public gaffes. Labour defence ministers have said that they will not tolerate discrimination and action will be taken to eradicate it. In April 1998 the Household Cavalry and five Guards regiments were given 30 months to recruit more than 200 black and Asian soldiers.[39] In 1998 only 323 out of a total of 32,625 officers in the armed forces were from ethnic minorities.[40] That was 6 more than in 1997.

Major Eric Joyce, a serving officer, wrote a pamphlet in 1997 claiming that racism, sexism and snobbery were integral parts of life in the military.[41] He said that the public schools provided the overwhelming majority of officers while the other ranks came from state schools. This criticism caused the crustier members of the military establishment to choke on their brandy. Colonel Mike Dewar of the Royal Green Jackets and editor of *The Officer* magazine said many felt Joyce had "stabbed his fellow officers in the back."[42] In February 1998 Major Joyce's commanding officer said that he was "unemployable" and issued him with his discharge papers. No officer had been expelled from the services for racism.

The Ministry of Defence was allocated £21.12 billion worth of public money in 1997-8.[43] The budget for 1997 was overspent by £246 million, including £16.3 million lost on advances on individuals' pay. These were never recovered. The Comptroller of the National Audit Office, Sir John Bourne said: "there was no central point within the department that had control over, or complete visibility of, all postings to the account."[44] The MoD spent £2 million on receptions and drinks parties in the first six months of the Labour government.[45]

If the MoD had spent its budget wisely, it could be argued that we were getting value for money. The evidence, however, points to gross mismanagement, waste and cover-up. William Pitt the Younger—Prime Minister at the end of the 18th century—created the first national income tax to finance the costly and largely unsuccessful Napoleonic Wars. Two hundred years later the British people continue to pay a high price for overblown military ambitions.

References

1 *Thatcher's Gold. The Life and Times of Mark Thatcher.* Paul Halloran and Mark Hollingsworth. Simon & Schuster 1995.

2 *The Time of My Life.* Denis Healey.

3 *Britain's Defence Procurement.* Ministry of Defence 1993.

4 *Ministry of Defence: Major Projects Report 1997.* National Audit Office. The Stationery Office.

5 *Ibid.*

6 *SIPRI Yearbook 1994.* Oxford University Press.

7 *The UK Trident Programme—Secrecy and Dependence in the 1990s.* The British American Security Council (BASIC) Report 93.5 1993.

8 *Ibid.*

9 *The Observer* 4 January 1998.

10 *Sunday Times* 16 February 1997.

11 *Sales of the Royal Dockyards.* National Audit Office. Stationery Office.

12 *Management of the Trident Works Programme.* House of Commons Committee of Public Accounts 1994.

13 *The Guardian* 6 October 1997.

14 *Jane's Defence Weekly* 25 March 1995.

15 *Defence Procurement: Certain Projects And Accounting For Inflation.* House of Commons Defence Committee September 1994.

16 *The Observer* 9 July 1995.

17 *Diaries.* Alan Clark. Weidenfeld & Nicholson 1993.

18 *Defence Procurement.* House of Commons Defence Committee September 1994.

19 *Ibid.*

20 *Ibid.*

21 *The Sunday Times* 28 January 1996.

22 *Ministry of Defence: Major Projects Report 1997.*

23 *The Mail on Sunday* 12 February 1995.

24 *The Times* 3 March 1995.

25 Letter from Roger Freeman, Minister of State for Defence Procurement, to Derek Fatchett MP 1 December 1994.

26 *Hansard* 8 December 1994. Written Answer from Roger Freeman to Dale Campbell-Savours MP.

27 *Daily Telegraph* 21 May 1998.

28 *Sunday Times* 22 January 1995.

29 *GEC Annual Report and Accounts 1997.*

30 *The Times* 25 January 1996.

31 *The Guardian* 23 November 1995.

32 *Ibid.* 6 March 1996.

33 *Ibid.* 14 February 1996.

34 *The Times* 3 October 1995.

35 *The Observer* 1 February 1998.

36 *Riding the Storm.* Channel 4 TV programme January 1996.

37 *Trust and Verify.* Bulletin No. 62 November 1995 of the Verification Technology Information Centre.

38 *The Times* 21 March 1997.

39 *Ibid.* 6 April 1998.

40 *UK Defence Statistics* 1998. Stationery Office.

41 *Arms and the Man.* Fabian Society 1997.

42 *The Sunday Times* 1 February 1998.

43 *UK Defence Statistics 1997.* HMSO.

44 *Financial Times* and *The Times* 30 January 1998.

45 *Independent on Sunday* 14 December 1997.

CHAPTER FIVE

THE HARD SELL

From now onwards, the average percentage that goes to export will have to be 50 per cent if we are to maintain the British defence industry in its current size and form.

Charles Masefield, head of the government's Defence Exports Services Organisation
September 1995.

Article 51 of the United Nations Charter states that every country has the right to manufacture or buy weapons to protect itself. Some countries do not have the means to produce even the most basic requirements and have to look to overseas suppliers to provide the necessary equipment. This presents both problems and possibilities for both buyers and sellers. For the buyer the first problem is money. Many importers of weapons do not have strong economies and defence inflation has consistently outstripped civil prices. If a country gives priority to buying arms, it will be at the expense of general economic development. A second problem is that heavy dependency on one major supplier can create political subordination, even between relatively large and independent countries.

On the other hand, if the buyer is sufficiently wealthy, it can boost purchases to a level where the supplier's military industries, if they are losing markets elsewhere, need those sales to survive. The buyer can then exert considerable political influence over the government of the supplier. That turnaround is now at the heart of the relationship between Britain and Saudi Arabia, our largest arms customer. The opportunities for the supplier lie mainly in the ability to increase overseas sales revenue to compensate for the loss of domestic orders. The danger is that over-reliance on foreign orders will be at the expense of efforts to create alternative civil products. This leads to frantic efforts to increase exports in a smaller world market that is increasingly crowded with more competitors.

Government as sales agent

By the mid-1960s, the British government had become worried about the growing US dominance of the arms markets of the pro-Western countries. The economic power of the Americans was easily outpunching Britain's efforts which were largely confined to areas of past influence and colonial rule. Washington had created a weapons marketing body called 'International Logistics Negotiations' headed by Henry Kuss, a Pentagon salesman who sold his products with "missionary zeal."[1] Such an organisation appealed to the technocratic instincts of the Labour government which under Harold Wilson was busily re-organising British industry and promoting the benefits of the: "white heat of the technological revolution."

The Secretary of State for Defence was Denis Healey, strongly anti-Communist, and possessor of a nasty right hook for those who got in his way. He was worried about the inefficiencies and contradictions between the political, military and industrial aspects of the defence business. He asked Donald Stokes, head of Leyland Motors, to enquire into the feasibility of a defence sales organisation. Unsurprisingly, Stokes recommended such a body and Healey nominated Raymond Brown of Racal, the electronics company, to become the boss of the Defence Export Sales Organisation (DESO) Brown wasn't keen on the name and suggested Export International Relations which, presumably, was an intentionally meaningless title. His point was taken years later when the 'sales' in DESO became the bland 'services.'

Healey's highly readable autobiography, so detailed in many aspects of less noteworthy events, passes quickly over the formation and activities of DESO. In an interview for a TV programme in 1995, he said that now he didn't feel "all that happy" about the organisation but that it was formed at the height of the Cold War. He also said that its main purpose was "to reduce unit costs of weapons by selling some abroad—I'll be quite frank about that."[2] In his formal statement to the House of Commons in January 1966, Healey said: "while the government attaches the highest importance to making progress in the field of arms control and disarmament, we must also take what practical steps we can to ensure that this country does not fail to secure its rightful share of this valuable commercial market."[3] Subsequent public justification was more to do with supporting allies, maintaining regional stability and fending off the Communist threat rather than selling more abroad to enable cheaper production at home.

The latter-day, avuncular Lord Healey, who opposes the expansion of Nato, seemed to have more doubts about the purpose of DESO than he did as Defence Secretary. It is now clear that arms sales never created stability and the scramble for a share of the weapons markets led to corruption, over-spending and, far from economies of scale, costs went through the roof. We seem to have learnt little as DESO still perpetuates the myth that this unstable industry can sell itself out of trouble. The bottom line is that its existence depends on military threats; real, imagined or invented, plus sufficient wealthy customers to buy the equipment. Defence budgets are shrinking throughout the world and the hard sell is becoming harder.

Surprisingly, thirty years later, the Labour Party document on the defence industry echoed Healey's Parliamentary words of 1966. It said: "the export of defence goods is vital for the long-term prosperity of the UK defence industrial base as it permits British companies to lower development costs through larger production runs and thus make savings estimated at £300 million per annum." It went on, however, to say: "Labour will not will not sell weapons to regimes which would use them for repressive purposes or to threaten or invade neighbouring countries."[4] Perhaps its policy-makers did not consider the full implications of the two statements, as in practice they could well be contradictory. The human rights record of Saudi Arabia is appalling but it buys half of Britain's defence exports. Which should take priority; opposition to repression or the "vital" export of weaponry? The Saudi connection has been crucial to Britain's credibility as a leading exporter of weapons. Of the top ten countries that bought British weapons during the period 1988-92, the Saudis took over 50 per cent of the total.[5]

Selling to the Saudis

The Central Intelligence Agency (CIA) World Factbook lists each nation in the world and its political system. Under the Saudi heading it says: "Constitution: none. Suffrage: none. Political parties and leaders: none allowed."[6] After the Gulf War 20,000 Iraqi refugees fled from Saddam Hussein to Saudi Arabia. The Minnesota Lawyers' Human Rights Committee and other organisations obtained evidence that they were placed in the Rafha desert camp in oppressive conditions with temperatures rising to 120 degrees in the shade. When they protested, demanding better conditions, they were fired on by the Saudi security forces. All requests by human rights organisations to visit the camp were refused. Trade unions in the oil industry were crushed in 1962 and their leaders disappeared.[7] There have been many more instances of repression, not to mention torture, public executions and the enforced servility of women.

It is not difficult to upset the Saudi rulers and they alarmed the defence exporters when they threatened to drop Britain from their list of favoured suppliers. What had enraged the House of Saud was that a group of pro-democracy activists based in North London had managed to pierce its blanket censorship by faxing bulletins to Saudi readers. The Home Office's attempt to deport the dissident Dr Muhammed al-Mas'ari for allegedly endangering British sales to Saudi Arabia was based purely on pressure from manufacturers anxious to cling on to a customer that represented their main but insecure foothold in the world arms market. The defence companies and visiting British ministers had been threatened by the Saudis that future contracts were at risk. The companies responded by working behind the scenes, using their informal contacts with the government to get al-Mas'ari expelled. Much to their dismay they found their discreet correspondence splashed across media headlines. Their memos were also interesting in that they revealed that King Fahd was not altogether unhappy about the London faxes as they mostly criticised his brother Prince Sultan, a possible contender for the throne.

The accident-prone Home Office Minister, Anne Widdecombe, was wheeled out to explain the government's position and, seemingly forgetting her departmental brief about the rights and wrongs of political asylum, blurted out that the decision had been taken on commercial grounds. Other Conservative ministers who had never been heard expressing concern for the 180,000 defence jobs lost since 1990 through government cuts, suddenly became advocates of full employment in the industry. The Labour front-bench response was muted as it worried about reaction in defence dependent constituencies. Jack Straw, shadow Home Secretary, said he couldn't comment as he "hadn't seen the (case) papers." The Prime Minister of the small Caribbean island of Dominica agreed to accept al-Mas'ari as a refugee but other parties on the island protested and the offer was withdrawn. Britain had increased aid to the country a few weeks beforehand.

The Chief Immigration Adjudicator, Judge David Pearl, threw out Home Secretary Michael Howard's application and told him to re-consider. He also accused him of trying to circumvent the United Nations Convention on Refugees for "diplomatic and trade reasons." What was intended as a smooth operation had blown up in the government's face. After further unsuccessful attempts to find a country that would accept al-Mas'ari, the Home Office gave up and allowed him to stay for at least four years. One of the consequences was that the BBC decided to close its Arabic television service broadcasting to Saudi Arabia as its partner company, Orbit Communications, based in Rome, had censored its reports on the al-Mas'ari issue. Orbit was owned by Prince Khalid, a cousin of the Saudi King Fahd. The result of the whole affair was that the British government had been made to look vindictive and foolish, the Saudis became even more angry and the Arab world lost access to an independent news source. Appropriately, the Arabic meaning of al-Mas'ari is "Lighter of Fires."

The dissident

For someone facing a death sentence in his own country and possible deportation from Britain, Dr Mohammed al-Mas'ari was in a surprisingly upbeat mood when I met him in the Westminster office of George Galloway MP on a freezing morning during Ramadan, the Muslim period of fasting. He and his then colleague Dr Saad al-Fagih, the General Secretary of the Committee for the Defence of Legitimate Rights, expressed no resentment about their predicament and answered questions frankly and with optimism. They did not attempt to hide their adherence to certain fundamental aspects of Islamic law, including the death penalty. Despite this, al-Mas'ari is regarded by the Saudi establishment as an extreme liberal. He was tried, found guilty of heresy by an ecclesiastical court and sentenced to death. One of the main accusations was his advocacy of the right of women to drive and to have improved access to education and jobs.

The members of the House of Saud are followers of the puritanical Wahhabi sect and he objected to their denial of the right of their people to have a free debate about the teachings and interpretation of Islam. He emphasised the point that the ulemas, the religious leaders, had become alienated from the rulers, not only because of the rise of the Islamic political movements in the Middle East but also because they believed that the royal family had under-funded and ignored the official religion. The Saudi flag contains their religious symbol and they felt that the rulers act without regard for them and the people.

He explained that the population had become extremely resentful as they have not received any real increase in basic wages for the past twenty years. Even King Fahd admitted, in a top secret telegram sent to the consultative assembly in August 1994, that the economic situation started to deteriorate rapidly after the oil surplus was exhausted in 1987. The ruler complained that Saudi citizens were paying too little for water, electricity, fuel and telecommunications and did not appreciate the difficulties. He raised prices, including those of Saudi Airlines.[8] Dr al-Mas'ari explained that average income had fallen from $17,000 per annum during the oil boom to around $3,800 in 1996. About 3,000 contractors were owed around $60 billion. The commissions and kickbacks were talked about openly, as were the Saudi dollar billionaires with their cash stashed safely in the Bahamas.

The mention of Mrs Thatcher's name rarely provokes laughter but it was clear that her involvement in his country's business was a source of interest and amusement to him. He told the story of when she first visited Saudi Arabia during the reign of King Khaled, Fahd's elder brother and predecessor. She had been tipped off that Khaled was not too intelligent and that Fahd was the man to watch. After the meeting, she said she was disappointed, Fahd had not impressed her and had hardly spoken. It was pointed out to her gently that he would not speak, it was the Saudi tradition of deference and respect for his elder brother that had kept him silent. She immediately requested an early meeting with Fahd which was lengthy and held in secret, with only an interpreter present. Al-Mas'ari believed that these were the preliminary discussions on the vast Al Yamamah arms deal.

When I raised the question of her son Mark's possible role in the deal, it again provoked a smile. He said that everyone in the country's business community believed Mark was involved and that he had received substantial payments. The offer of the services of the son of the British Prime Minister would have been impossible to refuse, even if he had no expertise in the arms business. From the Saudi view, it would have been improper not to have made him feel an important participant. Al-Mas'ari admitted freely that there was as yet no hard evidence to prove this, at least "not until someone obtains the key to a Prince's safe."

Dr al-Mas'ari and Dr al-Fagih have since fallen out. The latter formed a separate organisation and planned to set up a TV transmitter in his back garden to beam his message back to Saudi Arabia. A *jihad* of old religion and new technology looked likely to cause even more problems for the ruling family.

Relying on the Saudis

The power relationship between Britain and Saudi Arabia has shifted substantially since the kingdom was founded. Britain was instrumental in establishing Ibn Saud and his Ikhwan allies as the dominant force in the area during the period between the two world wars. One critical commentator estimates that 400,000 people, including women and children, were killed in the massacres of tribes opposed to Ibn Saud.[9] The ruler liked to display his military prowess by wielding the execution sword himself. Britain's covert support with arms and finance for Ibn Saud was in breach of the 1915 Treaty of Darea but was crucial to his success. A British representative, Lord Crewe, said: "What we want is not a united Arabia, but a disunited Arabia, split into territories under our suzerainity."[10] Saudi Arabia was established in 1932.

At first, Ibn Saud was militarily and politically dependent on Britain as oil had not yet been discovered in any great quantities. The country was poor. A British company, the Eastern General Syndicate, was granted the first oil concession in 1923 but did little to exploit it. Harry St John Philby, the father of the spy Kim Philby, was Ibn Saud's most trusted foreign advisor and tried unsuccessfully to interest other UK companies. Standard Oil of New Jersey eventually won the concession in an auction with a bid of $250,000 despite Ibn Saud's preference for the British. At the ratification ceremony the American company's representative presented the Saudi ruler with a box of Californian dates.

Subsequent US administrations must have regarded the initial investment of a quarter of a million dollars and some dates as extremely good business in a country that would eventually own 25 per cent of the world's oil reserves. Britain's attitude was typified by Winston Churchill who insisted on smoking and knocking back whisky when he met the abstemious Ibn Saud. Churchill explained that it was a "sacred rule of his life" that he should smoke cigars and drink before, after and during meals.[11] The king was shocked although he might have been even more surprised at the current antics of his descendants in the casinos and night clubs of Europe.

After the Second World War, the problems caused by Britain's lack of foresight and funds were compounded by the drive of the Americans to consolidate and extend their influence over Saudi Arabia. In 1950, the US oil company Aramco concluded a deal with the ruling family which split the oil revenues equally between them. This effectively removed Britain from any control over the Saudi economy and linked the House of Saud and the US government together in an alliance that was politically convenient for both parties. The Saudis saw it as a counter to Arab nationalism; the Americans as part of the crusade against Communism. The US became the main exporters of military hardware to the kingdom; the Saudis bought the most expensive stuff available. The only restraint on the shipment of American arms to the Middle East was the existence in the USA of the extremely powerful pro-Israel lobby. This pressure group was only too well aware of the anti-Semitism of the Saudi rulers and was able to block the export of equipment that could be used against Israel.

British defence company directors often referred approvingly to these restrictions as though they were part of their own export campaign in the Middle East. They were certainly a useful card in negotiations with potential Arab customers. However, US senators and members of Congress who were aware of Jewish sensitivities, particularly at election time, are now vocal supporters of arms transfers to the region. Unemployment in the defence industries is a big issue with the voters in California and other states. The Americans are determined to dislodge Britain, particularly in aircraft sales, and will use all forms of pressure, from the President to the Pentagon to achieve their aims. Post-Gulf War sales to the Arabian peninsula show that they have had some success. There is no love lost between the transatlantic cousins in the battle for defence exports.

Political restraints on the US arms trade allowed the British companies scope for major sales to Saudi Arabia. In 1985 the two countries signed the world's biggest arms agreement, named Al Yamamah ('The Dove of Peace'). After the rumoured involvement of Mark Thatcher in the deal, industry cynics suggested it should have been called "Who's ya mama?" Yamamah 2, a huge extension of the original agreement, was signed in 1988. The hardware on order included Tornado fighters, Hawk ground attack/trainers, Black Hawk helicopters from Westland, mine hunters from Vosper Thorneycroft, missiles and spares. There are no official figures on the value of the contracts, estimates vary between £20-£30 billion. Most arms deals consist of an order for a certain amount of equipment (with further options at the end of the contract), specified delivery times, firm prices at a fixed exchange rate and the currency in which it is to be paid (usually dollars). Al Yamamah is different. Payment is made in barrels of oil—about 400,000 per day[12]—which are then sold on the open market by companies acting as brokers for the British government. The revenue earned is placed in an MoD account. The ministry then pays British Aerospace, the prime contractor, a sum estimated at £2 billion annually.

How the deals are done

Commissions, paid by contractors to the go-betweens, middlemen and members of the Saudi royal family, are commonplace. British Aerospace is honest enough not to deny that they pay such commissions. United States legislation forbids this practice. Thorn EMI admitted paying 25 per cent in commissions to a Saudi and a British businessman on a £40 million order for 4,500 bomb fuse assemblies as part of the Al Yamamah agreement. The payments, which were lodged in an offshore bank in the Bahamas, were paid in three parts—two of just under 12 per cent and one of 2 per cent. Significantly, the Thorn EMI company handbook for senior staff stated in the section "Sensitive Payments" that any commission in excess of 12 per cent must be reported to the main board. The Bahamas payments were de-sensitised by each being kept below that limit. Sir Colin Southgate, company chairman, said that the payment of commissions: "is normal in some markets." Roger Freeman the Procurement Minister had previously stated: "the transaction between Her Majesty's Government and Saudi Arabia was on a government-to-government basis and no agents or middlemen were involved." John Hakes, former managing director of Thorn's defence systems, took a slightly different view. "Commissions make the world go round...I don't know of a (Saudi) royal who'll get out of bed for less than 5 per cent."[13]

Rolls-Royce, the aero-engine manufacturer, was forced in 1998 to offer £23 million in compensation after AEDC, a company registered in Panama, alleged that it had not been paid in full on commissions of up to 15 per cent as part of the Al Yamamah deal. The offer was rejected as too low. Jonathan Aitken was a director of BMARC, one of whose executives—the appropriately named Mr David Trigger—revealed during Aitken's High Court case against *The Guardian* and Grenada TV that he had been involved in the payment of commissions on Al Yamamah. The orders related to Royal Ordnance, part of British Aerospace. Mr Trigger pleaded confidentiality on the amount, saying: "my understanding is that all my work connected with that contract is governed by the Official Secrets Act."[14]

Graft, backhanders, bribes, fiddles and, of course, commissions are traditional methods of winning overseas arms orders. The National Audit Office investigated the Al Yamamah contract but the House of Commons Public Accounts Committee, chaired by the Labour MP Robert Sheldon, refused to publish the evidence, claiming that they had found no evidence of wrong-doing. If that was the case, why were they so reticent? A body so named might be thought to be accountable to the public.

The man who probably knows as much as anyone else—outside Saudi Arabia—about the workings of the Saudi system is Said Aburish, a Palestinian by birth and now resident in London. He is the author of the book *The Rise, Corruption and Coming Fall of the House of Saud*. This sold extremely well in the West and smuggled copies cost $150 in Saudi Arabia. He has first-hand experience of the Middle East arms trade and Saudi affairs and once worked for the pre-Saddam Iraqi government. I went to see him at his flat in West London.

We discussed future sales opportunities in the region for Western defence manufacturers and he had no hesitation in saying that "the bonanza days" of the past two decades are well and truly over. He said there is a consensus amongst oilmen that the price of oil will fall sharply, especially when Iraq returns to the world market. This will be a heavy blow to the economies of the oil producing countries. Saudi expenditure on health and education has been falling at between 10-15 per cent a year and the whole system is under strain. The cost per Saudi soldier is five times that of a US equivalent and the Saudi Air Force has the highest ratio of combat aircraft to personnel in the world.

Aburish explained that commissions paid on Saudi deals comprise three main types:

1. Direct payments from the supplier to his agent.
2. Those shared between the agent and his mentor in the royal family.
3. Indirect payments, which fall into two categories:
   a) Offset arrangements, where around 30 per cent of a contract is placed with a Saudi company for, say, maintenance, food, housing, etc. These will be charged to the overseas contractor at often double the real cost. They escape foreign anti-corruption laws as they are internal Saudi business.
   b) Barter arrangements, such as Al Yamamah, for weapons sold in exchange for oil. For example, 400,000 barrels of oil, as agreed between the parties, will be transferred in one day from Saudi Arabia to the military supplier's agent in Rotterdam. However, a delivery of 440,000 barrels will be recorded in the official Saudi books. The extra 40,000 barrels will be diverted and sold separately. The proceeds of this sale will be kept by the Saudi dealer and his friends.

Depending on the size and type of the contract, this flexible and lucrative system can provide for all or some of these types of commission. A big deal could comprise a direct commission *plus* money from the offset and sub-contracting programmes *plus* the difference between the real and the false (booked) amount of oil sold through a barter deal. Commissions can amount up to 40 per cent of the total price of a contract. Aburish said that the unspoken agreement between both sides engaged in these forms of corruption is that everybody becomes equally implicated in order to silence any likely whistle-blowers.

Payment to a relative of someone prominent in a Western government, such as the son of a Prime Minister, would be an effective means of ensuring silence even though that relative may have little direct involvement. He regards any British assertion that government to government deals do not involve commissions as "camel's dung."

Despite secrecy and a closed society, he said many Saudis are increasingly resentful of Western pressure to turn the country into an expensive arms dump.

They talk of the royal extravagance, the commissions and the fact that the armed services cannot handle the hardware already delivered. With only 62 per cent of the population over the age of fifteen able to read or write (48 per cent of women) it is proving difficult to obtain the people capable of meeting the training levels necessary for the high technology equipment. This problem is complicated by the fact that the ruling family, wary of a coup, recruit mainly relatives, friends and timeservers to the top positions in the armed forces. Haphazard purchases from a variety of Western countries means that there is little integration of equipment and common standards are rare. American, British and French tanks, all of different design and performance, were bought after protracted haggling and political pressure. They do not constitute an effective armoured corps.

Said Aburish emphasised his conviction that while the Saudi rulers may wish to sustain high levels of arms expenditure, the economy could not stand the strain. Islamic fundamentalism was now deeply rooted in the kingdom and would present a growing threat to both the royal family and the prospects for Western arms sales.

An economy in trouble

The Saudi economy, despite an image of unlimited wealth, is in increasingly bad shape. The 1996 budget of £26.78 billion forecast a deficit of £3.3 billion, compared with £2.67 billion in 1995. The cost of defence in 1995 was £8.76 billion— around one-third of the total budget.[15] In the period 1990-95, military spending took 57 per cent of the budget, three times as much as education and six times that of health and social development.[16] Saudi arms purchases in 1993 were 85 per cent of the combined total of Egypt, Iran, Iraq, Israel and the Gulf Co-operation Council countries (with the exception of the United Arab Emirates).[17] From 1988-92 Saudi Arabia took about 30% of all weapons delivered by Western suppliers to the developing world.[18]

Barter arrangements, such as Al Yamamah, are not shown in Saudi defence statistics. Although it was the Pentagon's largest customer with $30 billion in contracts between 1990-95, the country was unable to pay the $1 billion due in 1995. Repayment periods were negotiated and stretched from two to five years. The amount owed to external creditors rose to $32.2 billion.[19] In the past, Saudi Arabia and Kuwait have been resistant to raising the price of oil as they have had to consider the reaction of Washington to higher petroleum costs.

The National Guard, responsible for internal security, has 75,000 members and is larger than the army. It reports directly to the royal family and is stationed in key sites throughout the country, ready to repel any moves against the House of Saud. Foreign military experts have largely given up trying to create integrated armed forces and are resigned to the fact that despite all the expenditure Saudi

Arabia is incapable of defending itself against a strong enemy. The Saudi forces did not distinguish themselves during the Gulf War—there was a tendency to panic and fire weapons randomly in Wild West style. A Saudi soldier discovered drinking tea with his comrades during an Iraqi attack, expressed the general attitude. When told by a US officer that action had to be taken, the desert warrior shrugged: "The Marines," he said, "are here to protect us."[20] That remark neatly defines the Saudi situation. The US provides the protection, Saudi Arabia supplies the oil.

The previously stable situation is now in danger of unravelling due to the twin influences of militant Islam on the general population and the discontent of a growing middle class, often educated in the West, who are increasingly frustrated with their backward rulers. The Muslim leaders oppose the presence of foreign troops, the weapons extravagance and the hypocrisy of the drinking, smoking, womanising royals. They are a part of the wave of fundamentalism that is sweeping through the Arab countries and pose the same kind of threat to the House of Saud as the Ayatollahs did to the Shah of Iran. They are unlikely to view the countries and companies that now sell arms to Saudi Arabia with much brotherly feeling. The new breed of technocrats believe the ruling family to be out of touch and an anachronism in a global economy. Real business opportunities cannot be found through the labyrinthine system of favours, deference and commissions. They are impatient for change, albeit of a different kind from that demanded by the ulemas. These pressures have made the ruling family highly sensitive to any form of criticism, internal or external.

Growing American competition will also ensure that British defence manufacturers, even with government assistance, will find themselves increasingly squeezed in this once relatively easy and highly profitable market. The Chinese are now closer than they were previously to the Saudi leadership (neither ruling group spends too much time worrying about human rights) and have won some large orders for missiles. One of the main aspects of the arms trade is that it can transcend ostensible ideological and political divisions. In this case, members of the Wahhabi sect of the Muslim religion will happily buy weapons from the successors to Chairman Mao.

The growing instability of the Saudi situation makes it a bad bet for future military sales. The massive bomb explosion at Dhahran in June 1996 that killed 19 American servicemen was a violent warning of the growing internal resistance to the presence of foreign troops in the country. To categorise it merely as terrorism sponsored by Iran or Sudan would be to avoid reality.

Problems in the Gulf

Britain's performance in the Gulf War has since come under closer scrutiny. Sir

Peter de la Billiere, the British commander in the Gulf, openly criticised the MoD insistence on flying Tornadoes on dangerous low level missions against Iraqi targets. Britain's loss of aircraft, as a proportion of those flown, was the highest of all the Gulf allies. Four divisions of armour, transferred from Germany, were reduced to one as malfunctions, lack of spare parts and firing practice took their toll. General Schwarzkopf's request for British tanks to join the US Marines in leading the attack in the opening battle of the land war was refused by de la Billiere. He asked for a safer zone to the west of Kuwait. The new and expensive SA 80 high-tech infantry rifles jammed, reminiscent of US problems in Vietnam.[21] The performance of the troops was all that could be expected but despite the flag waving and cheering in the House of Commons, Britain's equipment had all the hallmarks of make do and mend. The extortionate cost to the taxpayer of modern weapons and their maintenance had come into conflict with the demands of the military. Despite Britain's high level of defence spending, much of its machinery and weapons were clapped out.

The government badly needed to be seen as the United States' most reliable ally during the war. Mrs Thatcher made this unavoidable when George Bush found her elbows in his ribs telling him it was "no time to go wobbly." Those in the know reacted with scepticism. Hugh Colver, then head of public relations at the MoD, said: "there is nothing wrong with punching above your weight in diplomacy—but not if you can't match it in military terms. The feeling was that our troops needed to do *something* to demonstrate that they were there, but without taking unacceptable risks like going in with the Marines."[22] Britain's military embarrassment was shortly to be followed by a new conflict in the region—the competition to win arms orders from the Gulf states.

Showpiece wars like the Falklands and the Gulf provide a brilliant opportunity for the marketing people to promote their products. There is plenty of video footage from news reports, in-plane cameras and enemy sources to demonstrate the pinpoint accuracy, lethality and speed of weapons in action. Pictures of bombs dropping into empty desert, friendly fire knocking out allied vehicles and collateral damage to houses and hospitals can be safely left out of the presentations. The men with arms for sale are banging on the doors of the defence ministries of their potential customers even before the clean-up operations have been completed.

Despite the British government's efforts to appear to be the Americans' most reliable friend, these counted for little when the Gulf states started to re-arm after the war. The MoD and the defence companies' hopes for a sales boom were dashed. All arms sales in the Middle East involve governments which has meant that both the British Foreign and Defence Secretaries have had to devote a good deal of their time acting as travelling salespeople for British military hardware. Unfortunately, the Gulf rulers remained largely unmoved by the persuasive talents of Malcolm Rifkind and Michael Portillo. By 1996 the US had received orders worth $22 billion, France $6 billion and Britain only $1.4 billion.[23]

At the time of the Iraqi invasion in 1990, Kuwait had armed forces totalling 20,000, including 16,000 in the Army. Its equipment included 275 main battle tanks, 190 desert reconnaissance vehicles, 220 anti-tank guided weapons, 23 patrol and coastal boats, 8 craft with Exocet missiles, 56 fighter and ground attack aircraft and 2 helicopter squadrons.[24] All were destroyed or captured within 24 hours. The Emir led a swift retreat to the border with Saudi Arabia, followed closely by government and defence chiefs. They did not return until months after the war was over.

Failing to exact revenge on the Iraqis, official anger was directed against resident Palestinians who had traditionally provided the bulk of the workforce that carried out the essential but often menial tasks disliked by Kuwaitis. Many were tortured and most were expelled from the country, almost halving the population. The Emir did not introduce the promised democratic reforms. Only 10 per cent of its citizens are eligible to vote. This privilege is confined to males resident in Kuwait before 1920 and their male descendants at age 21. There has been one reform—women are now allowed to enter Parliament—but only as visitors. The vice-president of the women's movement explained: "we cannot participate in the debates, but we are allowed to listen to what is being said. Also, we have had a number of meetings with Members of Parliament and they are always very polite to us."[25] Women-only shortlists are not an immediate issue in that part of the world.

Despite the evidence that its costly weaponry proved virtually useless, due to the less than stubborn resistance provided by the leaders of its armed forces, the Kuwaiti government has undertaken a new round of military spending. British and other suppliers are keen to sell. The population see little point in this policy. There is no enthusiasm for the nominally compulsory two years national service and few young men bother to enlist. The backbone of the army was formed by the non-Kuwaitis, most of whom have been expelled from the country. The target of a total of 30,000 in the armed forces is regarded as pure fantasy. Military strength stood at only 13,000 in 1996 and the high-tech equipment being bought is more of a status symbol than an integral part of a real defence force.

Even with limited powers, the Kuwaiti Parliament is restless and increasingly critical of the corruption that has permeated the ruling al-Sabah family's arms purchases. It has forced the leaders to publish the previously secret defence budget. Conscious of a weak and over-militarised economy, there is now popular pressure for cuts in arms spending.

Even in previously passive Bahrain, the al-Khalifa dynasty is under pressure to reform and is responding by rounding up and executing suspects to try to suppress opposition. Like Saudi Arabia, it has complained to Britain about the activities of dissidents in London. The old order is rapidly changing in the Gulf states.

Unpleasant friends

Britain's exporters of military equipment have two main requirements of their customers—payment and discretion. The former is obvious but the latter is equally important. Publicity is the enemy of the arms trade. Some of our best clients have a nasty habit of bombing, shooting or torturing their own people. The mandarins in the MoD would have undoubtedly sighed with exasperation when the Nigerian military government hanged Ken Saro-Wiwa. The public outrage that followed highlighted not only the nature of the regime but also the fact that we had shipped large amounts of weapons to Nigeria. Shell, still trying to polish up its image following its attempted dumping at sea of the Brent Spar oil rig, was also caught in the crossfire when its close relationship with the regime was highlighted.

After years of quietly fending off protests about weapons deliveries, Conservative ministers found themselves trying to urge restraint on the Nigerian military while publicly justifying past collaboration. The European Union had imposed an arms embargo on Nigeria in 1993 which the British government interpreted flexibly. In response to Labour criticisms over the shipment of tanks, missiles, howitzers and riot control equipment, a Trade Minister, Anthony Nelson, said: "It has been the practice of successive governments not to reveal details of export licences or applications for export licences unless the requirements of confidentiality are outweighed by the public interest."[26] He did not explain: "the requirements of confidentiality." The government knew what was being sent, the exporters and their employees knew, the Nigerian government knew and, very shortly after delivery, the Nigerian people saw the equipment on their streets. The rest of us, including Parliament, obviously could not be trusted with this information.

In 1990 Vickers sold 80 battle tanks to Nigeria. The following year British aid to that country was increased tenfold. The coincidence of an award of aid and large arms orders has been a common aspect of Britain's past relations with Third World countries. The tank contract escaped the EU embargo as it was placed before 1993 but world condemnation of the murder of Saro-Wiwa compelled John Major to tighten UK export rules. A reliable African customer had shown complete disregard for any elements of humanity or civilised behaviour. That was bad for business.

Indonesia was another country with an image problem. General Suharto seized power in a coup in which an estimated half a million people died. American and Japanese aid provided the economic support that enabled his government to buy large amounts of defence equipment. Nobody has been able to explain who or what was the external threat that made such expenditure necessary. The weapons have only been used against the people of Indonesia and in illegally occupied East Timor. The Indonesian government sent its tanks into action on the island in 1975 killing up to 200,000 inhabitants—one-third of the population. In 1991, government troops fired on demonstrators in the capital, Dili, and hundreds were killed. International reaction was such that the US Congress and other Western governments placed severe restrictions on arms sales to the Suharto government. The regime found no such squeamishness amongst the British government or defence suppliers.

'Jobs' were again the justification. Questions in Parliament, campaigns by human rights organisations and publicity in the media, particularly about the sale of Hawk aircraft, forced the Conservative government on to the defensive. Eventually, after arguments about whether the aircraft was technically capable of being used against the population of East Timor, the government announced that the Indonesians had given a commitment that they would not deploy it over the island. The Hawk 100/200 bought by the Suharto government is a counter insurgency/trainer aircraft ideal for military use over terrain in that part of the world.[27] Indonesia only gave this doubtful assurance because Britain had increased its credit to buy arms. According to the World Development Movement, the cover for Indonesia rose from £24 million in 1982/83 to £442 million in 1992/3.[28]

In 1997 the Labour government allowed the sale to go ahead. A year later the Indonesian economy had collapsed and protesters demanding Suharto's resignation were shot in the streets of Jakarta by troops using British equipment. Assurances had been given by successive UK governments that such equipment would only be sold on the condition it was not used for internal repression. Suharto's backers in the West realised that he was no longer a viable proposition and called on him to go. Madelaine Albright, US Secretary of State, asked him to step down "to preserve his legacy." On May 21 1998 Suharto resigned. His "legacy" did not include a shred of democracy but did consist of huge amounts of all the armoured equipment necessary to support a one-family state.

Who pays for the arms sales?

The risk of non-payment for such arms contracts is borne by the British taxpayer. The Export Credits Guarantee Department (ECGD) that underwrites the export deals is a strange organisation with an obscure title. Even its initials seem designed to be forgotten easily. It does, however, play an essential role in underpinning Britain's overseas arms sales. When it was established, it had the perfectly reasonable intention of allowing poorer countries extended credit to buy British goods. It guaranteed our exporters that they would be paid in full, despite any economic or political problems suffered by the country buying the goods.

The ECGD reports directly to the Department of Trade and Industry. To cover export risks, the system operates on three levels:

1. The ECGD unconditionally guarantees 100 per cent refunds to a British bank that lends money to an exporter whose customer fails to pay.
2. A company will be insured by the ECGD for up to 90 per cent of the value of a contract if it gives credit to an overseas buyer.
3. The ECGD will subsidise banks to allow them to provide favourable interest rates to exporters and overseas buyers. In return the exporter pays the equivalent of an insurance premium to the ECGD. These were reduced after industry complaints and pressure, even though it was incurring losses of over £3 billion a year by 1991. The National Audit Office found that the ECGD had probably overpaid by some £83 million.[29] The outcome was that the government privatised the short-term business and sold it to NCM, a Dutch insurance company. The ECGD retained the medium-term business.

Much of the credit extended by the ECGD has been hijacked by the defence exporters. The share of its budget devoted to arms exports rose from less than 10 per cent of total business in 1980/81 to 48 per cent in 1993/94. In 1995/96, 53 per cent (£446 million) of its defence business supported arms orders from the Far East, primarily Indonesia.[30] The ECGD and the DTI had again risked UK public money by underwriting a repressive and unstable customer. It is highly unlikely that the cheque to pay for the weapons will ever be in the post.

Oil-rich countries have received vast amounts of credit. One of them was Saudi Arabia with £1.5 billion. Bad news was to follow. In 1994, NCM, the privatised credit agency, said: "repeated promises from senior Saudi officials, including promises made directly to UK Trade Ministers, have not been fulfilled and there is no suggestion of an early improvement in the situation."[31] NCM had to explain itself to its shareholders; the ECGD only has to worry about the taxpayer, or, if very unlucky, a Parliamentary question or Select Committee.

The World Development Movement, which uncovered the facts behind the ECGD's operations, estimates that from 1989/90 to 1993/94, the British public paid about £250 million a year on claims, interest rate subsidies and bad debts on arms exports. That meant that we subsidised cash-rich British companies to export weapons to Third World countries that were unwilling or unable to pay the bill. Our arms exports 'success' turned out to be costing us money.

Aid or Arms?

In November 1994, a white-haired senior citizen—often seen around Westminster and Brussels—was found guilty of acting unlawfully. Not the usual fraudster, sleaze merchant or something more sinister, the guilty man was Her

Majesty's Foreign Secretary, the Right Honourable Douglas Hurd. Ignoring the advice of Sir Tim Lankester, his chief official at the government's Overseas Development Administration (ODA), he had given the go-ahead for £234 million of British money be spent on building a dam in Malaysia. The 'Pergau Dam Affair' as it became known, shed light on the increasingly close links between aid, arms purchases and expensive prestige projects.

Baroness Chalker, the Minister for Overseas Development, said that: "the central aim of the aid programme is to reduce poverty and to improve opportunities in the countries we assist."[32] The Pergau dam was a pet project of the Malaysian government but the ODA said it would have cost the country's consumers £100 million in extra charges. In the words of Sir Tim Lankester, it was "a very bad buy." Douglas Hurd over-ruled him on the grounds of "wider considerations" which he defined as: "the interests of British industry." It must have slipped his mind that the aid programme should have been designed to "improve opportunities" for the Malaysian people not those of the contractors, GEC, Balfour Beatty and the defence exporters.

Margaret Thatcher visited Malaysia in April 1985. She quickly struck up a friendship with the Prime Minister, Dr Mahathir, saying that she found him "tough, shrewd and practical." When she left they had established a "good understanding."[33] That understanding was eventually translated into a Memorandum of Understanding (MOU)—for military hardware valued at £1.3 billion. This followed another visit by Mrs Thatcher—not mentioned in her memoirs—to Kuala Lumpur in August 1988. Part of the MOU was confirmed when a contract worth £450 million was signed for 28 Hawk aircraft, a Martello radar system and two frigates from GEC Yarrow. The Tornadoes, which were part of the original order, were downgraded to Hawks due to a sharp fall in the price of oil that partly funded the deal. According to the biographers of Mark Thatcher, his partner, Stephen W Tipping, brokered part of the contract on behalf of Shorts of Belfast for Starburst laser-guided missiles worth £70 million. The Malaysian Ministry of Defence denied that Mark Thatcher was directly involved.[34]

The goodwill generated by the arms orders was reciprocated by an increase in British taxpayers' money in the form of aid to Malaysia. In March 1988, Lord Younger, then Defence Secretary, signed an agreement with the Malaysian government which promised aid worth 20 per cent of the arms contract. Overall British bilateral aid to Malaysia rose by 139 per cent over the ten years from 1980/82 to 1992/93.[35] This was double the average for all developing countries. There is a special Malaysia department within the Defence Export Services Organisation in the Ministry of Defence. Saudi Arabia is the only other country to enjoy this special attention from the MoD.

The future may not be so secure for those involved in this kind of business. Two major problems emerged. The currency crisis in South-East Asia in 1997 led the International Monetary Fund to clip the claws of the Asian tigers so severely that Malaysia had to cut its defence expenditure immediately by 10 per cent with a further 8 per cent to follow. Clare Short, International Development Secretary in the Labour government, made a break with the past when she published a White Paper in November 1997 which said that resources provided for development would be used "only for the purposes intended." This was intended as a clear sign that the linkage between aid and trade, particularly the arms trade, would no longer be government policy.

Many of the excesses of the arms business, such as the Pergau Dam affair, have been revealed by organisations such as the World Development Movement (WDM), the Campaign Against the Arms Trade (CAAT) and Saferworld. Staffed mainly by young, computer-literate researchers and volunteers, they have managed to create considerable discomfort for the defence exporters. Company annual general meetings, once soporific affairs only attended by compliant shareholders and fund managers, are now enlivened by awkward questions and demonstrations. Sometimes this has led to rowdy scenes and confrontations. These could have been avoided if the companies acknowledged that the campaigners had a legitimate point of view and offered them regular meetings where they could put their case to senior directors. The campaigners understand the difficulties faced by defence employees and don't propose easy solutions. CAAT has published a booklet *Killing Jobs* that analyses the link between the over-concentration on military exports and job losses.[36]

A success story?

Britain has made every effort to maximise the export of weapons since Denis Healey set up the government's defence sales organisation. The arms-to-Iraq furore was not the result of official policy being corrupted, it was the inevitable conclusion of official policy being implemented. Only those countries which have been designated as overtly hostile to our interests or international outcasts such as apartheid South Africa have been officially isolated. In the past there has been little difference in approach between past Labour and Conservative governments due to the shared acceptance that arms exports—even though they may occasionally end up in the wrong hands—strengthen, or at least support, a key sector of our industrial base. This bipartisan approach has lacked any proper cost-benefit analysis and has exaggerated its success.

The Conservative government proudly announced defence exports of £5 billion in 1994. The Labour Party echoed this in its policy document, saying: "In 1994 UK defence companies won orders worth £5 billion—16 per cent of the world defence market and second only to the USA."[37] Such cheering messages are misleading. "Orders" are often only statements of intent and are subject to alteration and cancellation—for instance, orders for the Tornado from Oman and Malaysia were reduced in value by substituting the cheaper Hawk. The price of oil had fallen and they could not afford the more expensive aircraft. The benchmark of real arms sales is the value of deliveries.

Over the four years 1992-95 defence export *orders* averaged £5.494 billion per annum but actual paid-for *deliveries* were worth only £3.439 billion—£2 billion a year less. Imports over the same period averaged £1.054 billion making the net balance an average of £2.385 billion a year. [38] It should also be noted that the export delivery figures include estimates by the Society of British Aerospace Companies (SBAC) of the additional value of military aerospace equipment that does not fall within official government classifications. The SBAC does not supply any additional figures for the import bill. The MoD also says that its export statistics cannot be taken as a reliable guide to the trends in exports and imports due to unspecified "changes in the coverage of the data."

The MoD Defence Export Services Organisation (DESO) produced a confidential list of targets and forecasts for British military exporters. These analysed performance during the period 1991-95 and set targets for 1996-2000. The main focus was on South Korea (estimated total market £6.9 billion); Turkey (£4.9 billion); India (£3.2 billion); Kuwait (£4 billion); United Arab Emirates (£4 billion) and Japan (£4 billion). Britain's past share of those markets has been small. Iraq is not included and no sales are forecast for Iran which has a larger market than India.[39] The Japanese and South Korean estimates later looked exceedingly optimistic in the light of the regional financial crisis.

France is usually depicted as the world's most aggressive and devious arms exporter. Its overt sales to Iraq—as opposed to Britain's covert efforts—earned it a reputation of unprincipled opportunism. In fact, like Britain, its overseas sales peaked years ago. In 1994, defence exports fell to their lowest level for 15 years. The figure of 16.8 billion francs was 20 per cent lower than the 20.6 billion francs of 1993. Orders also fell by 7.2 billion francs to a new five-year low.[40] It grapples with the problem that it might never be paid for some of its 'sales.' The Chairman of its Parliamentary Defence Committee, and an advocate of increased exports, said: "It is absurd that the Finance Ministry should hold up the sales of submarines and fighters to Pakistan because (the export insurance company) doubts its ability to pay." The French export insurers seemed to have a greater degree of scepticism than the ECGD, their British equivalent.

This is very different from the picture usually painted of a French government sending arms to just about anywhere with few questions asked. A French defence exports official stressed the need for: "increased support that would place French exporters on a par with their competitors in terms of political and financial backing."[41] Clearly, the French believe, as we do about them, that the competition is doing better. Despite all efforts, both Britain and France have been unable to come to terms with a declining market.

Over the past decade Britain has fluctuated between fourth and fifth place in the arms export league according to the Stockholm International Peace Research Institute (SIPRI), the acknowledged authority on world defence sales.[42] The three leading countries have been the USA, Russia and Germany. China is sixth. Global arms sales are predicted to fall by around 50 per cent between 1991 and the year 2000 according to a Pentagon study.[43] This makes depressing reading for non-American exporters as it sees the US maintaining its market share of between 53-59 per cent. With increasingly anxious suppliers, including the ex-Warsaw Pact countries and possibly South Africa offering special deals and cut prices, the other main Western exporters, like Britain, will stand to lose their share of a much smaller market. They now have to face the big hitters from the US who have the advantage of a much larger domestic market. The absurd intensity of the competition was highlighted when McDonnell-Douglas announced that it had accepted Thailand's request to pay part of the cost of 8 F-18 fighters in frozen chickens.[44]

In a far from perfect world it could be argued that other arms producing countries, particularly France, operate in precisely the same manner, so why shouldn't we? The simple answer is that for every marginal success achieved there is a price to pay. That price may be that the taxpayer has to subsidise the British contractor or the overseas buyer through export credits but it could also be the delusion that we can sustain jobs, profits and influence on the back of increased arms sales. Thousands of defence jobs have disappeared and the remainder cannot be secured through overseas sales. Profits are now heavily supported by revenue from orders placed in the past and buyers such as Saudi Arabia have made us so dependent on their goodwill that they believe can influence UK domestic policy.

The slave trade was an extremely profitable business for Britain. An 18th century writer on economics described it as: "the mainspring of the machine which sets every wheel in motion." Jobs in the port of Bristol were provided by the traffic in human beings. Liverpool, the other main port, also built ships for their transportation and rope for their captivity. Birmingham manufactured fetters, chains, padlocks and branding irons. Manchester was a centre for making the cotton cloth that was bartered for slaves.[45] Public opposition forced Britain to take the lead in boycotting this lucrative trade and to ignore the still familiar: "if we don't do it, someone else will" refrain.

Many British people have a moral distaste for the arms trade and, for once, morality is supported by hard economic facts. The longer any government ignores this, the heavier will be the price we eventually pay.

References

1   *The Arms Bazaar.* Anthony Sampson. Hodder & Stoughton 1977.
2   *The War Machine.* Interview with John Pilger. Channel 4 TV programme 1995.
3   *The Arms Bazaar.* Anthony Sampson.
4   *Strategy for a Secure Future—Labour's Approach to the Defence Industry* 1995.
5   *Gunrunners Gold.* Taken from SIPRI statistics. World Development Movement 1995.
6   *The World Factbook 1995-96.* Central Intelligence Agency. Brassey's 1995.
7   *The Rise, Corruption And The Coming Fall Of The House Of Saud.* Said K. Aburish. Bloomsbury 1994.
8   The telegram, translated into English, is published in full in *Saudi Arabia— The Political and Economic Situation.* Committee for the Defence of Legitimate Rights. January 1995.
9   *The Rise, Corruption And Coming Fall Of The House of Saud.* Said K Aburish.
10 *Ibid.*
11 *Ibid.*
12 *Jane's Defence Weekly* 6 May 1995.
13 *The Guardian* 14 November 1994.
14 *The Guardian* 23 June 1997.
15 *The Financial State of the Kingdom of Saudi Arabia.* Committee for the Defence of Legitimate Rights. January 1996. Report compiled by academic staff at the School of Oriental and African Studies, University of London. Figures calculated at rate of exchange 5.6 Saudi riyals to 1 pound sterling.
16 Ibid. January 1996. The figures quoted are from *The Middle East Economic Survey* January 1995.
17 Ibid. The figures quoted are from *The Military Balance 1994-95.* International Institute of Strategic Studies.
18 Defense News December 1994.
19 *The Financial State of the Kingdom of Saudi Arabia.*
20 *Crusade: the untold story of the Gulf War.* Rick Atkinson. HarperCollins 1994.
21 *The Observer* 14 January 1996.
22 *Ibid.*
23 *Ibid.*
24 *The Military Balance 1989-90.* International Institute of Strategic Studies. Brassey's.
25 *The Sunday Times* 10 March 1996.

26 *The Guardian* 28 May 1995.
27   *Military Balance 1989-1990*. International Institute for Strategic Studies Brassey's.
28 *Gunrunners Gold*. World Development Movement 1995.
29 *Ibid*.
30 *ECGD Annual Report and Trading Accounts 1995/96*.
31 *Gunrunners Gold*. Quoting the *Financial Times* 27 October 1994.
32 *Ibid*. Quoting speech at Royal Institute for International Affairs October 1993.
33 *The Downing Street Years*. Margaret Thatcher. HarperCollins 1995.
34 *Thatcher's Gold*. Paul Halloran and Mark Hollingsworth. Simon & Schuster 1995.
35 *Gunrunners Gold*.
36 *Killing Jobs*. Campaign against the Arms Trade, 11 Goodwin Street, London N4 3HQ.
37 *Strategy For A Secure Future*. Labour Party 1995.
38 *UK Defence Statistics 1997*. Ministry of Defence. HMSO. Figures at current prices.
39 Proceedings of DESO Symposium 1996. The dollar estimates have been converted to sterling at the exchange rate of May 1996 at 1.52 dollars to the pound.
40 *Defense News* October 2 1995.
41 *Ibid*.
42 *SIPRI Yearbook 1994*. OUP.
43 *World-Wide Conventional Arms Trade* (1994-2000) : a trade analysis. Quoted in *Jane's Defence Weekly* 11 March 1995.
44 *The Guardian* 21 August 1996.
45 *The Guardian* 17 December 1997. Article by Ronald Segal quoting the writer Postlethwayt.

CHAPTER SIX

THE JUDGE, THE MINISTERS AND THE
EX-ARMS DEALER

*"When I use a word," Humpty Dumpty said in a rather scornful tone, "it
means just what I choose it to mean,—neither more nor less."*
Through the Looking-Glass. Lewis Carroll 1832-1898

On Thursday 15 February 1996, the IRA planted a bomb in Charing Cross Road,
London. It was discovered and defused. The same day a 1,800 page document
weighing over a stone landed with a thump on the desks of politicians, civil servants and news editors. The reverberations were to rattle the windows of
Whitehall. After three years, during which time he heard 81 witnesses, read 278
written submissions and responded to mysterious leaks and attacks from government sources, Lord Justice Scott had delivered his report. It was blandly entitled:
*Inquiry into the Export of Defence Equipment and Dual-Use Goods to Iraq and
Related Prosecutions.* Anxious ministers and civil servants wondered whether the
green covers decorated with an indistinct map of Iraq and the insignia of government departments contained any politically explosive devices that might blow
away their careers. They need not have worried too much.

When a British government finds itself in trouble over an issue that has
widened to become a potential public scandal, it usually responds in one of a
number of tried and tested ways. It can try to keep discussion within the walls of
Parliament, knowing that few people outside have much interest in what goes on
in the chamber; it may attempt to remain silent, pleading national security, or—
as a last resort—it can set up an inquiry. To minimise critical or difficult conclusions, the inquiry's terms of reference should be set as narrowly as possible. The
person chosen to lead it must be qualified, honest, conscientious and, most
important, someone who will not rock the boat too much. The government can
then deflect awkward questions on the grounds that it would not wish to pre-empt
the findings of the inquiry. If the political opposition can be manoeuvred into
keeping within the limits of the investigation, the escape hatch is already half
open.

The government will put its own interpretation on the findings and recommendations and, if there are any it finds unpalatable, will promise to "take them
into account," and then do nothing. The Franks Inquiry, set up after the Falklands
war to look into the many military and political errors of judgement by the government, was a model of such an exercise. It was brief, limited and exonerated

Mrs Thatcher and her colleagues. Lord Carrington, the Foreign Secretary, had already done the decent thing and resigned. Its conclusions were entirely predictable.

John Major, however, made two deviations from the norm when he set up the Nolan and Scott inquiries. Their conclusions could not be predicted and were likely to cast the government and its supporters in an unflattering light. Nolan examined the ethical and political consequences of what are known as the 'outside interests' of MPs. These are the opportunities of elected members to make money and influence government on behalf of organisations that feel it worthwhile to retain their services. Several Conservative MPs had been caught with their hands in the till after putting down questions in the House of Commons on subjects about which they had not previously shown an overwhelming interest. This practice became known as 'cash for questions'. Nolan's proposal that MPs should disclose their earnings and paymasters caused outrage in Mr Major's party, not least from people like Sir Edward Heath and others, whose apparent lifestyles would have been somewhat constrained by a back-bencher's salary of then around £34,000 plus allowances. Both Sir Edward and David Mellor, who earned an estimated £200,000 a year from consultancies with the military firms British Aerospace, Racal, Vosper Thorneycroft and Shorts, refused to declare their outside earnings in the member's register of interests. Mellor has been described as a 'door-opener' for introducing companies to Middle East clients.[1] He claimed his Parliamentary connections had nothing to do with his consultancy fees.

Alan Clark spells it out

John Major faced an even bigger problem in November 1992. The directors of Matrix Churchill, an Iraqi-owned factory in Coventry that manufactured machine tools used in production of fuses for munitions, had been prosecuted by Customs and Excise on the grounds that they had sold these products to Iraq in breach of the export controls on the sale of military goods. The company's defence was that they had discussed the sale with the Department of Trade and Industry and had received no objections. Further, Alan Clark, DTI Minister, had told the trade association which covers machine tool manufacturers that if there was any doubt about the use of such products they should stress their peaceful uses on the 'nod and a wink' principle. In a newspaper interview he was asked if he had tipped off the manufacturers about how to get round the guidelines for trade with Iraq: "Yes", replied Clark flatly, "and I did it for two reasons. First, I was Minister for Trade, so it was my job to maximise exports despite guidelines which I regarded as tiresome and intrusive. Second, Iran was the enemy—it still is—and it was clear to me that the interests of the West were well served by Iran and Iraq fighting each other, the longer the better."[2] This report put the prosecution into a flat spin and phone calls to Mr Clark only elicited the information that he was "irritated" by being asked about the interview and it was "balls" that he would have said what the journalist had reported. He stood by an earlier statement in which he said he would encourage manufacturers to stress peaceful uses in the export applications for dual-use (i.e. military or civil) equipment.

It was too late. Mr Clark was cross-examined in court by Counsel for the defence.

"**Q.** You knew the Iraqis would not be using the current orders for general engineering purposes but would be using them to make munitions?

A. The current orders, yes.

Q. If you had said of course the Iraqis will be using the current order for general engineering purposes that could not be the case to your knowledge?

A. I do not see that the fact that they are using them, were using them, for munitions, excludes them from using them for general engineering purposes more than the other way round.

Q. But here the writer of this minute (the DTI note of the 20 January 1988 meeting) is attributing to you a statement the Iraqis will be using the current order for general engineering purposes, which cannot be correct to your knowledge.

A. Well, it's our old friend being economical, isn't it?

Q. With the truth?

A. With the actualité. There was nothing misleading or dishonest to make a formal or introductory comment that the Iraqis would be using the current orders for general engineering purposes. All I didn't say was 'and for making munitions,' if I thought they were going to be doing that...""

and:

"**Q.** You didn't want to let anyone know that at this stage these machines and their follow up orders were going to munitions factories to make munitions?

A. No.

Q. And the emphasis on peaceful purposes and so on would help keep the matter confidential?

A. I do not think it was principally a matter for public awareness. I think it was probably a matter for Whitehall cosmetics.

Q. A matter for Whitehall cosmetics to keep the matter ambiguous?

A. Yes, Yes."[3]

The brutally frank replies by Alan Clark had revealed the Whitehall methods of disguising the truth. The prosecution was now damaged beyond repair and the case collapsed. Senior ministers Michael Heseltine, Kenneth Clarke, Peter Lilley, Malcolm Rifkind and Kenneth Baker, together with Tristan Garel-Jones, had previously signed Public Interest Immunity certificates which, if the judge had agreed, would have prevented crucial evidence showing the government's complicity from being used by the defence. The judge did not agree.

The episode demonstrated not only the willingness of the government to allow innocent people to be prosecuted but also a lack of gratitude to an intelligence agent. Paul Henderson, the managing director of Matrix Churchill, had been recruited by the Special Intelligence Service (SIS) to inform on Iraqi manufacturing capabilities. The Matrix Churchill plant was closed by Customs and Excise, throwing 600 skilled employees out of work. They received only a few thousand pounds in compensation for many years of service. Unlike those responsible for their misfortune, many are still out of work.

The Iraqi Supergun affair had also attracted a great deal of media attention, not least because the gun's inventor, Dr Bull, had been shot dead outside his Brussels flat. The Israeli secret service, Mossad, was suspected although some in the arms trade point a finger at the Iraqis. Dr Bull's company, Space Research of Belgium, was working with Forgemasters of Sheffield to produce huge steel tubes for shipping to Iraq. Another UK company, Walter Somers, based in Bromsgrove, was also involved. It was known as 'Project Babylon.' Despite considerable scepticism and denials of any knowledge of military purpose for the tubes, news had leaked out that they were the barrels for a mighty piece of artillery that could fire nuclear tipped or chemical warfare shells over long distances. Customs and Excise launched an investigation, seized the tubes at Teeside Docks and brought a prosecution against the company's directors for breach of arms export controls. The only problem was that Somers claimed that they had kept the government informed of the orders and had sought advice from the DTI. They were backed by Sir Hal Miller, the local Conservative MP. He said that he had also told the department who informed him that licences were not required.

In 1990, the Trade and Industry Secretary, Nicholas Ridley, said that the DTI had only "recently" become aware of the real purposes of the tubes. The previous and more accurate wording "last year" had been deleted. The prosecutions were to go ahead. Sir Hal was not deflected and told Sir Nicholas Lyell: "Something must be done. I'll see Paddy" (Sir Patrick Mayhew, then Solicitor General). He told the Inquiry: "Accordingly I waited in the Aye Lobby to catch Sir Patrick when the vote came. We were standing in the queue to vote. I said 'You must stop the prosecution of the Somers people, I have evidence they were authorised to ship. I have checked that it is good evidence with Nick...' He replied 'I cannot do that, Customs are an independent prosecuting authority.' I said 'Paddy, I can't believe there is nothing you can do.' He replied 'There is nothing I can do,' so I said 'Well in that case I'll have to give the evidence in Court.' He said 'You wouldn't do that would you?' I replied 'Just watch me.'"[4] The prosecution was withdrawn seven months later.

Faced with these debacles, the Prime Minister had little choice but to agree to a public inquiry. He chose Sir Richard Scott, a bicycling, foxhunting judge with an independent reputation to head the Inquiry.

The leading actors

No public inquiry could ever have had a more interesting cast of characters— even though most appeared and spoke in various shades of grey. Quite a few suffered from stage fright. Only Gilbert and Sullivan could have done justice to its comic opera potential. The Scott Inquiry team had a star turn in Ms Presily Lamorna Baxendale QC, nicknamed the "giggler with the knife," due the disarming way in which she slipped the stiletto question between the ribs of the floundering witness. Lady Thatcher made a majestic entrance, only to leave somewhat confused by the amount of paper put before her. Answering questions was not her strong point. John Major, briefly Foreign Secretary, who pleaded that he had not seen important memos and letters from his department, muddled through, saying: "Something I was not aware had happened, suddenly turned out not to have happened." Alan Clark said that he encouraged the exporters to indulge in a "fiction" over the guidelines.

Lord Geoffrey Howe cried foul and spent the next three years complaining about the lack of legal representation for witnesses at the hearings. The public had paid £750,000 for Lord Howe and his colleagues to receive private legal advice. Sir Robin Butler, head of the civil service and cabinet secretary, and successor to Lord Armstrong who coined the phrase "economical with the truth," stretched the elasticity of language to the full. Under pressure from Ms Baxendale he assured the Inquiry that: "Half the picture can be true...it can be incomplete but not misleading." In his world the half-time score could be presented as the final result.

The British Ambassador to Saudi Arabia, David Gore-Booth, who seemed most put out by being dragged away from his duties in the desert kingdom, said that they had indulged in "a more flexible interpretation of a rigorous policy" in relation to the guidelines. Lord Trefgarne, procurement minister at the MoD, who was later to disappear from government and be appointed as chairman of the Engineering Training Authority, said that they "weren't changing policy, only implementing a more *flexible* policy." (Author's italics). That word was to occur frequently.

MoD senior civil servants, some appearing to be unused to daylight let alone the Inquiry spotlight, blinked and obfuscated. One DTI official tripped over himself, saying: "I think there was an element of mutual reinforcement of belief or misunderstanding...I quite simply misled myself on what I thought the situation was." Another, possibly a future Sir Humphrey, said reticently: "I don't think we should wish to encourage debate among ourselves as officials." The circumlocutory use of language was an art in itself. There seemed to be three rules: First: Avoid answering directly. Second: Use the passive rather than the active tense. Third: If caught out, use a phrase like "it would seem so" or "looked at that way, I suppose so." If a civil servant had been found holding a smoking gun over a corpse, he would have admitted that: "It might appear likely that the trigger was operated at about the time my finger was in its proximity."

Shrinking under pressure, William Waldegrave, Foreign Office Minister, and held to be one of the few intellectuals in government, mumbled, ducked and weaved. Confronted with a note written by an MoD official which said that "Mr Waldegrave is content for us to implement a more liberal policy on defence sales without any public announcement on the subject," Waldegrave replied that it wasn't the most brilliantly drafted note. He said it should have read: "Mr Waldegrave is content for us to implement the more liberal *interpretation* of the *existing* guidelines."[5] In other words, the policy (the guidelines) hadn't changed, only its interpretation. William Waldegrave also said, echoing Sir Robin Butler, that he believed that the definition of a "mature democracy" should include the principle that: "It is going to be necessary not for everything to be said in detail."[6]

Sir Nicholas Lyell, the Attorney General, and in the firing line alongside Waldegrave, was no more effective in his evasions. He was the man who had leaned on the ministers to sign the Public Interest Immunity Certificates. Michael Heseltine, showing more political acumen than his colleagues, had refused at first, saying that the documents might be necessary for a proper defence for the accused in the Matrix Churchill case. He later agreed to sign a re-draft on the condition that his reservations were passed to the prosecuting Counsel. Lyell did not do so, excusing his omission by saying that he thought the judge would notice the difference between Heseltine's certificate and those of the other ministers. He admitted that he hadn't read the documents which he believed were too sensitive to be disclosed in public. There was only a "tiny risk" of a miscarriage of justice.[7]

The missing evidence

And so it went on, for 80 days, and it included 15 members of the security and intelligence agencies who gave evidence in secret. It cost between £2-£3 million. Although the ground within the boundaries set by Sir Richard was covered exhaustively, the Inquiry was severely limited. Some of the most important players in Britain's arms business with the Middle East were not called. If he had questioned the chief executives and sales directors of British Aerospace, GEC, Rolls-Royce, Vickers, Vospers, Westland, Smiths Industries and Lucas, Sir Richard would have learnt a lot more about the realities of defence exports and the role of Iraq as a major weapons buyer. Ministers come and go (even though most are reluctant to go and have to be pushed) but the directors of the defence companies have a working lifetime in the business.

Their overseas agents could also have provided some insights on how the deals are done and the industrial streetfighting that is an integral part of the competition. It is world away from the wordbending and flexibilities of Whitehall. Sir Richard gave four main reasons for refusing to call such witnesses. First: It was primarily an inquiry into the role of government officials. Second: He had access to all the necessary government paperwork that dealt with the companies' activities in relation to exports to Iraq. Third: He would have had to put speculative questions to the witnesses. Fourth: Company documents would have had to have been subpoenaed and he was reluctant to take such drastic powers.[8]

It is easy to understand why he would not wish to take on a further mountain of paperwork. However some sharp questioning of the multinational executives about their dealings with the Iraqis—particularly during the Iran–Iraq war—together with their methods of operating in the Middle East would have given the Inquiry greater insight. They could also have been asked about the means by which they solicited support from their friends in the MoD and its Defence Export Services Organisation to receive export credit guarantees to sell arms to Iraq. Without the evidence of the defence companies the Inquiry became one dimensional, focused on government actions rather than the whole picture that would also include manufacturers and middlemen. Half the picture was inadequate.

An opportunity for the rest of us to scrutinise our decision-makers was also missed when Sir Richard prevented TV cameras from recording the hearings. The peculiar British snobbishness that believes that the electronic media should not be allowed access to quasi-judicial occasions prevented the public from gaining a full impression of the integrity, or otherwise, of the witnesses. The squirming contradictions of government ministers and their officials at the Inquiry could only be conveyed fully by visual means. Ordinary people are as competent as any judge of making up their own minds by listening to the evidence and watching the body language.

The report was difficult to read. The frequent use of double negatives and the kind of establishment phraseology used by politicians and civil servants, clouds clear, critical statements. Most long reports have an executive summary which clarifies and lists the report's main conclusions. Sir Richard declined this option, on the grounds that he wished people to read the contents for themselves and make their own judgement. That was unrealistic. It cost £45.00, was printed on heavy paper and needed a considerable effort to carry it for more than a few yards. Even the Bible, whose scope is somewhat larger, is easier to handle. The kind of thinking that believes that such weighty (literally) 'matters of state' should be read and discussed only by lawyers, journalists, politicians and other professionals is elitist and contrary to any spirit of open government. After all, the report was supposed to be dealing with public access to important information. It was no surprise, therefore, that six months after publication, the report had sold only 2,200 copies, apart from the 2,500 supplied free to MPs, civil servants and the media.[9]

The government's disinformation machine swung into action well before the report's publication. Hardly a month seemed to go by without Lord Geoffrey Howe, who bored for Britain in various roles for many years, issuing warnings about the biased and unfair nature of the Inquiry. The continual sniping may have influenced Sir Richard to an undue extent in his efforts to be seen to be impartial. He sent out drafts of parts of the report to those whose actions he felt merited criticism. However accurate or mild his criticisms may have been, it allowed the recipients to leak the main points to the media in an attempt build up the potential damage to themselves in the hope that the final report would let them down lightly. The power of anti-climax can dull any debate. To a large extent this worked, as did the lengthy written responses to his criticisms. This exercise in fair play meant that any of Sir Richard's original criticisms would be blunted if he accepted the replies as accurate. His seeming belief that politicians under pressure have a high regard for the truth runs contrary to the experience of those who come into contact with them on a more regular basis.

To what extent the drafts were changed after representations by the people he investigated, only Sir Richard and his team can know. Lord Howe was plainly relieved. He welcomed the report saying: "Obviously Sir Richard has approached his task conscientiously and in good faith and has come out with conclusions that acquit all ministers of any lack of integrity and substantially dismiss the charges."[10] That may have been Lord Howe's gloss but it was repeated elsewhere, notably by Tom King, ex-Defence Secretary who said that it was like the Bible— anybody could take what they wanted from it. Such was the consensus between government and opposition that while they drew very different conclusions, particularly on the question of ministerial resignations, hardly anybody criticised the report's scope or its lack of precision.

It would be wrong, however, to write off the report as just another establishment exercise in self-justification. Sir Richard and his team did provide a useful database that gave details of how, when and why we sent certain types of equipment to Iraq. What is more important, he unearthed some unpalatable truths about the way our elected leaders, and their unelected civil service advisers, regard the public's right to expect honesty in government.

Presenting policy

This seam of contempt that ran through most of the proceedings is clear in the evidence given by Lord Howe and the Foreign and Commonwealth Office (FCO) about the Iraqi leader's murder of hundreds of Kurdish villagers by chemical warfare in 1988. Pictures of people lying dead in the streets with babies huddled in their mother's arms had been received with horror around the world. This lodged a small piece of grit in the well oiled government machine that was preparing to flex the guidelines and sell equipment to Saddam Hussein. Mr Cowell, a FCO official, had written a paper dealing with both Iraq and Iran which acknowledged that "presentational problems" and "opposition from Parliament and public opinion" might cause difficulties.[11] The "presentational" question and the tying together of public and Parliament is interesting because it gives some idea of the mind-set of senior civil servants who believe that their superior knowledge reflects the realpolitik of the day. The rest of us, including our elected lawmakers, cannot possibly appreciate the finer points of policy. The problem wasn't presentational; the problem was genocide.

Mr Cowell's points impressed Lord Howe who decided that he was "reluctant to put this paper forward and thereby initiate a process whereby it will become known that our line on arms sales to Iraq has relaxed, while the Kurds/chemical warfare question is still hanging over us." Sir Richard spotted this for what it was—a cover-up—and quoted Howe's words: "It could look very cynical if, so soon after expressing outrage over the treatment of the Kurds, we were to adopt a more flexible approach on arms sales."

Lord Howe worried that "the extremely emotional way in which such debates are conducted in public" might impede the flexing of the guidelines "because the scope for misunderstanding is enormous." No doubt he felt aggrieved. There he was, attempting to support Britain's export trade, and the public had become concerned about a few poisoned Kurds. He did, however, have a kind of philosophy that took care of any qualms. Unlike Mr Waldegrave and Sir Nicholas Lyell, Lord Howe had no interest in twisting words to disguise the truth. He believed that no words should be uttered at all. The facts should be kept in the closed files of government. Sir Richard commented politely on the "compatibility" problem: "Lord Howe's mistrust of the public and unwillingness to run the risk that public debate might embarrass government policy was consistent with his evidence."[12]

The main points that emerged from the Inquiry provided a picture of bungled cover-ups, the liberty of innocent people put at risk in the name of 'national security' and some insights into the world of government arms dealing. Sir Richard's language was more charitable towards some of the participants than many people would feel they deserved. The implied assumption was that ministers and senior civil servants were, by definition, honourable. If they lied, well, it was because they had not been fully informed of the truth. If they misled, they were also inadvertently misleading themselves.

The deceptions uncovered

Some of Sir Richard's conclusions, if not his language, were very much to the point. They could be summarised as:

- Customs and Excise should not have prosecuted Matrix Churchill. Sir Nicholas Lyell was "at fault" for not forwarding Mr Heseltine's reservations about the gagging orders to the prosecuting Counsel. He also failed to recognise the important legal and constitutional issues involved.[13] The government's attitude to the disclosure of crucial documents to the defence was "consistently grudging."[14]

- The answers to Parliamentary Questions (PQs) in both Houses of Parliament were deliberately inaccurate. Sir Richard said: "I have come to the conclusion that the overriding and determinative reason was a fear of strong public opposition to the loosening of the restrictions on the supply of defence equipment to Iraq and a consequential fear that pressure of the opposition might be detrimental to British trading interests."[15]

- Letters signed by Mr Waldegrave and Lord Howe to MPs whose constituents had written expressing concern over sales to Iraq contained a fundamental untruth. The ministers wrote: "British arms supplies to both Iran and Iraq continue to be governed by the strict application of guidelines which prevent the supply of lethal equipment or equipment which would significantly enhance the capability of either side to resume hostilities." Further letters said: "The government have not changed their policy on defence sales to Iran or Iraq." Sir Richard stated that the letters were "not accurate" and the inaccuracy "should have been noticed by Mr Waldegrave who had been one of the midwives at the birth of this new formulation." The new formulation was the introduction of flexibility to the guidelines. He found the assertion that there had been no change in government policy "untrue" and that Mr Waldegrave knew the facts even though he said he still believed that there had been no policy change. This was in the face of "overwhelming evidence to the contrary."[16]

- The Prime Minister (Mrs Thatcher) and senior ministers had accepted that the "glittering opportunities" for defence sales to Iraq should entail a more "liberal" policy towards that country after the end of its war with Iran.[17] She gave an inaccurate and misleading reply in Parliament when she said: "The government have not changed their policy on defence sales to Iraq."[18] Sir Richard accepted that she had not been told of the changed interpretation of the guidelines but by not referring to "lethal" sales had made an unwitting mistake.

- Government ministers were usually careful to use the term "lethal equipment" in response to MPs when denying that they had allowed its export.

Occasionally they called it "military equipment" which Sir Richard said was wrong as the new flexible guidelines did allow sending military equipment and denials of such sales "should not have been made."[19] The difference is that 'lethal' stuff can kill directly while 'military equipment' covers anything used by the military but which can be used indirectly in support of killing. No such nice distinctions concerned the people who had written to their MPs to complain about British sales (lethal or merely military) to the man in Baghdad with genocidal tendencies. Sam Cummings, the famous arms dealer once said, ironically, "all weapons are defensive and all spare parts are non-lethal."

- The Supergun affair went "further than mere muddle" and the investigation by the Secret Intelligence Services was "inadequate." Neither Parliament nor the Trade and Industry Select Committee were told of suspicions that it was a military project. The DTI failed to keep records of crucial conversations between themselves and the manufacturers.[20] Nicholas Ridley's statement in 1990 that it learnt of the military purposes of the tubes "recently" was an "elastic" use of the word.[21] Intelligence services knew of the project at least six months previously. Ridley's assertion was, therefore, "inadequate or inaccurate." The Inquiry also reported that it "had difficulty in tracing all the relevant papers" from the DTI that were used to prepare the minister's statement.[22]

- Military exports to Iraq were falsely recorded as being supplied to Jordan. Prior to the Iranian revolution, the Shah had ordered 1500 Chieftain main battle tanks to be supplied by the Royal Ordnance Factories (ROFs), later part of British Aerospace. These needed Armoured Recovery Vehicles (ARVs) to rescue them in the event of a breakdown. Iran had ordered 250 and a small number had been delivered. The Shah was deposed in 1979 and all arms shipments to that country were stopped. A senior official of Millbank Technical Services (later IMS), the government owned business that acted as an agency in large arms contracts said: "When the revolution occurred something akin to panic broke out within the MoD/ROF (Royal Ordnance Factories) axis."[23] Jordan then bought 21 ARVs for its own use, leaving 29 still to be sold. During the urgent search for buyers, Iraq emerged but the vehicles had to be officially shipped to Jordan, a friendly customer. There was one slight hitch. Contractually, Jordan could not sell them on to Iraq without the permission of the MoD. Lord Strathcona, MoD minister, duly obliged and wrote accordingly. The IMS Project Managing Director was instructed by his Chief Executive: "to weed the IMS project file... of all papers referring directly to Iraq" and he (the Chief Executive) would: "personally shred them all with the exception of the Strathcona letter which he would retain in his safe in the Managing

Director's office."[24] A later head of IMS, Sir John Cuckney, told the Inquiry that the letter had been placed there to "protect its security."

A quick spin of the revolving door that linked the MoD, through its sales organisation DESO, to British Aerospace (BAe), the UK's largest defence contractor, was highlighted in the report. David Hastie, then at DESO but formerly with BAe, was found to have worn two hats. DESO and BAe were in continual contact in their attempts to persuade the government to support the sale of Hawks to Iraq. In April 1988, Mr Hastie was seconded for one year to DESO as 'Business Development Advisor' with his salary continuing to be paid by BAe. This was extended by a further six months in March 1989. What Sir Richard called the "ambiguity" of Mr Hastie's position came to a head in a little mystery of changed identity.

The Baghdad arms fair was scheduled for April 1989. British Aerospace and other British companies, including Matrix Churchill, and supported by DESO, were keen to obtain official government support for their displays of the latest hardware. The Foreign and Commonwealth Office (FCO) which was more sensitive to the public repercussion of sales to Saddam Hussein opposed it. Eventually, the MoD backed down and agreed that no DESO officials should attend. But Mr Hastie, a DESO official and an expert on the Hawk, did attend. It was obviously a clear breach of the ruling. Or was it? Not at all, according to the MoD, because Mr Hastie had swapped hats between London and Baghdad. He had been "de-seconded" back to BAe for the duration of the exhibition. He had, however, been warned "not to give out any MoD visiting cards."[25]

In one of his stronger comments, Sir Richard said: "It is as plain as a pikestaff that, so far as MoD advice to government on the Hawk was concerned, Mr Hastie was in a position of potential conflict between duty and interest."[26]

How the British taxpayer bankrolled Saddam

Britain, Saudi Arabia and the US supported Saddam Hussein before and after the war he launched against Iran in 1980. American satellite information on Iranian troop movements was passed to him during the conflict. A section of the Scott Report shows clearly how the British taxpayer, through the Export Credits Guarantee Department (ECGD), underwrote exports that propped up his regime in both the military and civil fields.

In October 1983, Britain and Iraq reached an agreement that an ECGD credit of £250 million should be made available. This was increased by a further £250 million in December 1984. Much to the annoyance of the MoD and the defence exporters, the first grant was intended for civil exports only. The British defence attaché in Baghdad, frustrated at seeing at what he believed to be a lucrative market being ignored, threw his weight behind the MoD. He quoted an old Arab proverb: "The man who does not visit me in time of war will not be welcome in time of peace."

The MoD made its move in April 1985 when it supported an application for a £17 million contract for radio communications equipment to be supplied to the Iraqi Ministry of Defence. The FCO agreed reluctantly but with the proviso that future military applications should be scrutinised on a case by case basis. There should not be a pre-determined allocation for defence exports. The MoD ignored this. Having placed a large foot in the door, they demanded that 40 to 50 per cent of the second allocation of £250 million should be earmarked for defence equipment, with a limit of £25 million on any individual contract. Supported by the DTI, the FCO responded with a counter-proposal of £25 million in total for defence, with an upper limit of £10 million on each contract. It argued that that any more allocated to the military would: "bring our neutrality into question."[27] This was agreed. These extended limits were not offered to Iran. Sir Richard pointed out that neither Parliament nor the public was ever informed of such a "defence allocation" to assist the Iraqi military machine. In the strongest word of his report he called the concealment of the bias to Iraq through the defence allocation policy "reprehensible."[28]

The government's generosity towards Saddam Hussein continued after the end of his war with Iran. A further £340 million of credit was allowed in September 1988, with up to 20 per cent for 'non-lethal' defence sales. The Treasury and the Bank of England were ringing warning bells as Iraq was falling well behind with the agreed monthly payments due, in part, to the collapse in oil prices. By the end of 1989 the UK taxpayer was bankrolling Saddam to the tune of £1.156 billion. By June 1990, the level was around £1 billion and a further £250 million credit was agreed. Non-payments had reached £140 million.[29] On 2 August 1990, Iraq invaded Kuwait and promptly defaulted on all debts. The potential risk to UK public money had become a reality.

After war, claims by British exporters to the ECGD for compensation for the non-payment of Iraqi debts were expected to reach a total of £652 million—more than the net cost to Britain of fighting the Gulf War.[30] In July 1996, the British government persuaded the banks that had lent the money to issue writs in the High Court against Iraq to attempt to recover it. The banks did not face the risk of loss; that was borne by the British taxpayer through the ECGD.

Parliamentary theatre

The government presented the Scott Report to Parliament on the afternoon of its publication. The drama of democratic debate was preceded by a warm-up act consisting of a cast of opposition spokespeople, drivers, minders and a large number of extras in the form of media people. The government, which had received the report two weeks previously, had decided to allow opposition nominees only three hours to read the full 1,800 pages, immediately prior to the debate. They ignored Sir Richard's pleas for fair play for all. Robin Cook, Labour's shadow Foreign Secretary, played to the gallery. Refusing to take the official government car to the DTI because he "was not confident where it might take me," he strode down Victoria Street surrounded by journalists. On arrival, he conducted a little ceremony of handing in his forbidden mobile phone before being escorted to a room to scan the report. Only sandwiches and soft drinks were available. The gourmet Lord Jenkins, Liberal Democrat spokesman in the House of Lords, had angrily refused to participate. Some thought that this could have been due to the poor quality of the food provided.

The three hours allowed to Mr Cook and Menzies Campbell of the Liberal Democrats were generous compared to the ten minutes given to MPs who queued and scrimmaged to grab their copies. As the Speaker called for order, they could be seen staggering into the chamber and heaving themselves into their seats. The visible effort of carrying the weighty report indicated that most did not appear to be regular visitors to the House of Commons gym. Once in their seats, many began a hurried search to find their names in the index.

Ian Lang, President of the Board of Trade, launched at once into a triumphalist attack on Robin Cook. Without a hint of irony, the former sketchwriter for the 1960s television satire, *That Was The Week That Was*, accused Mr Cook of slandering innocent ministers by alleging that they had knowingly allowed lethal weapons to be sold to Iraq and that they had lied to Parliament. Sir Richard had disproved this totally. Far from being an indictment of the government, the report condemned Labour as being irresponsibly prepared to sully the good name of ministers without a shred of justification. Mr Cook should apologise to the House.

Given the circumstances, Robin Cook's reply was nothing short of brilliant. By far the best Parliamentary debater and most forensic mind on the Labour front bench, he demonstrated a grasp of the report that few people could acquire in three days, let alone three hours. He had spent his allotted time, he said, studying the report and was unable to recognise it from the version presented by the President of the Board of Trade. The government had known about the Supergun a year before they took any action. They had turned a blind eye. In their evidence to the Inquiry, ministers had shuffled off blame for bad drafting onto civil servants but had instructed them to prepare submissions that protected members of government. He asked how could they give accurate replies when they knew their ministers were clearly to blame? His greatest anger was directed against William Waldegrave and Nicholas Lyell for their attempts to suppress evidence in the Matrix Churchill case. In one sentence, and looking directly at the government front bench, he summed up his own conclusions: "They misjudged Saddam, they misled MPs and they misdirected the prosecution." As he spoke, ministers looked down, turned the report's pages quickly and shuffled their feet.

If the exchanges of 15 February were the trailer, the full feature was due two weeks later in what was supposed to be the definitive debate. It was largely an anti-climax. Several MPs, including some independently-minded Conservatives, raised the constitutional implications of ministers misleading Parliament but even they struck a slightly hurt tone as if they were members of a much respected institution that had been by-passed. They were right but few pressed the point that the general public—which holds Parliament in much lower esteem than most MPs acknowledge—should equally have been informed.

Most of the debate centred on the question whether Waldegrave and Lyell should resign, a forlorn hope as John Major had made it clear that he had no intention of telling them to do so. A case of ministers caught behaving badly, or even dishonourably, was no longer a resignation issue. To reinforce this he had changed the rules on ministerial responsibility—his colleagues now had to be found to have *knowingly* misled Parliament—it was not enough for them to merely to have misled. The onus, therefore, was on those made the accusations to prove that ministers lied deliberately. If they denied it, then that was the end of the matter.

Even if Waldegrave and Lyell had resigned, they would have been replaced swiftly by people of like mind. It was difficult to see why resignations should have been the focal point of the whole issue. The finger pointing and shouting that carried on until late evening created the sort of Parliamentary noise that makes many viewers and listeners reach for the off switch almost as quickly as the Reverend Ian Paisley can rise to his feet. In fact, toward the end of the day, Northern Ireland began to eclipse the arms-to-Iraq question. The government, desperate not to lose the vote, were manoeuvring with the Northern Ireland Unionists around the system of elections that were to take place in the province. The intense media coverage focused on possible Conservative dissidents, non-resignations, votes being wheedled out of Northern Ireland politicians and, yet again, John Major's future. The arms trade, as an issue, was largely ignored.

The government scraped through by one vote. In the following hubbub, everyone claimed victory, moral or actual. The Reverend Paisley's Democratic Unionists, whom it was assumed would benefit from the new Northern Ireland electoral system, abstained. The official Ulster Unionists, who would not, voted against the government. Within two weeks the Scott report was off the front pages. The judge had done his job, the media had had their day and honourable men and women, after some anxiety, could sleep safely. The under-informed public, however, was not fooled. A MORI poll for *The Times* found that only 8 percent thought the government had handled the Inquiry well and by more than a three to one margin believed that the ministers named in the report should have resigned.[31]

A wasted opportunity

After the sound and fury, however, a substantial part of the picture was still missing. The whole debate, focused on personal integrity and Parliamentary procedure, had a hollow ring. The effects of deception were obvious but the cause was deliberately avoided. Nobody asked whether the essential nature of overseas defence sales did not demand of the participants that they should operate covertly, court unpleasant dictatorships and avoid the truth? Were Waldegrave, Lyell and the rest the villains of the piece or merely players in a game where Rule One is that there are no rules? Even in the heat of the party political accusations and counter-accusations there was a tacit understanding that defence exports were a good thing. All parties believed that Britain's sales effort was successful and so that success, real or imagined, should not be jeopardised.

The Conservative jibe that Labour had set up the whole government-sponsored arms export business in 1966 was accurate. Even effective and principled performers like Robin Cook were fighting with one hand tied behind their back as they were forced to concentrate on ministers' duplicity and incompetence, of which there was plenty. They could not question the whole edifice and culture of weapons exports that made that behaviour inevitable and predictable.

Evidence to the Inquiry also showed that it was: "the practice of *successive* governments not to make available details of export licence applications."[32] (Author's italics). The demand by the Opposition front-bench for more open government in relation to defence sales had not been put into effect by past Labour governments. The scramble to sell to Saddam in a shrinking market against equally unscrupulous foreign competitors demanded the very qualities displayed by the government ministers and their civil servants. The incidents that led to the setting up of the Inquiry were not aberrations but the inevitable consequences of operating in a strange, dangerous and secretive business where the only breach of professional ethics was to get caught.

The First Division Association, the trade union representing senior civil servants, demanded that its members should not be made scapegoats for the duplicity and evasions of ministers. That was entirely fair. However, the extent to which the machinery of government had become corrupted by one-party rule for 18 years and the supercilious attempts by top officials to fool the public were also issues. It was not surprising that ambitious fast-track civil servants took intellectual pride—whether for career or ideological reasons—in creating responses that used clever but essentially uninformative phraseology. Word games had replaced honest answers. Over fifty years ago, George Orwell wrote: "The great enemy of clear language is insincerity. When there is a gap between one's real and one's declared aims, one turns as it were instinctively to long words and exhausted idioms, like a cuttlefish squirting out ink."[33]

Speaking one month after its publication, Sir Richard said he had been depressed by the reaction to parts of his report. He asked: "What is the quality of civil servants or ministers who it is feared will temper their advice because of the possibility that the terms of their advice will become publicly known?"[34]

Any party in government that is anxious to distance itself from the past, including its own, might think it worthwhile to draw up a strict set of rules that makes ministers fully responsible for the answers they give. They should not be able plead ignorance of the facts. Their civil servants should also be instructed to draft accurate answers in plain English—the commodity that, along with the truth, was most lacking in the events surrounding the Scott Inquiry. Without those changes, it will be impossible to get rid of the culture of secrecy that buries the facts well away from Parliament and public.

Two years after the Inquiry a UK company called Sandline International was found to have supplied weapons and mercenaries to assist the ousted but British-backed President of Sierra Leone. There was a UN embargo on the export of arms to the country. The ultimately successful attempt to restore him to his elected position was led by troops of the unelected military dictatorship of Nigeria. Sandline said that its activities had been approved by the Foreign and Commonwealth Office. Robin Cook stated that he and the other FCO ministers had not been informed of any such approval. The issue, and the relevant civil servants, would be the subject of an internal inquiry. The FCO officials were not represented by the person who had spoken for them at the time of the Scott Report. Liz Symons, their First Division union general secretary, had become Baroness Symons, (unelected) Labour minister at the Foreign and Commonwealth Office. Her role in the Sandline affair was also part of the inquiry.

The wheeler-dealer

I finally tracked down Pat Benson in a wine bar in a quiet street near Kings Cross, one month after the publication of the Scott Report. A converted blacksmith's forge, it had a cosmopolitan clientele of lawyers, plain clothes police, publicans, journalists, and a sprinkling of those who don't disclose their jobs except for "doing a bit of this and that." The Channel 4 programme *Dispatches* had referred to his activities in a programme exposing Switzerland as the major European centre of arms dealing. He had refused to appear on camera. The story of his dealings with the Iraqis and British officialdom adds an interesting footnote to the Scott Inquiry.

Despite their colourful reputations, most of the private arms dealers are not men with forged passports slipping through airports and docks carrying suitcases full of Kalashnikovs. To a large extent they have to rely on the permission of the arms export bodies of the governments of the countries from where they operate. Those governments, therefore, can control most of the dealers' activities. Whether they choose to, or not, is another matter. Independent dealers supply only around 5 per cent of the world arms market. Official suppliers—the big manufacturers working through governments—provide the rest. Not all those independents involved in military equipment transactions are selling arms; many are acting as go-betweens. The British government knew very well that private middlemen were assisting the Iraqis during the late 1980s to build their high-tech military base with British equipment. This was the period when the government had secretly switched from its declared "even-handed" position to giving preference to Iraq over Iran.

Pat Benson did not fit the stereotype of people in his line of business. A lively man with a quick turn of phrase, he had a left-wing background. During the late 1970s, he was an active trade unionist working for a housing organisation. He and some colleagues, several of whom are now prominent in the law, the Labour Party and national trade unions, set up a union branch for the voluntary sector in London. Smiling benignly from his campaign leaflet for Hendon South in the Greater London Council elections of 1977 he says: "A Good Neighbour Votes Labour."

Ten years later, in a photograph taken in Sri Lanka, he looks like the neighbour from Hell rather than Hendon. Lounging back in an armchair, in a white silk suit, bright blue shirt, sun glasses, flashing gold ring, drink poured and a fat cigar between his teeth, he exudes new wealth. Despite being exasperated by the "middle-class barrack room lawyers" at union meetings, he decided to go to Birkbeck College as a mature student to take a law degree. After graduating, he was looking for work when he met an old friend who invited him to become a partner in a trading company called Bonaventure.

The firm traded as an intermediary in the buying and selling of military equipment. His job was to handle the contractual aspects of the business while his partner acted as the front man. In his words, he was not so much a salesman but more of a "facilitator" between the buyers and the sellers. He held three British passports so that visas showing the dates of visits to places regarded as unfriendly were not displayed at the border control points of certain countries. In the arms business, he believes that the British are regarded with much less suspicion than those carrying an American passport. From time to time, he said, a man from MI6 would contact him to ask him a few questions about where he'd been and if he'd seen anything interesting. There was no heavy pressure.

They moved the company to Geneva in 1986 for the simple reason that Swiss laws on arms trading were "lax to non-existent." Their business, which was mainly in the Middle East, India and Sri Lanka flourished until the Iraqi invasion of

Kuwait in 1991. They received an excellent banking service and extensive credit facilities from Barclays of Switzerland. Oerlikon's branch in Austria and smaller manufacturers supplied them with firing pins, fuses and artillery components which were sent on to Teheran for use by the Iranian armed forces. This type of equipment, together with mine detectors and machine tool parts that would be used in making heavy weaponry, was also sold to Jordan and India. Egypt acted as an agent for Iraq, taking 10 per cent commission, and shipped the equipment sold to them by Bonaventure from Alexandria to Iraqi ports.

Benson also dealt with China and he had a lot of respect for the Chinese authorities who he says were easy to deal with, relatively uncorrupt and reliable. He went to Beijing on four occasions, visited a fuse factory and bought surplus military equipment, including 60mm mortars, from the Chinese army. Delivery could be made within six days, if required, and the goods would be shipped on Chinese vessels direct to the customer.

He met the notorious Chilean arms dealer Carlos Cardoen who sold cluster bombs to Iraq. They tried to arrange letters of credit and banking facilities with the Egyptian banker Amar Sabry but were unable to reach a conclusion. Benson always stayed at the Al Rasheed Hotel in Baghdad as it was just across the road from the Ministry of Industry which was responsible for most of the arms purchases. The minister was Saddam's son-in-law, Hussein Kamel, who later fled to Jordan, returned and was murdered in February 1996 by members of the family. The hotel was badly damaged when a cruise missile hit the ministry during the Gulf War.

The Iraqis in Britain

After the end of the war with Iran, Bonaventure played a small but key role in helping the Iraqis buy engineering parts that were essential to their new weapons programme. The company offered the Ministry of Industry help in finding suppliers of linear accelerators used in the inspection of special tubing, rocket cases and high explosive artillery shells. They smoothed the path for senior Iraqi buyers in a number of European countries including France, Austria, Ireland and the UK. The Iraqis were all technical specialists with Masters degrees or PhDs. Some held senior military rank. The Home Office granted them visas without any problems as the purpose of their visits was known and approved by the government. They usually stayed at the Cavendish Hotel in Jermyn Street or the East India Club in St James'. MI5 kept an eye on their movements. In the evenings, Pat Benson would often take them to the now defunct Bristol Suite in Berkeley Square which was run by one of his friends. The club's hostesses provided the required hospitality.

Brigadier Azzawi, a senior member of the military section of the Iraqi

Ministry of Industry, was deeply involved with Forgemasters in negotiations over the Supergun. The Scott Report refers to his activities. Pat Benson arranged his visits and took him to meet the Forgemasters management in early 1988 at a hotel outside Sheffield. It was there that they met Christopher Cowley who was handling the proposed deal for Space Research, the weapon's designers. The company's founder, Gerald Bull had already been murdered. Bonaventure also established a manufacturing subsidiary at Brescia in Italy to make components for the Supergun. These included bolts and anchoring points. The Italian authorities confiscated all the production facilities when the tubes were seized at Teesside docks in Britain in March 1990.

Hadlands Photonics of Hemel Hempstead specialised in very high speed 'shadowgraph' photography and the Iraqis were interested in buying equipment that could track a Supergun shell in flight. In 1989, they asked Bonaventure to act as sponsors and arrange a visit to the company. This was convenient for them as although Bonaventure was a Swiss company, its staff were British and familiar with the local scene. Pat Benson obtained the visas, informed the Home Office as to the purpose of their visit and paid the bill for a good hotel in Hertfordshire. It was a seven man delegation—larger than most—from the Al Farouq establishment.

All were highly qualified technical specialists. Sir Richard Scott says that in June 1989, the British authorities decided that Hadlands did not need an export licence to sell the shadowgraph equipment to Iraq. The contract was signed in August. Three months later, they discovered the involvement of Brigadier Azzawi and that it was part of project PC-2 BABL, the Supergun.[35] The export licence was refused. It seems strange that although the shadowgraph equipment was clearly to be used in connection with Iraqi missiles or shells, it was only vetoed when the Supergun affair became public. Sir Richard wrote more about the Hadlands involvement but refused to publish his findings in the report, saying that it: "should not, in the national interest, be made public."[36] Why did Sir Richard, so scathing of government evasions, wish to conceal the precise role of Hadlands in the affair?

Crossed lines

Benson was extremely critical of the lack of contact between the British security services, who knew exactly what was going on, and other agencies, in particular, Customs and Excise, who did not. In a bizarre episode, he almost fell foul of the latter. In Spring 1990, Benson discovered that they were watching his flat in Sussex Gardens, West London, from a house opposite. Men with binoculars behind twitching curtains peered across; British Telecom and unmarked vans came and went. His secretary tried to phone the local grocers to place an order but all she heard was a recording of a conversation between two members of Bonaventure's staff that had taken place the previous day.

Benson contacted his solicitor who rang the Home Office to protest. At 9.30 am on a Tuesday morning, a senior official of the Customs and Excise Arms Control Division telephoned to ask him to come across to his offices in Central London. Benson claims that he was offered a deal. Although Bonaventure was a Swiss company and beyond British arms control laws, the official was prepared to offer immunity from public identification or any court appearances if Benson could tell him about the Forgemasters project. He pointed to some drawings marked PC-2 on his desk and asked what it was and how did it work. Benson says he replied: "What do you think it is? It's a bloody gun!" He also explained that the drawings were upside down. At that point he says the man lost his temper and went into a tirade about his department being expected to act as a policeman for the DTI but never being told what was going on—there was no contact with ministers—he was completely "pissed off"- and somebody should be held responsible for the cock-up. Benson made his excuses and left. The surveillance was terminated.

Bonaventure ceased trading in 1991 when Iraq invaded Kuwait. All its assets and money, which are held in several banks, have been frozen. Claims to the United Nations Iraqi Compensation Board from Bonaventure and companies in a similar position are being dealt with by the Foreign and Commonwealth Office. The US has been reluctant to allow Iraqi oil back on the world market so that the claims could be settled as oil prices would fall and provide less income for the Saudis and other allies to buy arms from the West. That was not good news for the Iraqi poor who desperately needed medicines and food.

Bonaventure's short history as an intermediary in the international military equipment business shows clearly how such companies operated with the full knowledge and permission of governments. The public may view them as sinister rogue traders but they fill the gaps regarded as too risky by the official defence suppliers. Pat Benson never bothered to read the Scott Report but he does wonder why Bonaventure, in view of its role in the Supergun affair, was not asked to give evidence. He believes that the degree of complicity between the government and the small dealers is not something that should continue to be ignored. His company is out of business, the multinationals carry on.

References

1   *Sunday Times* 12 May 1996.
2   *The Scott Report.* G8.1. HMSO February 1996. Interview in the *Sunday Telegraph* 2 August 1992.

3   *The Scott Report.* G17.29.
4   *Ibid.* F4.45.
5   *Truth Is a Difficult Concept—Inside The Scott Inquiry.* Richard Norton-Taylor. *The Guardian.* 1996.
6   *Ibid.*
7   *Ibid.*
8   *The Scott Report.* A.3.9.
9   *Knee Deep in Dishonour.* Richard Norton-Taylor, Mark Lloyd and Stephen Cook. Victor Gollancz 1996.
10 *The Observer* 18 February 1996.
11 *The Scott Report.* D3.18.
12 *Ibid.* D3.19.
13 *Ibid.* G13.125.
14 *Ibid.* G18.37.
15 *Ibid.* D4.42.
16 *Ibid.* D4.2—D4.7.
17 *Ibid.* D4.5.
18 *Ibid.* D4.30.
19 *Ibid.* D4.24.
20 *Ibid.* F4.80.
21 *Ibid.* F4.28.
22 *Ibid.* F4.31.
23 *Ibid.* D2.218.
24 *Ibid.* D2.220.
25 *Ibid.* D6.39.
26 *Ibid.* D6.35.
27 *Ibid.* D2.74.
28 *Ibid.* D2.120.
29 *Ibid.* D3.172-185.
30 *Gunrunner's Gold.* WDM. Quoting *Hansard* 1 January 1994.
31 *The Times* 29 February 1996.
32 *The Scott Report.* D1.26. Paul Channon, Minister for Trade, in response to a Parliamentary Question from David Howell MP on 11 June 1984 asking about current military exports to Iran and Iraq. The minister used the stock phrase.
33 *Politics and the English Language.* George Orwell. *Horizon* 1946. Reprinted in *The Collected Essays, Journalism and Letters Volume 4.* Penguin Books 1970.
34 *The Times* 22 March 1996 reporting the annual Public Law Lecture.
35 *The Scott Report.* F3.11-13.

CHAPTER SEVEN

UNCERTAIN TIMES

That is the land of lost content,
I see it shining plain,
The happy highways where I went
And cannot come again.
A.E. Houseman 1859-1936. *The Shropshire Lad.*

The Labour government inherited a strange and expensive contradiction when it came to power in 1997. The external threat facing Britain was far less than at any time since 1945, yet defence strategy was based largely on preparation for imaginary wars against unknown enemies. Unlike all its other European partners, except France, the country's main deterrent was centred on the deployment of nuclear weapons. John Major's government had presided over a costly muddle. Wishful thinking came into head-on collision with economic reality. Military chiefs complained that they did not have the right equipment or enough servicemen and women; cuts and abruptly cancelled weapons programmes caused redundancies in the defence industry and yet Britain remained a high military spender compared with most of its allies.

The 1997 official statistics show that UK defence spending fell by 28 per cent between 1985-1995 reflecting the sharp downward trend in world arms expenditure.[1] However in 1995 Britain spent £386 per head of the population on defence. Only four other Nato countries, the US, Norway, France and Denmark, spent more. Ten others, including Germany, Holland, Italy, Canada and Belgium, spent less.[2] A leading defence analyst, Dr. Neil Cooper of the University of Plymouth, examined the distorted priorities of the Major administration. The UK spent 3.1 per cent of national income (GDP) on defence in 1995, as did France. Germany, which had a larger and more successful economy, spent only 1.7 per cent. Britain was the fourth highest spender in the league table of 15 Nato countries. In 1993 Britain diverted 42.5 per cent of government research and development funding into military products, France 33.5 per cent and Germany 8.5 per cent. In the same year 48 per cent of all Britain's export credits underwritten by public funds were military related, France 21 per cent and Germany a minimal 1 per cent. Only the equivalent of 9 per cent of defence expenditure was granted in overseas aid, compared with 18 per cent for both France and Germany.[3]

The total UK defence budget for 1998-99 was £22.240 billion, with £9.78 billion earmarked for military equipment.[4] The latter represented an increase of £804 million over the previous year. A few large companies provide the bulk of this equipment. Although the Ministry of Defence (MoD) places over 70,000 contracts annually and more than 10,000 firms may be working on defence business at any one time, a study by the Centre for Defence Economics at the University of York showed that almost 50 per cent of MoD equipment expenditure in 1993-94 was awarded to only 18 companies. The top three companies (British Aerospace, GEC and VSEL) received nearly 25 per cent of the total.[5]

One of the many gaps in UK defence statistics is that the Ministry of Defence does not publish the *actual* amount paid to each contractor but divides the total of all expenditure into six bands—those paid over £250 million (10 contractors in 1997/8), £100—250 million (12), £50—100 million (19), £25—50 million (22), £10—25 million (51), and £5—10 million (67).[6] The top band is where the largest companies have flourished.

In the spirit of good financial housekeeping, Mrs Thatcher's government decided to abolish the old 'cost plus' form of defence tendering whereby the manufacturer would give an original estimate but the final bill would be based on stated costs (often artificially inflated) plus a mark up for an agreed profit margin that the contractor, in consultation with the MoD, decided was appropriate. It was a practice familiar to anybody who has received a builder's invoice. The contractors virtually wrote their own cheques and the taxpayer paid. The system was changed to fixed price contracts but there were loopholes. If the MoD, for whatever reason, decided to change the specifications of the equipment after it had been ordered, it provided the contractor with the opportunity to re-value the price upwards. If the technology didn't work properly (see Chapter 4), the contractor had to go back to the drawing board and labour costs rose. In theory, these latter costs should be borne by the supplier; in practice, the MoD has been generous with our money.

The Ministry of Defence has published *UK Defence Statistics* annually since 1992 and it does include information that was not previously revealed. There is still, however, a distinct lack of clarity and some important omissions. One section covers major equipment projects, under three headings. In the 1997 edition, the basic facts on the Eurofighter were given as:

1 Expected in-service date: 2001.
2 Cost: £4.289 billion (development costs only).
3 Year(s) of peak expenditure: 2002-04.

This provided a snapshot of the MoD estimate for one year only and did not include a comparison with forecasts of previous years.

For instance, three years earlier, in the 1994 edition, the MoD's Eurofighter calculations read:

1 Expected in-service date: Early 2000s.
2 Cost: £3.463 billion.
3 Peak expenditure years: 1999-2000.

In other words, over a period of three years, the development costs rose by £826 million and the peak expenditure was pushed back between three and four years due to programme delays. However, past estimates were not shown, thereby hiding the trend of sharply rising costs.

The statistics also do not show the full picture at first glance. It is essential to read the footnotes and small print. In the 1996 Defence Estimates, the definition of the 'In-Service Date' (ISD) of RAF equipment is given as "the date when the equipment is available in-service and supportable *in sufficient quantities to provide the desired capability.*" (Author's italics). However, the ISD of 2001 for the Eurofighter carries a small footnote saying that that date is for the delivery of the *first* aircraft only. One aircraft is hardly likely to provide "the desired capability."

Another method of blurring the costs is by "rounding" to the nearest £100 million "for reasons of commercial confidentiality." For instance, the cost of the mid-life update (modernisation) of the Tornado ground attack GR1 was given as £800 million in each of the annual statistics over the three years 1993-95. With the "rounding" to the nearest £100 million applied this meant that the real cost was estimated at between £751 million and £849 million. In fact, the actual cost, published in 1997, was £934 million, way beyond any previous "rounded" estimate.

A phone call to the MoD Defence Analytical Services Agency (DASA) to ask why their figures were rounded to such a large amount as £100 million, and quoting a similar example on the Sea Harrier, did not elicit an immediate reply. They contacted British Aerospace and later responded by saying that as all contracts were now competitive, rival contractors could set their bids at a lower level if the real (not rounded) estimates were given. That was understandable—at least from British Aerospace's point of view—but wasn't competitive tendering supposed to obtain lower bids ? The helpful official said he was confident that the public interest would be protected by the National Audit Office who checked the figures. The only problem with that is that the NAO can comment only *after* the money has been spent.

In 1997 the cost of the new Hercules C-130J transport aircraft disappeared from the statistics. Given as £1.1 billion ("rounded" to £100 million again) in the 1996 edition, the information had been removed from the following year's publication for "commercial or other reasons." The MoD was not keen on letting the British public know how much of its money was being spent on this huge project or what was going wrong. However, the financial watchdog, the National Audit Office, later revealed that the aircraft was £49 million over budget and will be delivered late. The US contractor Lockheed Martin had to pay £23.5 million to the Ministry of Defence in penalty charges.[7]

The MoD's figures also do not allow us to know the value of UK military exports to individual countries. The ministry divides the world into only five areas of destination: 1. Nato countries (including the US) and other West Europe; 2. Middle East and North Africa; 3. Other Africa; 4. Asia and Far East; 5. Latin America and Caribbean. By aggregating sales into these huge geographical areas the ministry hides, for instance, the reluctance of the US, our main ally, to buy military hardware from the UK. The British manufacturers estimate that it takes only half as much from Britain as it sells to this country. Also conveniently hidden is Britain's dependency on Saudi Arabia for exports. Nigerian sales are buried in "Other Africa" and Indonesia in "Asia and the Far East." Another phone call to the statistics people at the MoD to ask for the figures for exports to the US and Saudi Arabia received the response that this information: "was not in the public domain."

Company accounts are not very helpful. Some do not even distinguish between defence and civil orders. Their annual reports often list products by technology grouping rather than the use of the product. This obscures the boundaries between military and commercial applications. For instance, GEC includes radar for the Eurofighter, torpedoes and missile guidance systems in the same Electronics Systems and Defence Group as in-flight video entertainment, overseas telecommunications and radio communications. It is impossible for shareholders or the public to know the investment, income, profit or loss for each of the products, civil or military. In its 1995 Annual Report, in an oblique reference to the cost overruns and technical failures GEC said: "Higher profits were made on marginally increased sales, but were restrained by further costs arising from *extended development* of a few important contracts." (Author's italics). For extended development read problems. The facts are known within the companies, particularly to those who work on the projects or have to meet the customers, but there is a reluctance on the part of the directors to reveal them publicly.

Employment

A career in the defence industries was once a guarantee of a well paid job with excellent prospects. The big companies trawled the universities on the 'milk run' looking for the best and the brightest who would contribute to the task of sharpening Britain's leading edge of technology. The employers were well funded by high defence spending and were confident. The Warsaw Pact was the visible enemy and the sheikhs were prepared to spend their oil money on British-made weapons. Those days are over. The companies are nervous about the immediate future and the average employment horizon is about as far as the end of a current order. The employment statistics speak for themselves but the loss to the overall UK economy from defence redundancies is extremely costly as the majority of those dismissed possess advanced skills and qualifications.

- Total employment in defence (excluding MoD employees and Service personnel) fell by over 50 per cent in the period 1980-95—from 740,000 to 360,000—a loss of 380,000 jobs over fifteen years.
- Jobs related to MoD orders for equipment for the British armed forces fell from 600,000 to 270,000.
- Employment dependent on military exports fell from 140,000 to 90,000.[8]

In the early 1980s when defence spending was still rising sharply, the cuts were largely due to the introduction of new technology and materials. The latter years have been characterised by the shrinking market, increased competition and the search by government for spending reductions to hold down electorally unpopular tax increases. There was little re-deployment of people into suitable jobs and no overall planning in the run-down. In many instances staff made redundant were later discovered to be essential and had to be re-hired on contract through agencies. Many of those dismissed left the defence industry to take jobs where their qualifications were not required or appropriate. A limited survey carried out by the Strathclyde Defence Industries Working Group questioned redundant employees from four defence companies in Scotland. Their main findings included:

- 77 per cent were skilled.
- 62.2 per cent had college or university qualifications.
- The average age was 49 for males and 39 for females.
- 42 per cent found advice from their company "not very helpful" or "not at all helpful."
- The second largest barrier to obtaining new employment (after lack of alternative jobs) was lack of training opportunities.
- 50 per cent found alternative employment within one year but at an average income of £1500 per year less than in their previous job.
- 23 per cent of these in employment were in temporary jobs. [9]

A study of defence industry redundancies in the South-West of England in 1995 by the Centre for Defence Studies at the University of York confirmed a number of important points:

- Those made redundant in the defence industries were comparatively well educated and skilled. Around 40 per cent had formal qualifications. One-third had been technical staff, and a further third skilled manual workers.
- Qualified staff had a better chance of finding work than those who were unqualified. Nearly 60 per cent of these had obtained another job.
- Few people found new jobs of the quality of their previous employment or which enabled them to use their defence skills.

- A substantial majority of those with a degree or above found jobs that paid £15,000-£30,000. Around 40 per cent of those with ONC/OND or below earned less than £15,000.[10]

Employees in the defence industries are now very much part of Britain's 'flexible' workforce that suffers from lack of job security, re-training opportunities and suitable alternative employment. The Conservative government ensured that it was easier and cheaper to sack people in Britain than in any other European Union country.

Downsizing

The Strand Palace Hotel, just off London's West End, was busy, even at 8 a.m. People were heaving suitcases out of lifts, paying bills and large families of large Americans battled with 'Full English Breakfasts.' In the street outside, Japanese tourists took photos of their families and friends posing nervously next to the homeless slumped in shop doorways; symbols of modern life in central London. Our committee of trade union officials were there at the invitation of the defence company's Human Resources Manager. He had refused to reveal the purpose of the meeting. We knew, however, that they were going to declare yet more redundancies. The reporters and television cameras had arrived before us as their sources inside the company had tipped them off that another "Job Loss Shock" story was about to break.

This ritual took place about once or twice a year and rarely varied. As we arrived the reporters would ask us if the rumours were true; the chairman of our joint national trade union committee would reply in impeccable trade unionese: "on behalf of the colleagues present" that we would issue a formal statement later. We would then disappear downstairs to meet the company management. After handshakes and coffee, the door would be locked to prevent any of us slipping out to ring our brokers and indulge in some insider trading when the Stock Exchange opened. The company's shares always rose when they announced layoffs.

The main board director would then read the same announcement that was to be made later at the plants affected. Due to "market conditions," or "cancellation of the contract by the government" or "further reductions in the defence procurement programme," cuts in overall employment levels were, regrettably, inevitable. Jobs would have to go. The company was not to blame. Every effort would be made to keep compulsory redundancies to a minimum and outplacement advice would be available. We would make notes, ask questions and reply that we did not accept that the cuts were either desirable or inevitable. Any compulsory redundancies would be resisted. The director would say that he quite understood.

Back in the hotel lobby, our chairman would tell the reporters that the loyal and skilled workforce would feel betrayed. The focus would then shift to the local sites where the real negotiations would take place. In the vast majority of cases the original number of redundancies were reduced due to the ability and determination of union representatives and officials.

The engineer

A visit to an aerospace factory is a fascinating experience. The design teams grapple with complex problems on computers and electricians fix the electronics in cramped cockpits. Craft workers using hand/eye co-ordination that only comes with years of practice bend sheets of metal to within tiny fractions of an inch. These are some of the finest engineering skills in Britain. There are none of the assembly line robotics of the car factory or the routine continuous processes of other parts of the manufacturing industry. When the plane is rolled out and takes off for its first test flight, the workforce has a natural feeling of collective achievement and pride.

To have to negotiate the redundancies of the people responsible for such quality is not fascinating; it is depressing. For those who lose their jobs, it is much worse. Their careers have been ripped apart, many will suffer stress and their families will be affected. Despite their high levels of skills, qualifications and experience they were working in the wrong industry at the wrong time. A feudal ruler in the Middle East, an African military dictator or a British government cabinet meeting could have taken the decision to cancel the order that led to their dismissal.

Andy was one of the redundancy statistics. Born in 1952 in East London, he had a natural liking and aptitude for mechanical things. After his family moved to the West Country he managed to obtain an electronics apprenticeship with his Higher National Certificate at a large engineering company. The company was subsequently sold and the plant closed down in 1974. He moved to a nearby town where he found the local firms desperate for any type of skilled labour. It was even recruiting unskilled workers who, after completing a three-month training course, were offered a 'skilled ticket.' Andy became a quality engineer working on standards and process specifications for military products. It was 1983, the Cold War was alive and thriving and Mrs Thatcher's government was ensuring that defence products were well funded by public money.

He became active in his trade union and was elected as one of the plant's senior negotiators. As time passed and he learnt more about the company's prospects, he became increasingly concerned. Defence contracts were being cancelled or postponed. All the unions on the site launched a prolonged campaign to persuade the management to consider alternative civil products. The company listened but refused to act. Large numbers of redundancies were imposed on the workforce in 1989 and for the next two years both morale and productivity sank. No one, including the managers, believed they had any future with the company. They were right. In mid-1991 the government cancelled a major missile project and the employees were called in individually by managers from other sites— who could be trusted to be emotionally detached—to be told that the remaining work would be transferred to other plants.

At 39 years of age, Andy was out of work and out of the industry. He received no offers of alternative employment. His redundancy compensation was two weeks' pay for each year of service; an amount that would support him for about six months. The company was more enlightened than others and established a fund for redundant employees to set up their own businesses. The recession had bitten deeply and there were few prospects of success. The only one of those businesses that survived was a co-operative that was given some military equipment sub-contract work but, ironically, found it more profitable to concentrate on medical engineering.

Andy managed to obtain a place at university, successfully completed a degree course in sociology and went on to a PhD in new management techniques. He looks back with some anger tinged with wry humour on his short career in aerospace. Many of his ex-colleagues still keep in touch. Some of the younger ones have moved away from the area to find suitable work but most are still unemployed or in short-term contract jobs. Part of Andy's academic work is to lecture on the nature of contemporary management-labour relations and the requirements and motivation of employees in the manufacturing industry. He has a personal case history to illustrate how British management and government can lose people whose skills would be highly valued in almost any other country.

The manufacturers

The public voice of the defence industry is the Defence Manufacturers Association (DMA) whose offices are situated in the leafy Surrey town of Grayshott. The President of the DMA is Lord Gregson, the Labour peer and industrialist. One of its members is the NatWest Bank, which although it does not manufacture weapons, underwrites arms exports. The DMA has been quite unlike its American counterparts. The latter are highly visible, vocal, semi-political organisations who make no bones about lobbying and try, quite openly, to influence Washington. It has a much quieter demeanour, almost understated, but is influential behind the scenes. It operates on the basis of the consensus view of its member companies, which is a considerable task, given the open hostility between some of them. Its traditional position has been that it has accepted government policy without question and worked within it. There are signs that this may change.

I visited the DMA before and after the 1997 general election. On the first occasion I met the Director-General Brigadier Brian Lowe and Mike Evans his deputy. I asked them whether they were worried about the future order books of the companies. Not surprisingly, they echoed the export or die theme and admitted that the industry would have been in "deep, deep trouble" had it not been for the Saudi Al Yamamah order. About 40 per cent of military equipment went overseas. That percentage must be increased. But to where? The economies of the Middle East were stagnant, the Third World poor, Europe was re-structuring and the US had effective controls on imports. Their answer was the Pacific Rim and the countries of the Far East with their (then) rapid rates of growth and sense of national identity. They believed that there was not a new arms race but, paradoxically, the more prosperous a country became, the more threatened it felt.

They said there was a considerable conflict of opinion in the defence industry over Britain's relationship with the US and Europe. Despite being the great proponents of free trade, the American market was one of the most restricted and subject to more political pressure than any other. The US government would only buy equipment that they believed to be absolutely essential and could not develop themselves. British companies differed in their attitude towards the US. Some, like Rolls-Royce, were tied-in closely to US companies such as Boeing for their civil jet engine sales, others like British Aerospace were part of the European Airbus consortium and had different priorities. A more pro-European consensus was emerging to counter the paranoid view that we must never upset the Americans. Closer European integration would allow us to bargain with the US on more equal terms.

What was the role of government? This question proved something of a problem. Whilst wanting to minimise interference by the MoD, the industry required a more "educated" definition of competition. Although not stated, this seemed to mean preference for British manufacturers rather than buying off-the-shelf equipment from overseas. They said we were still living "off the fat" of the research and technology developed in the early 1980s but where, they asked, was the money going to come from over the next critical 10-15 years? It was one of the real issues still left unresolved. The Department of Trade and Industry should "come out of the shadows" and start to tell the MoD about the potential role of defence technologies in the civil sector. They did not expand on the apparent anomaly of welcoming public funding whilst at the same time rejecting any control by Whitehall.

One of Brian Lowe's final comments was that if Britain does not capture 20 per cent of the global arms market: "we are finished as a defence manufacturing nation." They did not fear a Labour government and reminded me several times that both the military and the industry believed that they had done better under

Labour governments than Conservative administrations.

I met Brian Lowe's successor, Major General Alan Sharman, six months after the election and there was a distinct feeling of unease in the air. Most of his member companies were wary of the forthcoming Strategic Defence Review and there was also a lack of enthusiasm by some for the government's decision to protect the Eurofighter programme. Although the aircraft had been promoted on the basis that it would benefit the whole industry, a significant number of those not involved believed that the ring-fencing of its extremely high costs could damage their prospects as it could take a disproportionate amount from the general pool of money available in the defence budget. He had mentioned this unbalancing effect to the Chief of Defence Staff whose reply was "very interesting" as he had said that that whilst the Eurofighter programme was really resolved, "the numbers (of the 232 aircraft ordered) are not."

I asked him what he thought of Robin Cook's ethical guidelines. He said that whilst on paper they were little different from the old rules, the main effect "has been a disaster" due to the failure of civil servants in the Foreign and Commonwealth Office (FCO) to risk "getting it wrong." The Department of Trade and Industry (DTI) which grants (or refuses) export licences takes advice from the FCO. Around 30 per cent of export licences were being referred to ministers by officials who didn't want to take decisions. The sale of an anti-mine flail to Canada for use in Bosnia had taken 15 months as the FCO civil servants had seen the words "Bosnia" and "mine" and had dithered. They did not appear to know that the flail was designed to clear mines. That was before and during the new guidelines. The average time to clear an application used to be 20 to 30 days. This had increased to around 100 days. The main sufferers were small firms, "the little chaps." He was sure that the outcome would be a lot of lost business which would show up in the statistics at the end of the year. He had been told of behind-the-scenes "shenanigans" between the DTI and FCO at the highest levels.

He was scathing about Robin Cook's decision to refuse to sanction the export of security vehicles to Indonesia. They were only the same type used by CNN and other news crews. The Foreign Secretary made the announcement when he was in New York, a week before the Labour Party conference. This was "extremely improper" as it effectively denied the companies their right of appeal. It was probably done to "appease Anne Clwyd (the Labour MP and anti-arms campaigner) and the rest."

How did his members now view the Ministry of Defence? This was extremely important, he said. The top people in MoD procurement (equipment purchase) are now making noises about "partnership" between government and industry. However, the culture below senior levels was going to take an "awful long time to turn round unless government brings in pretty drastic changes to kick things and make them go in the direction they want them to go."

Finally, I asked him whether his predecessor's view that the Asian countries would provide growing markets for his members' products now looked somewhat optimistic in view of the recent turmoil on their stock exchanges. He agreed and said that the ethical dimension would also cause problems. If we can't sell to Indonesia, what if Turkey wanted to buy 500 Challenger tanks? His organisation was going to become more pro-active than before and a new public relations officer was being appointed. The DMA was now in regular touch with the Conservative Opposition, providing them with information for Parliamentary debates.

My distinct impression was that if the DMA companies seemed temporarily dazed and confused, they were making every effort to get their act together. It was clear that they intended to intensify their lobbying up to the highest levels of government. Their past public reticence would be abandoned in favour of more active promotion of their products.

What about the workers?

The trade unions have always played a significant role in the defence companies. Organisation in the engineering industry throughout the automotive sector, shipbuilding and aerospace has traditionally been strong, partly due to high membership and networks of shop stewards in the blue collar areas. These sometimes operated outside their formal union structures and often attracted the disapproval of their National Executive Committees. These 'combines' eventually became accepted, and they played a key co-ordinating role in the successful 1989-91 campaign for a shorter working week in the engineering industry. The introduction of new technologies, particularly electronics, led to the growth of the white collar sector with a proportionate rise in the influence of unions representing supervisory, technical and managerial staffs. These tended to have more flexible structures which allowed local union representatives from companies or industries to meet centrally. They were able to research and co-ordinate claims and, importantly, discuss responses to their employers' wider corporate plans.

British industrial relations have traditionally been based on the confrontational model where both sides argued their case through agreed stages of 'procedure.' After procedure had been "exhausted"—an apt word—a compromise would be reached or a dispute begun. Given the time, energy and, often, heat involved, it might be thought that the defence employers would actively discourage union membership and organisation. In some areas this was true, particularly amongst senior staff, but managements usually accepted that their employees had chosen to be represented by a trade union. This continued even after Mrs Thatcher had made it easier for them to ignore that choice. One of the main reasons for the continued recognition was that local union representatives and officials, linked with their national officers, provided an extremely effective lobbying organisation. Most unions had Parliamentary Committees and sponsored MPs—almost entirely Labour—who could put down motions in the House of Commons. Many union representatives were also local councillors. Companies were happy to provide time off from work, paid travel, briefings and other facilities for lobbying for defence contracts. Those arrangements would not have been allowed for the preparation of a pay claim.

The most effective time to lobby is just before a general election when politicians pledge their support (for almost anything) and scramble to claim the credit. Ministers face pressure from their back-benchers to buy British and orders which have long been delayed are suddenly confirmed. In 1996 there were 27 Conservative marginal seats in areas which were at least partly economically dependent on British Aerospace.[11] The lobbies could be local, such as the campaign for the British Aerospace ASRAAM air-to-air missile in the Hertfordshire area in 1992, or Eurofighter, for which there has been both a national and international campaign.

A campaign that was not supported by the employers was the one that won the 37 hour working week in 1991. This started at the Tornado factory of British Aerospace in Preston. The Engineering Employers' Federation had refused to make any reduction in the number of hours worked despite negotiations that went on for many months. The union leaderships were hoping for a majority in favour of strike action at Preston but were not over-optimistic until a remarkable stroke of luck occurred. Admiral Sir Raymond Lygo, BAe Chief Executive, ignored the advice of some of his less gung-ho colleagues and decided to write to all employees at home telling them that: "British Aerospace has decided to stand firm on a policy not to reduce the working week." Angered by being written to by their ultimate boss for the first time at their private address—they had not been congratulated personally when record profits were achieved—employees voted decisively for strike action.

The company conceded after 18 weeks. Hundreds of other firms throughout the country followed. Despite all the threats of job losses and lack of competitiveness, a study of the campaign by the Employment Department subsequently found that productivity in the engineering industry had not fallen and, far from jobs being lost, potential redundancies were reduced as a result of the shorter working week.[12]

The trade unions have made specific proposals on key aspects of defence industrial policy, particularly on diversification to civil work. Their thinking on these issues has been well ahead of that of government and employers. One of the problems, however, is that the procedures of some larger unions, often created in the post-war years, are not always sufficiently flexible to take initiatives or react swiftly to events. Policy-making, in which few members participate, has to be processed through pyramid-like structures from local branch to region, national executive, annual conference and back again for action to be taken. It is a time-consuming system. The original pyramids were designed to bury the dead. Industrial issues such as redundancies can be dealt with more quickly but these are usually in response to employers' actions. It may be democratic but it is not always effective.

The European Works Councils have opened potential avenues of discussion on multinational defence companies' policies. Set up under European law to allow employee participation in management decisions, they were strongly opposed by the government of John Major. Many British and European companies ignored that view and are creating transnational Works Councils. Trade unions within the EU will be able to meet employers to discuss levels of employment, new products and investment. They will also be able to make proposals on issues such as diversification, civil technologies, re-training and new markets. The Works Councils will assume an increasing importance as more joint ventures and mergers are created within the European defence industries.

The boss

The history of British Aerospace is scattered with the names of famous companies that over the years were merged to create Britain's only manufacturer of fixed-wing aircraft. Sopwith, Gloster, de Havilland, Avro, Bristol Aeroplane, Hawker Siddeley, English Electric, Scottish Aviation and Vickers-Armstrong provided some of the world's finest designers and engineers. The post-war years saw US aviation taking many of the markets that were once dominated by the British. The declining Empire no longer provided a guaranteed monopoly on the long- haul routes and US national airlines bought American aircraft as a matter of policy.

It's a sad fact that British Airways has also traditionally bought from Boeing, refusing, until 1998, the option of the highly successful European Airbus. British Aerospace has a 20 per cent stake in Airbus and makes the wings at Chester and Bristol. UK defence spending protected the military aircraft sector during the Cold War years with BAe benefiting through the purchase of missiles, Tornado, Jaguar, Hawk and Harrier aircraft. Artillery, rockets and ammunition were supplied by its Royal Ordnance subsidiary which also owns the German company Heckler and Koch, one of the leading producers of sidearms and handguns. British Aerospace is ranked third in the league table of the world's arms manufacturers.

Its commercial aircraft division is now very much the junior partner in the company and significant parts of it have been sold to overseas competitors. All industry forecasts point to a rapid growth in sales of civil aircraft but BAe has relied on the once safer profits derived from the military sector. Much of its success has been due to the dedication and high levels of professional skills of its employees, especially during the bumpy period after the end of the Cold War. Despite this, it has insisted on reducing its workforce from 58,784 in 1991 to 41,800 in 1996—a loss of over 17,000 jobs—many of them professionals, engineers, scientists and technologists. The company's treatment of those made redundant was relatively fair in comparison with other defence employers, particularly GEC, who have rarely paid more than the legal minimum compensation. Cutting these labour costs it may have pleased the City but it lost the company some of the best people in the industry.

Sir Richard (Dick) Evans was the company's Chief Executive from 1990 until he was appointed chairman in 1998. Evans is probably the most powerful man in the European aerospace industry and was ennobled by John Major in 1996. A great survivor—he has seen three Chairmen come and go—he also provides a convenient target for campaigners against the arms trade. His slightly villainous appearance belies his personable affability. Having dealt with him for some years, usually over site closures, job cuts and mergers, I always found him blunt but likeable. British Aerospace paid him £727,879 including pensions contributions and bonuses in 1997. He also cashed in shares worth over £2 million.[13] He started work at the company's Warton site in Lancashire and was a member of one of the unions that merged to become Manufacturing, Science, Finance (MSF).

His rivalry with Lord Weinstock of GEC was legendary within the defence industry. GEC's massive cash reserves (£1.086 billion in 1996) fuelled the frequent speculation that it would make a hostile take-over bid for BAe. For many years the two men held diametrically opposed views on how the UK defence industry should develop. Evans wanted to create a series of joint ventures and Euro-companies with EU partners; Weinstock advocated a British defence 'national champion'—an enlarged GEC naturally enough—as the way forward. They exchanged blows in 1995 by competing to take over VSEL, makers of the Trident submarines. Their bids raised VSEL's share price to heights previously only dreamed of by that company's shareholders. After much public wrangling— GEC described BAe's financial performance as "deplorable"—the matter was referred by the Department of Trade and Industry to the Monopolies and Mergers Commission. The majority on that body recommended some restrictions on the GEC bid but were promptly overruled by President of the Board of Trade Michael Heseltine. A further brief flurry of punches took place before British Aerospace retired, claiming that it was far from hurt and well satisfied with the encounter.

Dick Evans believes in the working breakfast. As I waited to see him in the high-tech building in Brewers Green, near Victoria station, shirtsleeved men criss-crossed the reception area brushing flakes of croissant from their trousers. David Mellor rushed through clutching a bundle of newspapers. Several meetings were in progress, all scheduled to be attended by the Chief Executive. The timetable had slipped. Seemingly energised by the pressure he launched into a quickfire analysis of his company's world role.

He said that the main threat facing the UK defence businesses was the situation created by what he called the "gorilla" mergers of the US defence giants. The challenge, "without a shadow of a doubt," was how Europe as a collection of national defence entities could be made into something that could "harness the scale" to create a force to rival the Americans on a global scale. This was not a "fortress Europe" policy—both the US and Europe needed to buy and sell from each other—but on equal terms. The Americans had no compunction in using the mechanisms of their stock exchange to arrange protective mergers; in Europe it was much more complicated and involved governments. Overcoming that problem was the single greatest challenge.

I asked Dick Evans about past sharp differences between his more European approach and the British defence 'national champion' policy of Lord Weinstock. Apparently that was now all in the past. "Arnold has created international joint ventures in two-thirds of his business; in telecommunications with Siemens of Germany and in power generation with Alsthom of France". More recently he had linked up with Thomson, another French company, in defence. "Arnold's position is no different from ours." But weren't these joint ventures forced on GEC through its technological weakness? Wasn't it the case that both Siemens and Alsthom were more advanced? He waved the thought away. How you define weakness, he said, is a matter of opinion; the fact is that Weinstock took those decisions.

What about the war of words during the VSEL contest? Evans shrugged. In such circumstances, those sort of things happen. What virtually nobody understood was that from the BAe point of view the VSEL dispute and the amount of City support for the British Aerospace bid was "a major turning point." Arnold accepted the fact "that we were not the financial basket case they had tended to paint us." Until then the GEC argument had been that the BAe recovery was a mirage. Furthermore, the amount of financial detail both companies were obliged to supply to the Monopolies and Mergers Commission demonstrated that a lot of the claims GEC were making about BAe "were built on sand." A GEC takeover was out of the question. In any case, GEC was a very different company under George Simpson, the new managing director, who used to work within the British Aerospace group when it owned Rover cars.

The BAe boss stressed that government had an essential role to play in linking the industrial and defence interests of the country. Britain was unique in leaving its aerospace sector so unprotected. The export markets were now much tougher than in the past. The main reason was that the huge decline in the budget for military equipment in the United States had made the American companies "much hungrier" than they had ever been. The US political leadership had no hesitation in intervening in bids for overseas contracts. There was no doubt that Clinton had heavily influenced the Saudi Airlines contract won by Boeing and McDonnell Douglas. BAe was "bloody fortunate" in having an aircraft like the Hawk for which the Americans did not have an equivalent. The real crunch will come over the sales of the Eurofighter. The Americans only have the much more sophisticated and expensive F-22. For a single F-22, he said, it's possible to buy "half a squadron" of Eurofighters.

So, if all these planes are nearly ready to fly and to be sold on the world market, whom are they designed to fly against? This was not such certain ground for him. He said that although today's state of the art aircraft were designed fifteen years ago, at the height of the Cold War, there was still "instability" in many parts of the world. I wondered why the Russians were participating in the American JSF future strike aircraft project? Were they still the enemy? Neatly side-stepping, he said that was not his concern and suggested I talk to the strategic thinkers at the Royal United Services Institute who dealt with those sort of questions.

How did he feel about the company's dependency on Saudi Arabia? This was changing. About one-eighth of BAe's *total* (civil and defence) business was with that country. And in defence? One-quarter or more? Possibly. He said people should realise that BAe's defence business was a not a growth area and the Saudi contracts were nearing completion. Four-fifths of Al Yamamah had been supplied and there would never be another order of that size. Half joking, he said a lot more profit could be made out of the termination of contracts than out of their completion. Realistically, Saudi has a tiny population, and there could never be a revolution on the scale of Iran, and, in any case, there was a Western, that is, American, strategic interest involved. The Gulf War was fought on that basis.

Did he regret his part in the attempt to deport the Saudi dissident al-Mas'ari? There was no doubt in his mind that he was a genuine political refugee but he couldn't understand why we were "giving house room to this guy." He should not be able to conduct political activities from this country. Al-Mas'ari was a "one of the absolute militants of Islam" who was advocating violence and if "those guys ever get into control in Saudi Arabia it would make the people in Iran look like relative moderates." It seemed a good idea to change the subject. He was equally outspoken on the question of the sale of Hawks to Indonesia. There was no evidence that they were being used in East Timor, if they had been, he would have been "down at the Foreign Office" protesting along with the anti-arms trade campaigners. Evans had met the protesters and had nothing against them—as long as they got their facts right.

He did not think there was much of a sales challenge from the former Warsaw

Pact countries—the bureaucracy was "absolutely horrific." One of the biggest threats in a restricted market was the Americans dumping second-hand equipment. What were the employment prospects in BAe? *If* the UK aerospace business as a whole was to maintain current levels of employment, it must claw back from 9 per cent of the world market to at least its previous level of 13 per cent. He was hopeful that employment numbers had stabilised at British Aerospace: they were trying re-build their graduate base through recruitment from the universities. The company was in good shape.

The Chief Executive had been in a typically bullish mood. This had served him well in grimmer times when the City analysts needed some convincing that the company was not in financial free fall. He accepted that while defence remained big business for the company, it was not growing and that the civil sector represented a better chance of success. It was obvious that like other defence industry leaders had had no clear idea of who the 'enemy' was, but in the meantime the defence bandwagon should be kept rolling. Ironically, most of his worries were not about military enemies but the danger to his business from our old ally, the United States of America.

Dick Evans had emphasised the importance of politicians taking the right decisions so it seemed appropriate to go and talk to some of them. It would also provide an opportunity to compare their views before the general election with decisions taken afterwards.

The Conservative Minister

It took some time to arrange a meeting with James Arbuthnot, Minister for Defence Procurement in John Major's government. The MoD is British industry's largest customer and as the man with the huge responsibility of overseeing £9 billion of military equipment purchases, it was perhaps understandable that his Press Office would want to check, double-check and check again the questions that I intended to ask him. We talked in his office, sitting on a battered leather couch next to the table first used by the War Minister Lord Kitchener in 1914.

Our meeting took place on the day before a £4 billion package of orders for cruise missiles, anti-tank weapons and patrol aircraft was announced. The Chancellor of the Exchequer, Kenneth Clarke, had been trying to block the deal on grounds of cost but Defence Secretary Michael Portillo had pushed the cabinet to give the go-ahead. I asked Mr Arbuthnot whether the justification for buying CASOM, the air-launched cruise missile, was the poor performance of the Tornadoes in the Gulf War. There was a pause. It had become "pretty plain to everybody" he said, not just to the service chiefs, that smart weapons were essential to reduce collateral damage, particularly in Bosnia. The Gulf experience had showed us that aircraft had to get near the target and were vulnerable but laser-guided bombs were extremely effective. It would be far better to use a missile that could be launched 100 miles away from the target. As far as the patrol aircraft was concerned, he stressed its air-sea rescue role. But why had the American defence press described its prime task as spying on Russian submarines? "It does lots of different things, following the Russians or anything else." Making sure the "integrity of our defences" were intact was its most important role.

Mr Arbuthnot said that whilst he agreed: "we had lost an enemy," the world was not a more stable place. Wasn't it problem though that in the late 1990s we were buying equipment designed to fight the wars of the 1980s? He said that there used to be something in that point but our procurement programme had now changed to allow us to "fight more flexibly." Did he have any thoughts on the future JSF (Joint Strike Fighter) programme being organised by the Americans. The Russians are also participating. Who had authorised the payment of £133 million of our money to allow us to take part? He explained it wasn't just the MoD who took the decision: "We had to convince the remainder of the government that it was just as sensible a use of taxpayers' money as opposed to buying a hospital, building schools, universities or whatever. It was possibly one of the best investments of our money that we could have made." Other countries were looking to join.

I was confused. If this is a club that anyone can join, what purpose does it have? Who is the enemy? The minister patiently explained the logic of it all. Looking at things as they were at the moment "it might be possible" to say that there was no obvious threat but we saw how important technology was during the Gulf War. Countries can change their intentions: "within twenty minutes." If a country changes its attitude towards us and is equipped to defeat our armed forces, the fact that twenty minutes ago they were friendly towards is no comfort. Quite. Point taken. Perhaps a fellow Joint Strike Fighter consortium member or someone like Saddam Hussein, to whom we sold military equipment? Wrong. Mr Arbuthnot corrected me. The conclusion of the Scott Report was that we didn't sell him military equipment. I changed the subject.

I admitted I had never really understood how the MoD came to a firm conclusion on what new weapons should be bought and from whom. He explained that it was the job of the MoD to ensure that the country was defended effectively and his job, as the purchaser for the armed forces, was to buy the equipment at least cost. "Operational requirements" were determined by research and those requirements were then bought by his department. Some were long term and some were short term, such as in Bosnia. Like what? Boots. Boots? Yes. A new type had been designed. "For the first time, the British armed forces are making use of the clothes they are issued with and not going out to buy their own at their own expense. That is an example of the way in which we respond to the sort things the armed forces tell us."

Should we buy British and why do our defence manufacturers complain that we don't get a reciprocal deal from the US? The minister spoke very clearly and deliberately. I was obviously a slow learner. "We-believe-that-competition-is-the-best-way-of-doing-our-basic-job. We don't want the Americans to give us orders as of right but we do need access to their markets. There is a worrying tendency in the US, and in Europe as well, to buy from the home base simply on the basis that it must be the best." Yes, but isn't that connected to the jobs argument? Well, that may be attractive in the short term, but it leads to protectionism, lack of competitiveness and reduction in free trade. We must remember it was free trade that got the economies of the world to take off.

How do the Americans block our potential defence exports? Well, the US administration is sympathetic to our point of view but it is harder to get it across to the more "widely spread" American politicians that protectionism through the 'Buy American' policy is damaging their interests. Did we buy the US Apache helicopter, upsetting the French and Germans, to influence the Americans? No, we had recently joined the Franco-German Armaments Agency and were part of the European multi-role armoured vehicle project. The vehicle is known as the "battlefield taxi." I asked whether the driver would demand a tip or refuse to pick up people in the rain. The minister looked blank then joined his advisers in discreet laughter.

How about the projects where things had gone badly wrong, both in terms of vast cost overruns and technical failure? We were told they were essential for our defence but they had been long delayed and we did not appear to have been vulnerable without them. He said this raised two points: the first was that the armed forces should be properly equipped to provide a credible deterrent. "If you try to equip yourself after the enemy has declared war, it's too late." The second was that the MoD is transferring the risk to the prime contractor as the ministry "is not frightfully good at managing risk." The supplier should take on that responsibility, co-ordinate the sub-contractors and bear any cost overruns. So the taxpayer won't have to fund the cost of any future mistakes? Ah, well, the minister felt it was not quite as black and white as that, but every effort was being made to minimise that risk.

I pressed him a bit harder. Why were the development phases so long and often delayed that the equipment was out of date on delivery? If companies in the commercial sector operated like that, they would have lost market share and have gone out of business years before. What was different about the MoD and the military manufacturers? If we said to a civil supplier: "Look, this is what we want and this is when we want it" for, say, battlefield communications, there is a strong likelihood that they would meet their targets. Did he agree? Well yes, but then we would have to ensure that our communications systems "meshed in" with those of our allies. I didn't ask why one of the main complaints of the Services is the current lack of common standards and compatibility of equipment within Nato.

I enquired what he thought about the ethics of MoD staff and Service chiefs going to work for their suppliers through the 'revolving door' system. He believed the rules were strict and the inside knowledge they would bring to their new employers would be "rapidly perishable." His assistant popped her head round the door and smiled. Watches were scrutinised, my time was up. Mr Arbuthnot retained his seat at the election and was appointed Opposition Chief Whip.

The Labour Party

I had no problems in meeting Dr David Clark, the defence spokesman for the party prior to the election. He is an extremely nice man with a genuine courtesy that is rare in the Parliamentary arena. A keen gardener and ecologist, he blends almost invisibly into the hedgerow of politics and is noticed only by those with a trained eye. Rumours were already circulating that he would be moved to another job if Labour gained office.

I wondered why he thought the Defence Manufacturers Association had objected so strongly to the party's decision to undertake a major defence review when in government. He too was puzzled. After all, he said, the military chiefs were in favour and had gone so far as to conduct their own review. But wasn't this their attempt to try to keep politicians off their patch, stop spending cuts and pre-empt a new government? He didn't think so. It would make the task of a new Labour government much easier. However, his party's review would be wider. It would fit the defence strategy within its overall foreign and security policy. This would be in the *long term* interests of the defence industry because then everyone would have a "fair idea" of where Britain would be going in defence terms and in our relations with Europe and America. We would know what sort of equipment would be needed.

We moved gently on to the question of arms exports. I raised the question of the party's emphasis on the importance of overseas sales. Wasn't Saudi Arabia, our biggest customer, a bad economic bet for the future? Were the rulers repressive? He had clearly given considerable thought to the matter and his conclusions seemed firmer than on some other issues. The United Nations endorsed the right of every country to self-defence and "you don't make judgements about the particular form of regime in a country" unless the UN specifically says so. It's quite legitimate to trade with these countries. It's difficult for Westerners to come to conclusions about different cultures. East Europeans, for instance, do not share our view of what constitutes human rights. But, I asked, if we sell them *our* equipment surely *we* should have the right to make a judgement about what they did with those weapons? OK, he had no doubt whatsoever that we should have that right but he had come to the conclusion we should carry on and trade as we have done. There was no problem about trading with the Middle East countries except for, of course, Iraq and Iran. There should be a common European approach although the French were problematical.

What about the scenario where a powerful customer like Saudi Arabia could interfere in the internal affairs of the supplier's government? He believed the Conservatives had "completely mishandled" the al-Mas'ari deportation affair but the bulk of British exports to Saudi were civil not military. A Labour government, "as far as one can see because things change very quickly in that part of the world," would continue to trade with the Middle East and Saudi Arabia. That would include military equipment.

How would Labour's defence review avoid the pitfalls of the past when hugely expensive equipment was ordered, only to find that a few years later a change in world politics meant that it could no longer fulfil its original purpose? Why was there so little discussion, in Parliament or public, as to whether these projects were necessary or not? He agreed that was "fair comment," wrong decisions had been made, although Eurofighter was so far down the line that there was no going back. Whether or not a specialist Parliamentary committee should be established to debate and monitor new projects was an open question but he had been very impressed with the joint working party of the House of Commons Defence and Industry Committees which looked at the links between the two areas. So that was a body which could scrutinise proposed defence contracts? Possibly, but unfortunately it had concluded its work and was not due to meet again. Could it be revived? That could be part of the new defence review alongside a "more open dialogue" with the manufacturers.

What about opening up the Ministry of Defence? He believed a Freedom of Information Act was essential. The real problem with the ministry was that just about every job was duplicated; a civil servant looked at something, then passed it on to someone in the military, who then passed it back. Everyone looked over each other's shoulder. The organisation has got to be slimmer and more devolved. How did he feel about the revolving door and jobs for the boys? What concerned him most was that people working for the MoD on buying items for a specific contract leave and then go and work for the contractors on the same project. That could not be right. OK, what should be done? We must try to look at it. The rules must be tightened. How? We've got to be pragmatic. Maggie tried but she was polemical rather than pragmatic.

David Clark denied that the Labour Party had backed away from its promise to help defence companies diversify into civil opportunities. He said, however, that we made a mistake in the past by believing that a Defence Diversification

Agency (DDA) was all that was needed. Part of his job had been to educate the party to demonstrate to them that it was not the *whole* answer. After the Labour Party won the election there was going to be such pressure on time that legislation on the DDA would not be forthcoming in the first session of Parliament. It would take *time*.

What kind of structure would the DDA have? A structure would have to be worked out. And the funding? He couldn't be too specific—we joked about Gordon Brown listening at the door—but it would definitely come out of the MoD budget. Although major changes "won't get a slot" in the first year, the DDA principles must be established within two years. The trade unions would definitely be involved, together with the industrialists. The people who run, research and develop the company products must be consulted. The work will really start after the defence review.

Given the reluctance of the party leadership to talk openly about defence, whether the military or economic aspects, David Clark had been helpful. I had the feeling, however, that a large number of the pieces of the jigsaw were still missing and those that were on the table didn't quite fit together. While there may have been a determination to change things, the specific means were not yet part of Labour Party policy. In fact, it was not clear that there was much that could be termed a policy other than a wish list of desirable actions that *might* be given some priority.

As I left the House of Commons the mid-day newspapers were carrying Tony Blair's statement that the laws on the sale of guns should be tightened. Easy access to weapons, he said, made it inevitable that some would be used against innocent people. He was referring to the shootings at Dunblane.

I next met David Clark some months after the general election. He had been appointed Chancellor of the Duchy of Lancaster and was in charge of drafting the Freedom of Information Act. I told him that the Ministry of Defence had refused to provide the figures on British weapons exports and asked if these would be available under the new Act. He said he wasn't sure but I should apply and, in future, the MoD would have to give specific reasons, in writing, for any refusal.

David Clark was dismissed by Tony Blair in July 1998 in a cabinet re-shuffle. He had been pursuing the new legislation quietly but vigorously. Some powerful ministers, including those at the Ministry of Defence, were nervous. They did not want their little empires opened up to the public gaze.

The Liberal Democrats

Menzies Campbell is the highly-respected defence spokesman for the Liberal Democrats. I wanted to seek his views on the effectiveness of the Defence Select Committee on which he has sat for a number of years. However, he was determined that I should see the whole of his party's policy and gave me a copy of *Shared Security,* a 1994 document drawn up by a committee chaired by Lord Bonham Carter. The section on 'Controlling the Arms Trade' was considerably stronger than that of the Labour Party's pre-election policy. Its first sentence read: "For a world beset by poverty and disease, the international arms trade constitutes a great evil."

Menzies Campbell also said that he opposed the sale of British Aerospace Hawks to Indonesia. He felt that the company might be upset with him but, on the other hand, he was a strong supporter of the Eurofighter. Unlike Labour, he was not in favour of a major defence review as he envisaged already demoralised senior military staff: "jumping off the 13th floor at the Ministry of Defence." The problem was that there had been no strategic thinking by the Labour Party because "what they have done—no pun intended—is to try to defuse defence."

The booklet said that all companies should be required to publish in their annual accounts the amount invested in research and development and the breakdown between civil and military production together with any government subsidies received. It was more ambivalent on levels of overall UK defence spending, saying that it would like to see it fall, as a proportion of national income (GDP), but that we should be prepared for an increase if the international situation worsens. It did not mention any of the MoD overspending that could be eliminated to ease the burden.

I had previously heard Menzies Campbell criticise the inability of the Defence Select Committee to deal with issues as they arose and he confirmed this. "We operate in a kind of *ex-post facto* environment. In the main we are reactive rather than creative. If people start complaining about Gulf War syndrome and getting nowhere with the Ministry of Defence, they then start writing to us and at that stage we then institute some sort of investigation." There was also a problem with time and lack of resources. "There are only eleven of us (MPs) on the committee, almost all with other responsibilities, and our support is only one clerk and three assistants." The situation in the United States is "totally different." He had a friend on the US Senate Armed Services Committee and their resources were much greater. There was a clear "tension between the Committee and the Ministry of Defence on what Parliament should be told in the national interest." Its role was more of a "watchdog or scrutiny committee rather than an initiating committee." It would take a "sea change for that to alter, together with a massive increase in resources." It was unlikely that government would make those changes as Select Committees "have the capacity to embarrass them."

I wondered why the defence debates were so low-key and largely unreported. He explained that two Parliamentary days a year were spent on the Defence Estimates and three single days for each of the armed Services. I was surprised when he told me that the main two-day debate had taken place, a month before I met him. I had heard nothing about this. He tried remember "anything that was said that was of any moment." He paused. "I can't think of anything." There had been no real debate and, therefore, little or nothing had been reported.

He argued strongly that we should not continue to pay over £1 billion a year to keep troops in Germany and said that he "was laughed at" by Conservative ministers when he had raised it two years previously. In keeping with his party's pro-European stance, he fervently believed that as the pressure was downwards on all West European defence budgets, the logical conclusion was greater integration. The French had previously had a "go it alone" policy and had annoyed the whole world with their nuclear tests. He said that they had been persuaded by the Americans to reduce the number of tests originally planned in return for the release of US classified computer simulations of nuclear explosions.

Within a more cohesive Nato that included the French, it was "absolutely nonsensical" to have 8 nuclear submarines (4 British and 4 French) without any operational integration between the two countries. He said that whoever won the election there would have to be a review of the nuclear deterrent but he firmly believed in the British independent deterrent as a "form of insurance." But how independent is it? It relies entirely on US technology and re-fitting. He still felt that "as long as there is any threat to the integrity of this country it is right to retain the deterrent." Finally, I asked whether if we didn't possess nuclear weapons, would we need to develop them? "No. Obviously we couldn't afford it but the real problem is what will succeed Trident."

Eighteen years is a long time, especially in politics, and those to whom I spoke to had been conditioned by the prolonged period of Conservative government. However, I did sense a feeling that if given a chance, most would be prepared contribute to fresh thinking, particularly about how to harness defence resources to the country's efforts in the civil markets. The arms manufacturers, often painted as the villains of the piece, were worried and saw their American counterparts as the real threat. They were reluctant to take risks but knew that their traditional profits could no longer be guaranteed and that in the longer term they had little to lose by a change of direction. They needed the mechanisms for that change to be put in place. The politicians, conscious of the media and public opinion, wanted to appear positive and innovative. The people who worked in the defence industry required re-training and career development. All believed that the *status quo* was not an option.

References

1 *UK Defence Statistics 1997*. HMSO.

2 *UK Defence Estimates 1996*. N.B. The Defence Estimates were not published in 1997 due to the change of government.

3 Paper *The Cost of UK Defence Exports* based on his book *The Business of Death*. I.B. Taurus 1997.

4 *UK Defence Statistics 1998*. The Stationery Office.

5 *Study of the value of the defence industry to the UK economy*. Centre for Defence Economics, the University of York December 1995.

6 *UK Defence Statistics 1998*.

7 *Ministry of Defence: Major Projects Report 1997*. National Audit Office. The Stationery Office.

8 *UK Defence Statistics 1997*. HMSO. The MoD changed the basis of calculation of the figures for 1996, moving to Standard Industrial Classification (SIC) 92. This showed an increase in the number of people employed (415,000 in total) but cannot be used in comparison or to calculate a historical trend until future figures are available.

9 *Redundant Defence Workers Survey*. Strathclyde Defence Industries Working Group. March 1996.

10 *Defence Industry Redundancies in the South-West Region*. Centre for Defence Studies. University of York. January 1996.

11 *Sunday Business* 21 April 1996.

12 *The Economic Effects of Reductions in Working Hours. The UK Engineering Industry 1989-1993*. Ray Richardson and Marcus Rubin. Employment Department 1994.

13 *The Guardian* 28 March 1998

CHAPTER EIGHT

PEOPLE AND INNOVATION

Change is in the blood and bones of the British.
We are by nature and tradition innovators, adventurers, pioneers.
Tony Blair. Speech to the Labour Party conference October 1997.

It costs the British public £3 million to train one RAF jet pilot or navigator. That is more than the entire annual training budget of many companies. The intellectual and organisational skills needed by aircrew in a highly advanced technical environment are expensive but necessary. The RAF understands clearly that the individual in charge of millions of pounds worth of equipment must know exactly what he, or more rarely, she, is doing and why they are doing it. Our armed forces are among the best trained and most effective in the world. Unfortunately that is not true of many people employed in British industry.

The fact that Britain has concentrated so much on defence at the expense of the civil sector is reflected in the contrast between the levels of achievement of those in the Services and the general workforce. Even the most lowly-ranked infantry soldier has to have a good working knowledge of complicated weaponry, communications and geography. This involves a great deal of intensive training. Unemployment is one of the main recruiting agents for the armed forces and many of those who sign up initially have few skills, low levels of literacy, numeracy and, increasingly, are physically unfit. There is no doubt that by the time they leave the Services, their abilities and potential will have been improved considerably. Whether they will then find suitable employment is another question. The number of Service personnel fell from 274,800 in 1993 to 210,100 in 1998, a fall of almost 65,000.[1] As they exchanged their uniforms for P45s, it would have been little consolation for them to know that their levels of competence in electronics, mechanical and electrical engineering, and other skills, were higher than most of the rest of Britain's unemployed.

The leading edge?

Towards the end of 1987 a seminar was held at Ditchley Park in Oxfordshire with participants from the Soviet Union, the USA and the UK. It was chaired by ex-Prime Minister James Callaghan and was called, somewhat intimidatingly: 'End of Century Tasks: Coping with High Technology, Industrial Transformation and Economic Interdependence.' The Cold War was thawing and it was the first such quasi-official meeting during the Gorbachev period to be attended by scientists, business leaders, politicians and commentators from the three countries. The Foreign and Commonwealth Office held a prior briefing for the UK participants. It was held under what are known as 'Chatham House Rules,' a very British arrangement which allows everyone to speak freely on the understanding that nothing can be attributed to individuals afterwards. I was there to present a short paper on education and training.

The common theme that ran through most of the contributions on science and technology was the need to find ways to free research from the Cold War dependence on defence funding. The Soviet experts spoke forcefully of the overt dominance of the military establishment; for the West the problems were as acute but more complex. This issue linked directly with the paper from Richard Foster of McKinsey, the US consultants, which was based on his book *Innovation; The Attacker's Advantage*.[2] He addressed the question of 'discontinuity' in the process of change. His main conclusion was those who rely on a steady, continuous rate of development will lose out to rivals who can handle the leap from one type of technology to another. To stay ahead of the pack, organisations (and their governments) should anticipate change and act before they are swept aside in a highly competitive environment. To react is to be too late. The specific example he gave was the transformation caused by the switch from old electromechanical equipment to fully electronic systems. He said that NCR, the American company, had announced that $140 million worth of newly designed cash registers had been written off because they had failed to foresee the advent of electronic machines, many made in the Far East. The Chief Executive Officer was sacked along with thousands of workers.

The point he made then about the changing nature of technology is now a commonplace but the question of managing discontinuity remains a key issue in British industry as a whole and defence in particular. Neither government nor most companies have acted to anticipate change and now face problems in two main areas: the economic dislocation caused by the end of the Cold War—evidenced by thinner order books—and the challenges posed by the need to switch technological priorities into the civil sector. Britain's recent record in science and technology suggests that the latter issue must be addressed swiftly.

Until 1983/84 government-funded research and development (R&D) directed at military requirements exceeded that for the total of *all* civil objectives. The Ministry of Defence is still by far the largest single recipient of funds from the total government R&D budget. In 1995 it took 38.9 per cent of all the money made available. Industrial development received 9.6 per cent, health 7.6 per cent and environmental protection 2.3 per cent.[3] At a time when Britain desperately needed to develop world-class products and with the defence market in decline, the government spent over four times as much money on military research as it did on civil industrial development. In the league table of the 'Group of Seven' industrialised countries, Britain is bottom (together with Italy) in investment in research and development (as a percentage of sales).[4]

The extent to which government has supported research in defence companies at the expense of civil enterprises is clear. In 1993, companies involved in civil R&D drew 5 per cent of their funding directly from government; defence companies received 50 per cent.[5] The effect of the bias of successive governments towards defence has been to starve the productive civil sector of the funds essential for the intellectual and technological base of industrial innovation. This had three main results:

- Military R&D absorbed large amounts of scarce resources, including scientists and engineers, that could have been used to advance civil technologies.
- Expenditure on defence research created the potential for new weapons, thus justifying more military spending.
- The internationally competitive nature of military research helped to drive the arms race.

Despite being the largest single recipient of European Commission research funding, Britain's overall research effort has been flagging badly in recent years. This is hardly surprising as companies in this country still insist on paying their shareholders twice as much in dividends as they invest in R&D. Their overseas competitors spend three times more on R&D than on dividends.[6]

Re-skilling the people

Most British manufacturing employers, including the defence companies, have adopted a *laissez-faire* attitude towards training. It is easy to find firms where there are both redundancies and posts unfilled due to a lack of appropriate personnel. It often does not occur to management that, for instance, word processor operators or junior technical staff can be trained to become computer programmers or software engineers, occupations where there are severe shortages. They do not understand that cross-training from a career path limited by obsolescent technology to one which has a long-term future will benefit both company and the individual. The technical press is packed with advertisements for qualified staff offering relatively high salaries. Most employers look to this type of recruitment to solve their problems rather than seeking to improve the skills of their current workforce. Ushering employees out of one door towards the dole queue while opening another for new starters clutching large remuneration packages is not a sensible policy.

The nebulous term 'human resources' was imported from the US and depicts people as passive beings, to be turned on or off like a water main or an electricity switch. People are creative and, if permitted, able to generate ideas at all levels, even in the rigid hierarchies that still form the basic organisational structures of most British companies.

Britain's record on training and career development is poor compared with that of other competitor countries. In 1964, the Conservative government under Edward Heath was so unimpressed with the country's training performance that he proposed to establish 27 Industry Training Boards (ITBs) through an Industrial Training Act. These covered 15 million employees. They were statutory bodies based on the firm principle that companies would be required to spend enough money to train sufficient employees to agreed standards. This policy was supported and eventually implemented by the following Labour government.

The largest of these was the Engineering Industry Training Board (EITB) which included most of the defence sector. The main board was tri-partite, comprising employer, government and trade union representatives. Academics and specialists also participated. A financial levy was introduced which could be waived through a rebate if the minimum requirements were met by the employer. Area Manpower Boards, which also included local authority representatives, were established to shape regional initiatives. Training advisers, who were among the best in Europe, were appointed to assist the companies in reaching their targets. The system was rather rigid in some respects but, by and large, it worked. The Department of Employment said that the number of workers undergoing training increased by 15 per cent between 1964 and 1968.[7] The EITB's main drawback was that it related mainly to traditionally male craft and technician areas and did not cover adequately the later computer-related skills of information technology. It also involved too much form-filling and paperwork.

Rather than make the necessary changes to bring it up to date, Mrs Thatcher's government decided to abolish it, along with most of the other training boards. Her narrow ideology was unable to comprehend that, unlike other countries, Britain had so neglected vocational training, it had been necessary to place a legal responsibility on the employer. She was supported by a campaign run by the 'Group of 14' personnel managers from some of the large engineering companies who believed that they could look after their own training needs and did not need the stimulus of the EITB. The Engineering Employers' Federation eventually concurred with its abolition, although within one year it was complaining of "the delay between perception of a need and development of trainers and training programmes to meet it."[8]

The EITB was abolished in 1991 but its real influence effectively ended the previous year. Its successor body is the Engineering Training Authority (Entra) whose powers are limited to information and exhortation. It was no surprise to those of us who survived the transition from the EITB to the Entra Council that voluntarism (later re-defined as 'partnership' under New Labour) produced no better results in 1994 than prior to 1964. After only 3 years, an Entra survey revealed that the number of trainees in the engineering manufacturing industry had fallen from 64,200 in 1990 (3.4 per cent of total employment) to 42,300 in 1993 (2.6 per cent). The number of trainee professional engineers, who should represent the best hope for the future, dropped by 5,000—from 8,300 to 3,300. In any case, all these figures were pitifully low in a total industry employment of 1.59 million in October 1993.[9]

Nearly 50 per cent of the people working in the British engineering industry have no vocational qualifications. This compares with 23 per cent in Germany.[10] The survey also showed that the greatest source of untapped potential was women. Despite all previous initiatives, such as 'Women into Science and Engineering,' the number of women employed as professional engineers (as a percentage of that category) had remained static at 5 per cent. They did, however, constitute 36 per cent of administrative and clerical jobs and 42 per cent of operators and assemblers. These were the lower paid, non-career jobs. There is no 'glass ceiling' in the defence or general engineering sectors, it remains solid and very visible.

There is also a lack of young people. More than one-fifth of the 9,000 engineering apprenticeships on offer in 1996 were unfilled due to lack of interest and high-calibre people.[11] In early 1998 Britain's largest car maker, Rover, advertised vacancies for 250 routine production-line jobs at its Solihull factory. Over 3,000 people applied. It also announced the creation of 150 well-paid skilled engineering posts. There were 20 replies. The company said: "we want skilled British workers but if we cannot get them we will have to go to Germany, France and Italy."[12]

Britain's low-skill, low-wage economy is a major handicap in the quest for innovation. We have neither the high pressure education system of France or the planned work-based training of Germany. Only in Britain is the subject of training a guaranteed mind-closer in any discussion about jobs. Unemployment is a hot political topic but one of its main causes—the lack of appropriate skills—is deemed to be a worthy bore. To the young unemployed, it has meant yet another discredited 'scheme' with little money; to the better educated it seemed irrelevant until the time came when their knowledge and skills were outdated. France has a training levy on employers and Germany ensures that extensive workplace training takes place through its 1969 Vocational Training Act. Young people in this country leave school or university, try to find suitable work and, if they do, are largely left to make career progress through their own initiative. The Labour government has said that it is determined to change this passivity into a pro-active training culture.

The Thatcher government launched 82 Training and Enterprise Councils (TECs) in England and Wales in 1990. They were designed to be run by local business people with a first-hand knowledge of the type of training appropriate for their companies. However, the rules on the funding of TECs ensured that the stated purpose of ensuring high quality courses would not be achieved. Public funds paid the TECs by the number of trainees cleared off the unemployment register up to 13 weeks after the end of their courses. This virtually guaranteed that the courses were aimed at filling the more available job vacancies in the low paid, less skilled areas of employment.

The TECs contract out the running of the courses to suppliers, some of whom have taken the money and supplied little relevant training. The National Council of Citizens Advice Bureaux reported hundreds of complaints of fraud, bogus qualifications and cheap labour being used for such jobs as shelf stacking. Hairdressing is by far the most popular course. The National Audit Office estimated that the TECs overpaid suppliers by £30 million in 1993/94.[13] The TECs total budget was cut by the Conservative government from £3 billion to £1.4 billion. If training in the armed forces had been organised on the same basis most units would comprise cooks, storekeepers and waiters. The TECs do have potential but they need to be re-structured, better funded and tailored to providing worthwhile jobs.

Labour policy

The Labour Party has always had a long term commitment to a national training culture. Tony Blair made it clear that this aim, linked with education, was to be at the heart of his government's efforts to transform Britain into a modern economy based on opportunities for all. This was widely welcomed. When shadow employment spokesman he forcefully advocated a key element of this strategy. A compulsory levy on employers was to be enforced to make them spend a reasonable amount on training. Unfortunately that principle was abandoned just before the general election when the Labour Party policy paper said only that "we would expect" that all employers should invest in training and learning.[14]

Given that the document was called *Labour's Plans For A Skills Revolution* and quoted the fact that Britain was ranked 40th out of 48 countries for "motivation to retrain," it was difficult to see how employer motivation would be achieved merely through government expectations. Such wishful thinking has not borne fruit in the past. Despite the evidence, Labour believed that: "a training system with a top down approach, levies and rebates, all through government, is simply not appropriate for the majority of industries."[15] The political search for consensus with business had removed the main stimulus to the industrial re-skilling that would help keep businesses alive. In its anxiety to grasp something 'new' and non-confrontational, the party had returned to the very old pre-1964 principle of government allowing many companies to ignore the needs of the very people that could bring them success.

The Labour government accepts, however, that that statutory training is appropriate for the engineering construction industry which is involved in major projects such as building oil rigs, but not for engineering as a whole, particularly the defence sector, which is responsible for multi-million pound aircraft, tank and submarine programmes. The reason is that the Engineering Construction Industry Training Board escaped the Thatcher axe and lobbied Labour leaders demonstrating a record of success. It still retains levies and rebates. Many of Britain's best companies do support this principle because they are fed up with their trained staff being poached by less scrupulous employers.

The Department for Education and Employment introduced a new programme 'The Learning Age' in 1998. It included proposals for a University for Industry and was aimed at those seeking to upgrade their skills. The programme had four priorities: skills for managers in small businesses; information technology courses for the unemployed; greater access to engineering theory; improved literacy. These were admirable intentions but again depended entirely on the goodwill and participation of the employer. This would be absolutely crucial to the success or failure of such an initiative. The initial funding came not from new government money but from raids on the funds of the TECs. People would receive £150 paid into an 'individual learning account' and would be required to top this up with at least £25 of their own money. A £175 account could fund a year of evening classes to get an 'A' level; an introduction to word processing; a three day initiation on the Internet or an eight week course in setting up a small business. The programme received a boost after its launch when the European Union agreed to pay £164 million towards its costs.

The 'Learning Age' publicity brochure provided the example of 'Kate' who works in a supermarket and has a husband and children. She speaks to her careers advisor, sets up the Learning Account with an electronic Smartcard and enrols on an IT skills course. Her manager is enthusiastic and agrees to contribute to her account. She goes to classes run by the local further education college on Saturday afternoons at the local library and gets on-line access to the course on her children's computer "in the comfort of her own home." She can also learn during the supermarket's "usual Tuesday morning training session." After five years 'Kate' has achieved National Vocational Qualifications (NVQs) in management and financial management, has been promoted and even persuaded her husband to start a course in French.

Unfortunately this is an unrealistic view of working and home life for someone employed in a supermarket, particularly if she is on, say, the checkout counter. Wresting the computer (if they have one) away from the kids after a long day at work would be no mean feat. Does the supermarket really have a *weekly* half-day staff training session? Is the local library still open? Does the college have the lecturers to run the courses? Around 18,000 posts of lecturers in further and higher education were axed between 1993-98. How many of the supermarket staff would be allowed to have time off on busy Saturday afternoons? According to USDAW, the shopworkers' union, that scenario gave a "distorted view" of life in a supermarket. In their experience there was unlikely to be a half-day a week training programme, time-off with pay would probably not be allowed and 80 per cent of retail jobs were part-time.

After five years of such difficulties 'Kate' might find that her previously supportive husband was learning French in order to emigrate. As a lone parent she would then have far less chance of continuing access to the 'Learning Age.' Such a view may be pessimistic but when the Open University, created by Harold Wilson's government, found itself facing a funding crisis in 1998 with the prospect of operating with 200 less staff and 5,000 fewer students, the government blamed the previous Conservative administration for under-spending while pledging to remain within its limits.

If a skills "revolution" did start immediately, it would need at least ten years for the benefits to feed through to the national economy. The Industrial Training Boards cannot be re-established but legislation could be introduced to *require* employers to enhance the skills of their workforce. Trade unions have proposed that a legally enforceable amount equivalent to 2 per cent of a company's payroll should be devoted to employee training.

The government has quite rightly placed considerable emphasis on getting young unemployed people into work and backed its commitment with £3.2 billion funding from a one-off 'windfall' tax on the privatised utilities for its welfare to work programme. Part of this is the 'New Deal' for 18-24 year olds who are offered the options of paid work, voluntary activities, education and training, improving the environment or self-employment. Those who refuse to take part risk losing up to 40 per cent of their benefits. Lazy employers who neglect to train their employees are not penalised.

British governments accept that military personnel need clear guidelines, commitment at all levels (not just among the lower ranks) and the right equipment to achieve their goals. They should equally realise that those principles apply to training people for civil employment. After its Strategic Defence Review, the government could profitably turn its attention to a strategic training review that would examine all the existing schemes, practices and relevant bodies. It could make proposals that would help to boost Britain's flagging performance in the provision of new skills and career development.

Does manufacturing matter?

The manufacturing industry in Britain does not have a good image. It's spokespeople, often earnest men with strange haircuts, complain frequently that young graduates prefer the law, financial services or the City rather than join them in the real world of making things. The contrast between the imagined world of smoke-stacks, assembly lines and flat caps compared with that of shirt-sleeved dealers, power-dressed women and computers is stark. In fact the image is false; much of what remains of modern manufacturing in Britain takes place in clean, purpose-built centres. Many high-tech business offices are so cramped and unhealthy that if calves or lambs were trapped inside, animal rights campaigners would be protesting in the street outside. Engineers grumble that their profession does not convey sufficient status in comparison with their counterparts in other countries. They often refer to the large number of engineers on the boards of directors in Japan and Germany. Many would like to have 'Engineer' as a title before their name as it is in some other parts of the world.

Much of this search for approval is due to the fact that they are often badly paid and have little influence at their place of work unless represented by a professional organisation. They know that in France, Germany, Italy, Japan and the USA their talents would be valued much more highly than they are in Britain. It can't be easy for a qualified metallurgist or aerodynamacist to watch news clips of young men in red braces shouting into a dealing room phone and know that the dealer's pay and bonuses are many times greater than their own. Just under 19 per cent of the UK total workforce is employed in manufacturing, only 1 per more than in Ireland.[16]

Britain's problems with the lack of qualified staff will worsen as the pace of the movement of labour within the countries of the European Union quickens. These will be particularly acute in the defence sector as it re-structures through cross-border mergers and joint ventures. Employers here will be even more likely to fill the gaps with people from continental Europe on fixed term contracts with better salaries than those paid to British employees. The standardisation of qualifications between the EU countries is now well advanced, particularly in the professional areas, making the old barriers legally and practically redundant. The superior language skills of those coming to work here allow them to be much more mobile than their UK counterparts. If some of the shortages can be allevi-ated—even in the short-term—by the employment of overseas staff, our employ-ers will be even less motivated to train their British employees.

Within the joint ventures, British employees will be at a distinct disadvantage compared with their overseas colleagues. Very few UK companies offer language tuition. While English is the common technical language in the aerospace indus-try, to be able to perform competently in the wider aspects of employment (and socially), it is necessary to speak the language of the host country. When British Aerospace was planning to merge its missiles division with that of Thomson of France, it was forced to send key personnel on crash courses in French to enable them to establish a working relationship with their opposite numbers. The merger was subsequently called off after a disagreement about whether the company's Chairman and its Chief Executive should be British or French. At a more basic level British Airways revealed in 1996 that they had been forced to recruit cabin staff for Gatwick Airport from France and the Netherlands due to the lack of foreign language skills in Britain.

There are about 115,000 qualified accountants in this country, only slightly fewer than scientists. Many science graduates are choosing accountancy as a career because the pay and conditions are often better. From 1985 to 1993 salaries for male scientists in the private sector fell from 15 per cent to 10 per cent above the average for all white collar employees. For scientists in engineering, which includes most of the defence companies, it fell from 14 per cent to 10 per cent. Pay for accountants rose from 11 per cent to 17 per cent above the average. Solicitors earned 34 per cent more than scientists.[17] In 1992/93 nearly 19,000 university science graduates found employment in the UK. The vast majority went to work in the public sector. Only 5,000 took jobs in manufacturing while 4,000 were attracted into commerce and other non-science related employment.[18] Those statistics spell decline for Britain's industrial future.

The defence companies have traditionally paid the highest salaries in the engineering industry. The downside is that stress is a major factor for many of those working on military products. Due to the often closed nature of their work and the restraints of the Official Secrets Act, they cannot talk about their jobs, even to their families. They are unable to share their worries and problems. Defence employees do not agonise about the morality of lethal products. They take pride in contributing to something that is usually interesting, often ingenious and sometimes physically impressive. If asked, however, they almost always agree that they would prefer to work on a product that would directly assist human progress. Engineers often mention new types of hospital and medical equipment.

If successive governments had diverted some of the money spent on military production into civil manufacturing—particularly towards research and development—Britain could have developed far more world-class products. Those successes would have provided real motivation for young people to seek well-paid careers in the wealth-creating sectors that support the provision of good public services. Unfortunately, the exaggerated demands of the defence lobby were always given priority.

Changing course

New and profitable areas of civil manufacturing could be found within defence companies by using military-related technology. This type of initiative has had a number of names: arms conversion, alternative production, diversification or, in the US, economic conversion. All are imprecise and have at various times been promoted either as a quick fix for defence companies in trouble or ridiculed as wishful thinking. Diversification is probably the most accurate description as it indicates a planned move away from traditional military production towards civil opportunities, while keeping some defence capacity, rather than the sudden wrench of conversion. Pinpointing the most appropriate term, however, is less important than finding new production opportunities. Simply withdrawing money from the defence budget without planned alternatives has already caused economic hardship for those people who have lost their jobs in the industry.

The best known initiative was the Lucas Aerospace Corporate Plan. Drawn up in considerable technical detail in 1976 by a trade union committee of shop stewards and white-collar representatives, it said that Lucas would have difficulty in finding sufficient new defence orders and proposed specific alternatives. Included in its ranks were senior technologists and engineers who believed that it was perfectly feasible for the company to design and produce medical equipment; transport vehicles and components; new braking systems; energy products and undersea devices. They placed strong emphasis on the social use of the products. Many academic staff and researchers also assisted the project. The obstacles they faced were formidable. The hostility of the company, the indifference of the then Labour government, inter-union rivalry and, possibly the main problem, the fact that they were ahead of their time. The defence industries were relatively prosperous in 1976 and few people believed that they would decline to today's level of jobs and orders.

The campaign lost its momentum after the dismissal of Mike Cooley, a union activist and one of the key technologists behind the plan's priorities. Strikes aimed at his reinstatement were not widely supported. Nevertheless, the ideas sparked by the Lucas initiative struck a chord well beyond this country's borders. It is still possible to meet trade unionists and others who work in the defence industries of many other countries who have not only heard of the campaign but have also attempted to emulate it.

Diversification, once derided as the dreams of peaceniks, is now taken seriously by the defence industry even if it is not often put into practice. The general attitude is that expressed by GEC in its evidence to the House of Commons Trade and Industry Committee in 1993 when it said that: "a UK Defence Diversification Agency with adequate funding wisely allocated could give rise to immense benefits, but it would be no help at all to establish a bureaucratic organisation offering only advice."[19] Even the Department of Trade and Industry issued a booklet of good cheer to companies caught in the trap of making military equipment that was no longer required. The problem with this publication was that it was strong on advice but lacked any offers of practical assistance.[20]

Mrs Thatcher's government recognised the wealth of technology in the defence sector and knew that very little of it was finding its way into the commercial field. Michael Heseltine launched Defence Technology Enterprises (DTE) with a loud fanfare at Lancaster House in 1985. Venture capital was provided by eight consortium members in partnership with the MoD. Its purpose was to transfer technology from the government defence research establishments to develop products that could be sold in the civil market place. By 1988 it had attracted 260 member firms and 32 licences had been taken out to use ideas that were previously locked behind closed doors in the military research establishments. It was estimated that £60 million of business could have been created over the next ten years.[21] Five years later Defence Technology Enterprises had disappeared. The government made no official announcement and refused to give reasons. The Defence Manufacturers Association said that it had been poorly publicised.

The understanding of the need for alternatives has reached a wider political audience than could have been imagined at the time of the Lucas Plan. The Scottish Arms Conversion Project organised a fringe meeting at the 1994 Conservative conference and the room was packed with delegates worried about local defence factory and dock closures. Roger Freeman, the Minister for Defence Procurement, came along to listen. Unlike his predecessors, he understood the effect that MoD decisions had on industry and took steps to establish a point of contact by setting up a joint body of the House of Commons Industry and Defence Committees. Unfortunately, it only produced one report before it was disbanded. Mr Freeman was subsequently re-shuffled upwards. The political consequences of constituency job losses and spending cuts has concentrated the minds of those who once would have brushed aside the idea of using defence technology for alternative purposes.

Trade unions, whose members stand to lose most if the current drift continues, have continued to pursue the issue vigorously. In 1990, three defence unions with a membership that covered jobs from senior aerospace managers to dock and factory workers published *The New Industrial Challenge*, an analysis detailing the specific steps that could be taken by government, companies and employees to move from military to commercial production.[22] The unions were Manufacturing, Science, Finance; the Institution of Professionals, Managers and Specialists (the technical staffs' union within the Ministry of Defence) and the Transport and General Workers' Union. It was widely welcomed and its rationale was not disputed. The problem of how to overcome government (then Conservative) indifference and the over-optimistic view of the companies about the state of the export market was not solved, however, and blocked any practical progress.

Diversification from products no longer needed in the military arena to bring benefits to the civil sector is nothing new in Britain. Substantial funding was provided for scientists and engineers during the last world war to research new weapons and technology. They applied their knowledge subsequently to develop non-military applications. Some examples included:

- Antibiotics. Alexander Fleming discovered penicillin in 1928 but it was never mass-produced until it was needed to protect allied troops during the war. Scientists at Oxford University persuaded the American pharmaceutical companies to produce it on a large scale, thus cutting its price tenfold. It then became readily available to the public.
- Computers. Programmers at Bletchley Park, near Milton Keynes, developed the Colossus, a code-breaking machine with 1,500 valves that could read 25,000 characters a second. It was instrumental in intercepting German High Command messages. Much of the technology was later used at the University of Manchester to develop the first electronic computer.
- Radar and Microwave Technology. The invention of radar gave early warning of enemy aircraft attacks on Britain. It is now used in the civil aircraft sector, for collision avoidance and storm warnings. Amongst its many other spin-offs are microwave and communications technology.
- Space research. Hitler's V-2 rockets brought devastation to London towards the end of the war. Many of the Nazi scientists who worked on them were captured and taken to the United States and the Soviet Union to pursue their careers designing missiles during the Cold War. The technology was also used for more beneficial purposes including weather and communications satellites that greatly improved our knowledge of the environment and transformed inter-continental telephone systems.[23]

There are those in the defence industry who argue that such examples were only possible in times of forced change. They say that in switching from a war economy to peacetime production, demobilisation and government intervention were necessary then but such needs and mechanisms no longer exist. It is quite true that the modern scale of the problem is smaller, but the waste of military technology and people's skills is just as acute. The main difference is that there has been no recent collective determination to deal with the issue. Governments were unwilling to intervene, the defence companies searched desperately for new sales in a smaller world market and employees hoped that fresh contracts would turn up.

Another argument against planning is that that military science *automatically* produces tangible benefits, thereby providing some return on the money spent. This is sometimes known as the 'non-stick frying pan theory.' It uses the example of the spin-off from the US inter-continental ballistic missiles (ICBMs) which produced the technology that allows us to fry eggs without having to scrape the pan afterwards. It is said that the Teflon type material developed as a low resistance surface for the ICBM led to a breakthrough in the manufacture of kitchen utensils. There are many more recent examples, including the redundant Soviet SS missiles which now provide the titanium for some of the latest American golf clubs. These products may indeed enrich our lives but it would not have been beyond the ingenuity of scientists to have developed them without first having to spend billions of dollars on missile programmes. The scientific breakthroughs of the last world war were picked up and used in the civil field but unlike later military technology they were out in the open. The government was also prepared to play the leading role in ensuring that their application would be spread more widely and beneficially.

The hands-off optimism that declares that defence technology will inevitably move across to be used in commercial products is paralleled by a pessimistic school of thought that believes that diversification is impracticable. This extends to some defence academics, one of whom, Professor Ron Smith, who has frequently argued for defence spending cuts, has written: "Trying to convert arms factories to alternative production is as sensible as trying to convert coal mines to alternative production. In one case the problems are geological, in the other cultural. Dependence on military contracts appears to induce attitudes and practices, such as performance-maximisation rather than cost-minimisation, which inhibit adaptation to profitable commercial production. When you have put a lot of your life into learning how to do one thing well, it is very difficult to switch to doing something completely different. Such a switch is hard for individuals, though they can manage it; it is almost impossible for whole plants or organisations."[24]

The analogy between coal mines and defence production is misleading. It is true that geology is largely unchangeable in the short term—unless by earthquakes or explosives—but working practices, old habits and obsolescent products do not need such a dramatic shock. They have been transformed in the civil sector. Even people in universities who have spent much of their lives learning "how to do one thing well" now find themselves working within an environment that has switched from an academic to a more business-orientated culture. There is no cultural or practical reason why a diversion away from defence production could not be implemented through re-training and capital investment. It could be at plant or regional level, depending on the nature of production and the technological base.

Many countries, including Britain, are experiencing varying degrees of de-industrialisation and it could be asked what makes the defence industry so special that it should be granted state assistance. There are a number of factors which distinguish it from other declining sectors and make it a clear government responsibility:

- Production and research has been related entirely to military needs determined by government. The state has often been the main or only buyer, thus making normal commercial marketing activities irrelevant and linking supplier and customer in a unique relationship.

- The defence industry has taken a disproportionate amount of professionally qualified staff and technological developments have been funded by government to a far greater extent than those in the commercial field.
- The concentration of production in certain regions has caused particularly acute local problems. Around 77 per cent of the employees in Britain's main defence contractors are based in only four regions—the South-East, the South-West, the North-West and the North.[25]
- Governments negotiate disarmament treaties that may cut production and result in job losses.

In Britain possible solutions to a problem are often met with the standard counterblast that demands to know immediately from where the money is going to be found. Any opinion that says that the government might just have some financial responsibility—especially if it created the difficulty in the first place—is met with incredulity. For defence diversification, however, there is money available. It comes from the most obvious source—the cash saved through defence spending cuts. The fact that so far it has been frittered away by government—like North Sea oil revenue—only emphasises the need to allocate it to specific targets. A realistic defence diversification programme could have been funded, even under the random defence spending cuts made by the Conservative government.

In 1992, the MSF, TGWU and IPMS, the unions that have led the debate, undertook an analysis of defence spending reductions based entirely on official government (Treasury and MoD) figures and forecasts by City analysts. They calculated that after a ten year period (1990/91 to 1999/2000) a total of £30.5 billion would be saved. This would be the equivalent of £21.9 billion at 1990/91 figures. The savings would increase gradually, year by year, from £800 million during the first year to £6.8 billion for the tenth year.[26] Given that there is money available, the opportunity is there to be seized by a government that believes it has an active rather than a passive role to play. This does not mean a return to centralised planning or re-nationalisation. It does mean, however, that just as a government is elected to determine the defence needs of the country, it should also support its civil industrial requirements.

Blue skies

"One of them carries his laboratory files and books in a wicker basket, balanced African-style on his head. Another is always seen running between buildings. A third wears Wellington boots indoors... Eccentricity, ruffled hair and gawky movements in worn tweed jackets are part of the landscape."[27] David Shukman, the BBC's defence correspondent, found the stereotype of the British boffin to be accurate when he visited one of the country's top research establishments at Malvern in Worcestershire. He was also aware that he was amongst 1,500 of Britain's most brilliant scientists and engineers. Unlikely as it may seem, those cerebral types were in the same business as the uniformed men in the marquees at the Farnborough and Aldershot exhibitions. Shukman was visiting the Defence Research Agency (now re-named DERA—Defence Evaluation and Research Agency) where many of the people were involved in what is known as 'blue sky' research. This allowed freethinking, imagination and invention without limits or deference to conventional methods.

One of the most important results achieved by DERA was the development of thermal imaging, the technology that allows the human eye to see through cloud or at night. Heat, generated by the object, rather than light, creates the image. The invention has been crucial to the development of night-vision for military reconnaissance and weapon sights. Firefighters also use a civil version to discover living creatures buried under rubble after an explosion or a natural catastrophe. By far the greatest amount of DERA's work, however, still remains tied to the restrictive requirements of the MoD where the 'blue sky' concept is rare except for when officials and ministers dream up reasons for extra funding. There are 8,000 scientists and engineers employed at the various establishments of DERA. The technologies covered include:

- Acoustic, electromagnetic and electroscopic sensing.
- Aerodynamics and hydrodynamics.
- Electronic devices and components.
- Energetic materials.
- Propulsion.
- Guidance control and navigation.
- Signal and information processing and computing.
- Structures and material sciences.

These are all leading edge technologies and their development would be immensely useful in the civil sector. DERA made a technological breakthrough which can replace bulky television sets with flat, wall-hung, high-definition screens. It can also project 3D images. The potential world market for this is vast. The manufacturing license was negotiated with a Japanese company—there are no British-owned television manufacturers. It is not difficult to imagine how Britain's industrial performance would have been improved if the collective intelligence of DERA had been released earlier to work on inventing products that would sell in the commercial markets.

The Defence Research Agency was formed in 1991 as part of the MoD. It brought together the four previously separate establishments of Signals and Radar, Admiralty, Aerospace and Armaments. DERA is an umbrella body also covering chemical and biological warfare, defence analysis and test establishments. It is the largest defence research agency in Europe. In 1997 DERA had a turnover of over £1 billion and an operating profit of almost £76 million.[28] It was turned into a Trading Fund in 1993. It now 'sells' research to the MoD and other government departments who provide the bulk of its income. Customers in the civil sector are also sought but they constitute less than 10 per cent of its turnover. A programme known as Pathfinder is the agency's main outside initiative and is aimed at stimulating the defence industry to make proposals that can be included in DERA's research work. In theory this can also include projects for civil work but in practice it has been almost wholly military-orientated.

The Labour government has decided that DERA will incorporate the new Defence Diversification Agency (DDA). It is intended to assist defence manufacturers move from purely military production to innovative civil products. If this is to be successful, DERA will have to change its military-industrial culture to a much more commercially accountable approach.

The problems it will have to overcome were shown clearly in a Channel 4 television documentary on the agency in early 1998.[29] DERA had been given the task of producing the battlefield equipment for 'the soldier of the future' within the programme known as Future Infantry Soldier Technology (FIST). Its customer, the Ministry of Defence, was represented by the Brigadier in charge of Army Requirements. He was clearly impressed with the prospect and explained that "firepower," "communications" and "situation awareness" were the key aspects of FIST. About £3 million had already been invested.

Out in the field, Dave, the FIST trials manager, was more sceptical. He had been with DERA for thirty years. A group of specially selected infantrymen and DERA staff grappled with the complex technology of a soldier's huge bulbous helmet that contained a TV screen and satellite-linked communications. One of the watching squaddies observed that there was no need for the enemy to aim at the man anymore: "just go for the fuckin' contraption—what a target!" The experimenting soldier no longer had to jam the rifle in his shoulder as it was not aimed by conventional sights. A 'Video Aiming System' would automatically find the target. Unfortunately the sun was shining and the TV screen—worn like a pair of spectacles—became invisible to the soldier. He had no idea if his aim was accurate or when to squeeze the trigger. It was decided that the system wouldn't be of much use on sunny days. The Brigadier had explained how troops in the deserts of the Gulf would find FIST a great advantage. "Disaster," said Dave.

It went from bad to worse. The team decided to demonstrate how the future soldier would no longer need to communicate by voice in the old-fashioned way but would receive orders through pictures in his helmet. The old and the new were to be compared to prove the superiority of technology. Thirty infantrymen charged across the scrubland shouting "fuck" and "dickhead" at each other in the time-honoured manner. The two high-tech FIST soldiers wandered around with blank screens and no sound. The video link only operated within line of sight.

Finding the enemy proved no more successful. The Brigadier had said that maps were outdated and of no use in places like the Gulf. A 'Global Positioning System' would receive messages from satellites. Pink dots on the soldier's screen would then indicate the position of the enemy. It didn't work. The soldiers, who could see their destination clearly with the naked eye, were told by the pink dots and a £20,000 digital compass to travel at 90 degrees in the other direction. "As a navigation aid it made a good ashtray," concluded Dave and his colleagues.

The senior managers of DERA working on the FIST project assembled three weeks later. There was clearly a problem of how this was going to be reported to the customer, the Ministry of Defence. Future funding was at stake. It was decided not to discuss the outcome of the trials. Something called a 'first impressions report' had not been submitted "for obvious reasons." The team leader concurred. He thought: "We should play down the report and the scientific side to as low a level as possible. Minimum circulation. That OK?" Heads nodded. "What about the first impressions report?" "Might be best just to keep quiet."

Back in London the Brigadier was thrilled with the results. DERA had astutely sent him a CD-ROM showing how the 'future soldier' would dominate the battlefield. He believed that the trials had shown how the soldier was performing "infinitely better" with the new technology. The information would be fed into mathematical models that would give "even greater confidence" that this was a worthwhile investment. He said another £4 million would be spent on further research and trials. FIST carries on but with the work now being contracted out to an industrial consortium. It hopes to have positive results by the year 2008. Meanwhile the money pours out.

DERA also established Dual Use Technology Centres (DUTC) to develop products that can be used in both the military and civil spheres. This was a useful move but as the whole of the past direction of DERA's work has been military it will be extremely difficult, without prior planning and training, for the researchers to give equal emphasis to the commercial field. The business methods are entirely different. The power of the Ministry of Defence compared with that of the Department of Trade and Industry has ensured that the gap between publicly-funded military and non-military R&D is greater in Britain than any other EU country with a large defence industry.

If discontinuity created by new technology is to be managed and turned to advantage, the first requirement is that we have to recognise that it exists—in all aspects of people's working lives. It can extend or limit choice. Defence is no exception. There is no problem persuading people that progress is essential, the difficult part is making the necessary changes. These can be disruptive and painful. Any effort to harness technology, improve training and promote innovation will face many obstacles. Proposals, particularly on defence diversification, will be greeted with scepticism by those who don't accept that change is necessary or those who genuinely don't think it can be achieved. Such pessimism is not easily overcome, but government, co-operating with companies and employees, could put in place a series of mechanisms and structures that would enable the problems and possibilities to be analysed and action taken.

References

1 *UK Defence Statistics 1998.* The Stationery Office.
2 *Innovation: the Attacker's Advantage.* Summit Books, New York 1986.
3 *Forward look of government-funded Science, Engineering and Technology 1994 and 1995.* HMSO.
4 *The Guardian* 26 June 1997. Taken from the DTI UK scoreboard figures. The percentages are: Canada 10.8, Japan 4.9, Germany, 4.6, US 4.3, France 4.0, Italy 2.3, UK 2.3.
5 *Forward look of government-funded Science, Engineering and Technology 1994 and 1995.*
6 *Contract or Career?* Association of University Teachers, Institution of Professionals, Managers and Specialists, Manufacturing Science Finance, NATFHE. March 1996.
7 *Training Levies in Four Countries: Implications for British Industrial Training Policy.* Peter Senker. Entra 1995.
8 *Industrial Strategy.* Engineering Employers' Federation 1992.
9 The Labour Market in the Engineering Manufacturing Sectors 1993. The Engineering Training Authority 1994.
10 *Productivity, Education and Training—An International Perspective Volume 2.* National Institute of Economic and Social Research 1995.
11 *Financial Times* 2 September 1996.
12 *The Guardian* 5 February 1998.
13 *The Independent* 15 January 1995.
14 *Labour's plans for a skills revolution.* The Labour Party 1996.
15 *New Labour New Life for Britain.* The Labour Party 1996.
16 *The Guardian* 31 December 1996 quoting the Eurostat LabourForce Survey.
17 *Contract or Career?* AUT, IPMS, MSF, NATFHE.
18 *Ibid.*
19 *British Aerospace Industry.* Report of the House of Commons Select Committee on Trade and Industry 1993.
20 *Changing Tack. New Perspectives for Defence Suppliers.* DTI 1993.

21 *Relationships Between Defence & Civil Science and Technology.*
    Parliamentary Office of Science and Technology 1991.
22 *The New Industrial Challenge.* IPMS, MSF, TGWU 1990.
23 *Sunday Telegraph* 7 May 1995. Article by Robert Matthews.
24 *About Turn, Forward March with Europe.* Chapter by Ron Smith. Institute
    for Public Policy Research. Rivers Oram Press 1996.
25 *UK Defence Statistics 1995.* HMSO.
26 *Defence Employment Briefing.* IPMS, MSF, TGWU 1992.
27 *The Sorcerer's Challenge.* David Shukman. Hodder and Stoughton 1995.
28 *DERA Annual Accounts 1996/7.*
29 *The War Machine.* Channel 4 TV programme 23 February 1998.

CHAPTER NINE

THE INTERNATIONAL DIMENSION

*We cannot bring ourselves to believe it possible that a foreigner should in
any respect be wiser than ourselves. If any such point out to us our follies,
we at once claim those follies are the special evidence of our wisdom.*
Anthony Trollope 1815-82.

The end of the Cold War had a massive effect on the main arms-producing countries. The number of jobs in the defence industries fell sharply in nine out of the
top ten military producers. Between 1987 and 1995 they were down by 48 per
cent in the former Soviet Union, 21 per cent in China, 34 per cent in the United
States, 36 per cent in the UK, 24 per cent in France, 60 per cent in Germany, 62
per cent in Poland, 46 per cent in South Africa and 36 per cent in Czechoslovakia.
In India, which was conducting an arms race with Pakistan, they fell by only 1
per cent.[1] The only countries where defence employment increased were
Indonesia, South Korea, North Korea, Syria and Turkey. In the areas where the
industry was state-owned, governments were able to intervene more directly to
attempt to deal with the problem. Little was done by those that believed that the
mechanisms of the market would ease the situation by forcing defence companies to diversify into civil products with better sales potential. Britain was a
prime example of this unrealistic school of thought.

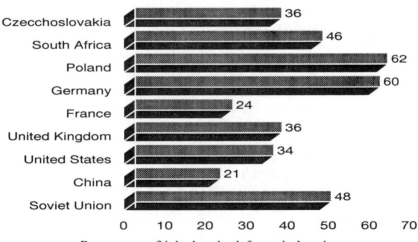

Percentage of jobs lost in defence industries
between 1987–1995

Globalisation is the much publicised phenomenon of the late 1990s. We are told that the convergence of information technology and finance capital has produced an economic whirlwind before which national governments can only run for cover. Huge chunks of pension funds are shifted instantly from country to country; unaccountable transnational financial institutions can determine where investment is placed and jobs created. In the West, many of the jobs involved in moving money around are not well paid and interesting but of the battery hen variety. People sit at small desks in long rows, their eyes focused on computer screens. Telephone headsets are plugged into their ears and their fingers flicker rapidly over keyboards. Repetitive strain and 'work-related upper limb disorders' are the modern industrial injuries. In the Far East, young women working for a few dollars a week ruin their eyesight testing the chips that power the electronic networks.

Ministers accountable to the public for the management of the UK economy have handed over responsibility for the fixing of interest rates to a committee of financial gurus with little knowledge of the manufacturing industry. If George Soros could make millions by outbidding and outwitting Norman Lamont in 1992—when Britain was forced to eject itself from the European Exchange Rate Mechanism—what can governments do? "We must all realise that we live in a global economy..." is the soundbite of politicians promoting inertia as a philosophy. The corporate Daleks say resistance is useless.

It all carries the heavy implication that the markets have a life of their own and human activity—particularly politics—is peripheral. The old theory of economic determinism is promoted as a new science. The financial soothsayers, investment pundits and economic tarot card readers play with other people's money and promise a bonanza return—subject to the small print—on our Peps and Tessas. Optimism is essential. The 'feelgood factor' is part of the system. Such rigorous logic ensures that share prices rise if England are set to win a Test Match or when the bells ring for a Royal Wedding.

Countries in the Far East adopted globalisation enthusiastically. Malaysia, Indonesia, South Korea, Thailand and the Philippines were held up as models to over-regulated economies, particularly those within the European Union. In 1997 these showpiece economies collapsed, revealing very shaky foundations. Short-term money left the region like air from a punctured tyre. Japanese executives wept and apologised on television. The Prime Minister of Malaysia who had spent so much of his country's money on armaments blamed George Soros (again) and President Suharto of Indonesia was forced to reveal his nepotism and corruption to the International Monetary Fund. As if to make some form of recompense, members of his family handed in bits and pieces of their jewellery to a national salvation fund.

As usual it was ordinary people who suffered most with previously loyal company 'salarymen' out on the streets protesting about the disappearance of their promised jobs for life. With no proper social security or compensation they had very little reason to thank globalisation. In effect their governments had declined to govern. Decisions that radically affected their economies had been left to the men in the boardrooms. This abdication of political responsibility had disastrous results. The dumb acceptance that those moving transnational capital cannot in any way be questioned, diverted, controlled, taxed or, on occasion, stopped is not modern thinking but a political excuse, sometimes dressed up in blurry philosophising about the 'Third Way.' Such phrases may sound deeply perceptive after the third bottle of Chardonnay but they have little meaning in the world outside the dinner party.

Global operators like Rupert Murdoch know this. They spend considerable time and effort trying to influence political leaders in order to allow them to evade controls on media ownership, or any other area of business. Their funds and political support—though temporary—are on offer to those who are willing to help them over the barriers. They have had some success in new Britain.

The forces of globalisation were initially weaker in the international defence manufacturing sector than in the civil markets. This was mainly due the industry's close links with governments, involving research and development funding, national security and policies of buying primarily from the home-based producer. Some years after the collapse of the Warsaw Pact official perceptions shifted radically. Less priority was given to the defence industries producing equipment for protection against external attack and more emphasis was placed on them as players in the international market place. This was partly due to necessity as the defence ministries in arms-producing countries were buying far less, but also in the hope of increasing overseas sales. As any major new defence project outside the USA was too expensive for one country alone, it was envisaged that cross-border mergers and joint ventures would be necessary. The companies understood the necessity but were slow to act. They had been locked in combat with each other for far too long to become sudden and natural allies.

The British, French and German governments told their manufacturers to make specific joint multinational proposals by March 1998. "They need to do it for their own survival," said George Robertson, the Labour Defence Secretary.[2] The companies responded by proposing a single aerospace and defence conglomerate comprising BAe, Daimler-Benz of Germany, Aerospatiale of France, CASA of Spain and the possibility of the Swedish firm Saab joining later. The catch was that this was only agreed "in principle." British Aerospace later bought a 35 per cent stake in Saab.

These dilemmas were reflected in Russia but in a different form. Some of the newly-privatised military manufacturers and design bureaux set up a network of banks and investment funds to attract capital. The Moscow Aircraft Production

Organisation (Mapo) formed Mapobank in 1993 to avoid a plant closure and in an attempt to start some non-defence production. The company had produced more than 3,000 MiG fighters in over 30 years. The head of development, Mr Smirnov, said that they were seeking foreign investment. "We are ready to co-operate to produce fighters or components for aircraft such as the Eurofighter," he said. "We want companies in the United States, France and to know who we are and what we can do—that we can produce technology that is competitive."[3] Mapo will, of course, continue to produce technology for the Russian military. Mr Smirnov's statement was a plea for help but if he and others like him are successful in attracting foreign investment to Russia it would add another interesting and potentially dangerous dimension to the international arms economy.

The large financial conglomerates obtain their capital from a variety of sources at home and abroad. They invest substantial amounts of that money in Western defence companies whose products are currently designed to be deployed against Russian equipment. If some of that money was diverted to Russian companies such as Mapo, the investor could be financing projects on both sides of the military divide. The advocates of globalisation would support such a move, arguing that national governments should not interfere with the free movementof capital.

A British reconnaissance aircraft tracking a Russian submarine could be manufactured by a company partly financed by the same institution that has a stake in the submarine's producer. The investor would benefit from maximum sales of both aircraft and submarines. The best way to achieve that would be through the existence of a high level of international tension and mistrust. Those with a direct interest in the profitability of such investments could persuade politicians in one country that more money should be spent by its government, not only on orders, but also on research so that the other 'side' could not gain a sudden advantage in detection or anti-detection devices. The military would undoubtedly concur and add its voice. The pressure to crank up arms production would increase.

Arming both sides in a war has long been the dream of the disreputable arms dealer. Financing both sides in making the weapons would be equally attractive to the morally neutral corporate investor. It has been done before but mostly by covert methods. Globalisation could provide new, legitimate opportunities. The Department of Trade and Industry, in consultation with the Foreign and Commonwealth Office, decides on what military equipment can be shipped to customers overseas. This is checked by Customs and Excise. What controls are there on UK money being invested in weapons production in Russia? The Department of Trade and Industry said in May 1998 that: "the short and simple answer is that there are no restrictions on UK companies investing in whichever overseas market they want, subject to there being no UN sanctions prohibiting such investments."[4] There are no UN sanctions against Russia.

When President Eisenhower warned of the dangers of the military-industrial complex he was talking of a collusion of *national* entities that drove his country to adopt a confrontational posture. The Soviet Union had its own vested interests with the same intentions. The global economy could create huge *transnational* military-industrial-financial complexes that would make Eisenhower's fears seem over-optimistic. At worst it could be dangerous, at best a waste of public money.

The United States, Russia and Western Europe are the main areas of arms production. South Africa is a recently liberated Third World country with a highly militarised industrial base inherited from the apartheid years. The problems and possibilities that face governments, companies and people in these four areas show how deep have been the roots of the arms economy.

The United States

The United States of America, founded on Thomas Jefferson's principle that "all men are created equal and independent" is the last remaining superpower. It has military expenditures of around $280 billion dollars (£175 billion) a year.[5] By 1996 its arms exports exceeded the total of those of Russia, Britain, China, France and Germany together. In 1995 half of all government-sponsored research—£23 billion—was spent on weapons development. In 1996—seven years after the end of the Cold War—it was planning the production of 30 Centurion nuclear-powered attack submarines at a total cost of £25 billion; 442 F-22 advanced tactical fighters at a total projected cost of £45 billion; 120 C-17 Globemaster transport planes at £212 million each and 20 B-2 Stealth bombers at £1.375 billion per aircraft (3 times their weight in gold). At the same time one American child in five lives in poverty (even after allowance is made for cash welfare, food stamps and tax relief). That is the highest poverty rate for children among 18 industrial nations. Ten million children do not have health care and 15 children a day die of gunshot wounds.[6]

It has often been said that the United States is a land of contradictions. Its constitution is a model of democracy but the stated good intentions of its foreign and military policies—backed up by overwhelming force—often produce a dire result. Many are devised for domestic consumption. There are 9 million people of Polish origin in the United States. Their organisations lobbied Bill Clinton during the last presidential election campaign demanding that he advocate an enlarged Nato. This should include Poland. Their main motivation was antipathy towards Russia. The campaign succeeded and he included the proposal in his election speeches. Loyal allies, including Britain, adjusted their foreign policies accordingly. There was little debate.

When Madelaine Albright, US Secretary of State, was advocating the bombing of Iraq in February 1998 in retaliation for Saddam Hussein's non-compliance with United Nations arms inspections, she said: "If we have to use force it is because we are America. We are the indispensable nation. We stand tall. We see further into the future."[7] She was expressing an attitude that much of the rest of the world, particularly in the Middle East, sees as typical and offensive.

Unfortunately the desire to intervene to bring 'stability' to a region has often brought with it the absolute belief that the imposition of American values on cultures many hundreds of years old is not only beneficial but essential. Mishaps and blunders in Cuba, Vietnam, Lebanon, Somalia and other areas have cost the lives of American troops and those of the indigenous population. Shock and bewilderment, mixed with anger at the ingratitude of the natives, follows each episode. The search for the culprits is expressed in ideological terms, particularly the hostility towards Islamic politics.

The problem with a foreign policy that is mainly focused on the need to search out and destroy the bad guy is that it can encourage fixed perceptions of evil rather than become a means of understanding and dealing with other peoples' political priorities. Some huge errors of judgement have been made in the demonising of foreign regimes. The secret decision of the US government under Ronald Reagan to support Iraq and Saddam Hussein when he launched his war against Iran was a classic example of a bad choice of friend.

This highly personalised foreign policy based on heroes and villains—even though they may swap roles overnight—helped to keep international tension at a high level. It guaranteed that there were few American voices heard opposing expenditure on faster, smarter and stealthier weapons. Only when the prospect of peace was visible did the demands decrease. The end of the Cold War in the early 1990s raised real problems for the US defence manufacturers and it took them some time to react.

The general response in the United States to the need to re-structure and adapt to the new circumstances can broadly be divided into two phases. These were not entirely separate and to some extent have overlapped. However they demonstrated different types of thinking. The first was Federal and State government initiatives; the second was the rush to mergers and acquisitions by the large defence corporations.

While the US is the spiritual home of the free market and the ostensible enemy of protectionism, its governments have not been slow to spend money and pass legislation to assist industries in trouble. US military bases have been closing since the 1960s and Federal intervention was used to ease the pain of the loss of employment. The President's Economic Adjustment Committee, working with local communities, established the Base Realignment and Closure Programme (BRACE) and from 1961-1993 succeeded in creating 171,777 new jobs to replace the loss of 87,557 civilian jobs at 97 closed bases. Vocational training courses for 37,953 trainees were held at 21 of the former bases.[8]

The Technology Reinvestment Project (TRP) was introduced in 1992 by Congressional legislation on conversion (diversification). Its aim was to promote the increasing use of dual-use technologies—those which have both military and civil applications—to create an increasingly integrated high-tech industrial base. The Departments of Defense, Commerce, Energy and Transportation were all involved. It was divided into four parts:

- Technology Development—assistance for specifically identified dual-use technologies.
- Regional Technology Alliances—assistance to enhance regional industry in dual-use areas.
- Manufacturing, Education and Training—grants to support the creation of a flexible workforce that could operate in both defence and commercial fields. The emphasis was on re-training defence industrial employees.
- Small Business Innovative Research—assistance in introducing manufacturing processes and technology to small firms.

All the funds were granted on a competitive basis.[9]

The Clinton administration allocated more than $13 billion out of the 1994 defence budget of $250 billion to fund conversion projects and clean-up operations at former military bases. The latter represented a large amount of business and defence contractors such as Lockheed Martin, Raytheon, TRW and Hughes, all of whom had laid off thousands of employees, competed for the contracts. The amount was more than triple that provided by George Bush in 1990.[10] While the United States has not undertaken a national commitment to become directly involved in assisting the large military manufacturers to diversify, its federal structure does allow state funds to be used to assist defence dependent communities.

The United States' best known contribution to the principle of allowing defence technology to move into the public domain is the Internet. With over 30 million subscribers it has been the communications phenomenon of the past decade. It has grown so quickly that national and international regulatory authorities, who regard cross-border, unlicensed contacts between individuals and organisations with suspicion, have been unable to control it. The Internet was created in 1969 within the Department of Defense (DoD) by the Advanced Research Projects Agency. Its purpose was establish computer links between universities and research sites working on military projects.

The DoD was the largest single fund provider for US universities. Other networks were set up in the 1980s, including a National Science Foundation network. All the networks were connected so that one computer could communicate with all the others. It was released into the public domain when the need for a purely military system declined. The Internet spread to over 146 countries, providing nerds with an outlet for their obsessions and access to information for millions of ordinary people to such an extent that it worries governments. Many thousands of commercial organisations who have never given any thought to the problems of the defence industry, let alone diversification, now use one of its creations as a matter of course.

The second phase of US adjustment to the end of the Cold War, and the one which is giving great concern to British and European defence manufacturers, started in 1993. William Perry, President Clinton's Defense Secretary, invited the country's largest defence contractors to dinner. It subsequently became known as 'The Last Supper.' Later, Norman Augustine, the boss of Lockheed Martin, spelt out the logic of their conclusions. "There will come a moment of awakening for the Pentagon," he predicted. "They may have to say to themselves that the free market system has no forces within it that ensure the survival of a viable defence industrial base..."[11] As a consequence there were 21 major mergers and acquisitions between 1993 and 1996. Boeing acquired McDonnell Douglas in 1996 in a $28 billion venture after the latter had been eliminated from the Joint Strike Fighter project. In 1997, Hughes Electronics, worth $9.5 billion, was sold by General Motors to Raytheon, manufacturers of the Patriot missile, which had previously acquired the defence interests of Texas Instruments for $1.8 billion. There are now only one or two producers in some areas of US weapons procurement.

The mergers between these hugely rich corporations were also partly subsidised by the American taxpayer. Under what became known as 'payoffs for layoffs' the companies could claim reimbursement for legal costs for court cases against employees in disputes over the mergers, costs for eliminating productive capacity that could have been sold to a competitor, severance payments and costs for moving people and machinery to lower-wage or union-free areas. Lockheed Martin and Boeing applied for over $1 billion from the Federal government.[12]

This strategy will mould a US defence industry that is both defensive and aggressive. As jobs continue to be lost, domestic pressure will grow to "buy American" from both the unions and the contractors. Government will be receptive as it is spending money to subsidise the mergers. At the same time, in order to compensate for the decline in the home market, the manufacturers will fight ruthlessly for a much greater share of overseas sales. Beneath the surface of Nato military co-operation there will be increasingly bitter and intense rivalry between the European and US defence suppliers. Smaller and new Eastern European Nato members will be propositioned with financial incentives or coerced through political pressure to buy from the big suppliers. Governments in unstable parts of the world will face competing offers of weapons from countries who could also comprise multinational peacekeeping forces in their region. Unless European companies regroup swiftly they may well find even their diminished market opportunities lost to the heavy hitters from the US.

Russia

By 1989 the Soviet economy was in deep trouble. It was spending 19 per cent of its national income on defence and running a budget deficit of 13 per cent of total expenditure.[13] The drive against alcohol consumption had sharply reduced government income from taxes and investment in computers and new technology was expensive. The end of the Cold War caused the collapse of its arms manufacturing industry. The slump was greater in Russia than in any other country.

Gorbachev had been ousted, the Soviet Union dismembered and President Yeltsin—with his belief in free market shock therapy—was President of Russia. The total value of defence equipment orders fell from $23 billion in 1987 to $1.8 billion in 1993.[14] One of the more bizarre examples of military decline was when troops forced engineers at gunpoint to restore electricity to an Arctic nuclear submarine base. There was a danger that the submarines' reactors would meltdown due to the lack of power. The regional electricity authority had cut off the supply because the base had not paid its bills.[15]

The Russian government planned to privatise about 1,500 of the previously state-owned defence enterprises that were not regarded as essential to national security. These were opened to investment and diversification projects. About 250, known as 'treasury enterprises,' and regarded as strategically important, would remain as before, fully funded and controlled from the centre. A further 250 continued to be majority owned by the state but under local management control and able to carry out both civil and defence work.[16] The government has stated that it wants to limit its stake in any new investment project to 25 per cent. The Russian government has been reluctant to pay the wages of defence employees. Workers in Ekaterinburg and Murmansk protested in 1995 and demanded payment of back wages. The main sectors where these were not paid were defence, mining and agro-industry.

The need for some form of planned diversification became clear in 1992. During that year defence factories worked flat out to produce weapons for export. The official idea was that the profit from these sales would fund attempts at conversion. As in the West, there was a grossly over-optimistic expectation that customers would be lining up to buy the products. Not only did the enterprises produce a vast surplus of unwanted equipment but many actually exceeded their contractual obligations. Much of this was dumped on the market at rock-bottom prices, damaging the attempts of both Russian and Western companies to earn money to compensate for the lack of domestic orders.

The Russian Government was forced to re-think and set up a special fund for conversion. It also listed 14 priority areas for commercial development using defence technology. These included civil aviation, telecommunications, consumer durables, electronics, medical equipment and desperately needed measures for environmental protection. The non-state enterprises were able to apply for special grants from the fund. Previous attempts at conversion in the old Soviet Union had not always proved successful. The Central Committee of the Communist Party severely reprimanded one defence factory when it started to make television sets that exploded when switched on.[17] Given the quality of Soviet TV programmes it was perhaps not an entirely inappropriate technical error.

The Russian Government established an arms export agency in 1993 in order to avoid the mistakes of the previous haphazard attempts to capture a greater share of the world market. They set up an agency called Rosvooruzhenie, under General Shapashinikov. He was previously commander of the strategic forces of the Commonwealth of Independent States (CIS). The agency started off with high hopes. It established offices in more than 30 countries with press offices and an English language magazine, *Military Parade*, printed in full colour. The use of colour was regarded as a breakthrough in Russian military marketing techniques. The magazine's deputy editor said: "The world is accustomed to high-quality advertising. If we try to sell a piece of equipment costing $10 million with advertising printed in black and white, a client might think that the quality of what we are selling is the same." The client might well have been right, of course, and not only in relation to Russian products. Echoing the principles that underpinned the setting-up of the UK Defence Export Sales Organisation (DESO) in 1966, the head of the Moscow Aircraft Production Organisation (Mapo) said: "it finally united all military sales activity in our country and established prices that are in the Russian national interest."[18]

Despite the colour printing and sales co-ordination the government carried out a swift U-turn two years later and abolished the Rosvooruzhenie monopoly in order to allow manufacturers to sell their products independently. The deputy chief designer of one major enterprise said: "It was an absurd system. Profits from the company's sales went to Rosvooruzhenie while we were left without money to pay our employees." The agency was reduced to a loose overseeing role and export licence applications from the manufacturer are dealt with by the Ministry of Foreign Economic Relations.[19]

The new rulers of Russia have proved to be no more transparent than the old Communist regime when it comes to reaching international agreement on arms exports. In 1996 Russian officials refused to agree to a provision in what is known as the Wassenaar Arrangement that would require one government to reveal sales to any country that had been previously declined by another government. In other words, if Britain refused to supply Iran, and that contract was taken up by Russia, the Russians would have to tell the Wassenaar secretariat. A

Russian official said that: "we favour a reasonable degree of transparency and mutual co-operation but these measures should not be detrimental to our national security interests."[20] He did not explain how the disclosure of overseas arms sales would damage the defence of the people back home.

One international military analyst believes that the Russian defence industry of the future will be characterised by a nucleus of large groups owned by the state. They will be surrounded by small and medium size private companies comprised of the most profitable parts of the former defence industry together with production facilities for civil use. The defence industry will lose its traditional privileged position within the economy.[21]

The political future of Russia is uncertain but there is no evidence of an upsurge of public opinion demanding more military spending. Like their counterparts in the West, the various lobbies and interest groups will continue to press for bigger and better weapons but ordinary people who have had eighty years of guns before butter seem to prefer higher living standards to more military parades. During the Communist years people watching the latest Soviet missiles in Red Square used to wonder why such ingenuity and investment couldn't be used to manufacture a decent pair of shoes. It remains to be seen whether the Russian government will actively promote and fund diversification as a realistic alternative to weapons exports.

South Africa

Although it has a completely different background and history, South Africa found itself facing a similar situation to Russia after winning freedom from apartheid. Both countries had been ruled by unpopular governments who had over-militarised the economy at the expense of basic necessities for their people. The manufacture of military equipment was also the largest industry in both countries. Discrimination was formalised by law in South Africa. By 1994 the income of the white population was ten times greater that that of blacks and 4.5 times that of coloureds. One quarter of the black labour force was unemployed.[22] For both countries the dilemma was whether to try to export more weaponry to earn desperately needed revenue or to take steps to switch to commercial production.

During the apartheid years in South Africa, all aspects of the country's life were distorted by a mixture of paranoia and repression. This provided fertile ground for the advocates of high levels of weapons production. It also produced institutions and practices that were peculiar to South Africa. For instance, it did not have a Ministry of Defence that was even theoretically accountable to the public. That responsibility was handed over to a single minister who oversaw a department run by uniformed staff. Another distinction was that a large amount of government military purchases were designed for use against its own citizens. This meant that expenditure on internal security was relatively much higher than elsewhere in the world. Not surprisingly, South Africa became a world leader in the manufacture of riot control vehicles. Other types of products that in most countries would have been used by the armed forces for protection against external attack were deployed by the South African police and internal security forces. These were not calculated as being part of 'defence' spending but were counted in the police budget. That kept official defence expenditure artificially low.

Armscor is the central agency of the South African arms industry. It employs around 1,000 people, 400 of whom are scientists and engineers. Until 1990 it was also a production company but then hived off those activities into a new enterprise, Denel, which operates as a private company with a major government shareholding. Armscor became an 'acquisition' (procurement) agency but was also responsible for promoting overseas sales. This role caused considerable controversy in the country with many in the South African churches and peace movement arguing that a newly liberated Third World country should not be in the business of exporting weapons. Those previously in the armed wing of the African National Congress and most politicians believed that South Africa could win lucrative orders that would provide money to support economic recovery. President Mandela said that overseas military sales would assist domestic reconstruction and development.

Some of those who attended an Armscor seminar at King's College, London in 1994 were surprised at the 'business as usual' approach of the agency's senior planning manager after the political changes. He said that while South Africa's share of the world's defence market was only 0.4 per cent, Armscor intended to increase this to 2 per cent. Jobs were the priority and he estimated that 20,000 would be created. It was clear that that while he acknowledged the government of the country had changed, he believed that his job would be very much the same. Top executives from many of the large British defence manufacturers and the Ministry of Defence attended the meeting.

A year later Armscor was discovered to have illegally sold shipments of AK-47 assault rifles to South Yemen without the knowledge of the government. The Cameron Commission, which was set up to review the agency's activities was scathing in its indictment and recommended that Armscor be stripped of its export role. An independent body would take over this operation. The Commission also found that the agency had continued its operations in the same covert manner as it had under the old system. This involved the use of 130 front companies, numerous agents and middlemen, false end-user certificates and 'free on-board' shipments where the buyer took over the responsibility as soon as the equipment was loaded. The buyer could then than determine the destination of the arms and Armscor could plead ignorance of the final user. Ronnie Kasrils,

Deputy Defence Minister, and former head of the intelligence section of the armed wing of the ANC, said: "we will have to clean up our arms industry."[23] Armscor officials resigned, no doubt hurt that they had been prevented from playing their usual role in an agency that regarded itself as autonomous from government and public accountability. Their counterparts in many other countries have not been so unlucky.

The South African government banned the export of all mines in 1994, several years before the West took similar action. It also has a clear commitment to defence diversification and has established a Diversification Council, comprising government, industry and trade unions. This body is responsible for information, analysis, financial incentives and general support for those enterprises wishing to free themselves from total dependency on military production.. The Council has organised training programmes to help provide the necessary skills for this process.

There is no doubt that South Africa faces considerable difficulties, moral and practical, in balancing its real defence needs against pressures to make money by arming other parts of the world. There are also demands from its own military for money to be spent on buying equipment from overseas. This was underlined by reports that Britain had offered four submarines—mothballed since the 1980s— at a price of £200 million. These had cost the UK taxpayer £930 million when they were manufactured in the 1980s. The good news for the South Africans was that no payment was required as the cost was planned to be offset through 'industrial participation' (aid) from Britain. This special offer was part of an estimated £5-10 billion worth of arms purchases by South Africa. Other European governments were also lobbying vigorously on behalf of their manufacturers. It did raise the question of whether aid for trade—which Labour had previously condemned—was back on the agenda.[24] It was not immediately obvious who or what provided the seaborne threat that made South Africa require such protection.

Whether the maintenance of a large military-industrial base will assist or restrict the growth of essential civil industry and social programmes should prove an interesting question. Investment from abroad, linked with diversification programmes and the growth of its civil skills base, could make some of its choices easier. The country is better placed than many others in the Third World as it is partly industrialised and has earned a huge amount of goodwill due to its post-apartheid policy of reconciliation and the personal bravery of its leaders during the years of political repression.

The European Union

The scenario for the start of the Third World War was centred on a small area 60 miles from Frankfurt on the borders of East and West Germany. It was known as the Fulda Gap. Warsaw Pact tanks supported by aircraft and troops were thought to be prepared to sweep through at this point until slowed and, hopefully, halted by the combined Nato forces led by the Americans. The West was ready to use nuclear weapons if the attack could not be stopped by conventional forces. The Fulda Gap was a strange place, completely unheard of by most Europeans, but absolutely critical to those that planned the battles that would storm across their countries. In 1987 it was guarded by the 11th Armoured Cavalry Regiment ('the Blackhorse') part of the US V Corps.

Our trade union group were there as guests of the US Embassy in London who had arranged a tour of Berlin and US bases in West Germany. It was obvious that the latter possessed nuclear weapons but the base commanders would "neither confirm nor deny" their presence when asked. It was impossible to see the exact location of the East-West border at Fulda but there were tall fences with watch-towers a few hundred yards behind it on either side. The tank crews at Fulda were a cheerful bunch who said, quite openly, that if the attack came their position could only be held for a few hours at the most. They cracked the joke about their armour having three reverse gears for rapid retreat and one forward gear in case the enemy attacked from behind.

Their commander told us that his border guards, like their opposite numbers, used East German Zeiss binoculars which were superior to those made in the West. Soldiers on both sides occasionally waved across at each other, technically a military offence. He confirmed his troops' view that his unit was there to delay the enemy forces as long as possible. The Americans said that they had much more respect for the East German forces at Fulda than they had for the Soviets who kept their tanks in poor condition. After a good lunch, we were presented with scrolls which made us Honorary Members of the Border Legion and commended us for "having undergone the hazards of a journey to the border of West Germany and the Communist World and visiting the Blackhorse frontiers of freedom."

The attack never came and the Fulda Gap has now returned to well-deserved obscurity. Most of the countries that were designated as invasion targets are now members of the European Union and a number of those who were believed to have been the potential invaders are waiting to join. Given the recent military history of Europe, it is hardly surprising that a combined defence policy has been difficult to achieve. Its military industries have taken a battering since the end of the Cold War. EU equipment production slumped from over $40.5 billion in 1988 to $28.4 billion in 1992.[25] The fear that is now driving European military manufacturers into urgent consideration of cross-border joint ventures and mergers is not that of war and the need to have better weapons but fear that the US giants will mop up the shrinking opportunities for arms sales.

The sales onslaught of the American companies has already begun in Europe.

US manufacturers now appear among the top ten suppliers to the British Ministry of Defence. In 1997 Lockheed Martin was paid over £250 million.[26] The European companies (and their governments) also worry that they could be targets for takeover from across the Atlantic. Those that have been squeezed out of recent large contracts could be particularly vulnerable.

European defence integration has been slowed by the continuing anomaly of Article 223 of the Treaty of Rome. This states: "Any member state may take such measures as it considers necessary for the protection of the essential interests of its security which are connected with the protection of or the trade in arms, munitions and war material." The rationale behind this, when it was signed, was that Brussels should not be able to intervene in the sensitive area of national security. This allowed national governments to prop up and subsidise their defence industries, a practice not allowed under the rules of competition in the civil sector. When the Common Market was established by the Treaty of Rome in 1958 it was a much smaller organisation than the present EU and its powers were limited. The Cold War was also well under way.

Nearly forty years later the Maastricht Treaty hinted at a possible change when it confirmed the Western European Union (WEU) as: "the defence component of the European Union which will formulate common European defence policy and carry forward its concrete implementation..."[27] The WEU is a fragmented organisation. Not all EU partners are full members and there are four levels of membership with 'associate partners' who include former Warsaw Pact members. It also participates in an even looser body, the Conference on Security and Cooperation in Europe (CSCE) which includes most European countries and is dedicated to the protection of human rights, conflict resolution and the market economy.[28]

If member states wish to take joint action to rationalise military manufacturing costs, Article 223 will have to be amended. Defence technology and its possible civil uses will not be safeguarded or advanced by protectionism. That kind of policy, however well disguised, will often mean the purchase of inferior and expensive equipment without any stimulus to the supplier to research and provide more appropriate and less expensive products. Genuine competition within Europe and a pooling of resources to confront the external challenge from the United States will not only provide better value for money but also weapons and materials relevant to the present situation rather than the Cold War.

While that will restrict the power of national governments to assist companies by direct financial hand-outs, there will be a need for a provision that will allow some public money to be spent on assisting companies to diversify. It would also mean that the various national groups, including rival companies, manufacturers' associations and trade unions, who have traditionally lobbied for their governments to buy 'British,' French' or 'German' etc. will have to accept that decisions on what type of equipment should be manufactured would not be taken by individual governments. The establishment of some joint ventures and the buying-in of components from other countries have already made the national interest argument much more complicated. Defence ministries would need to come to a common conclusion on the type, amount and cost of the equipment when European defence needs were agreed. The Eurofighter experience would provide a helpful warning on how to avoid past mistakes.

There is no reason why British defence companies who are, on the whole, relatively competitive compared with most of their rivals, should not succeed in a smaller but better planned European market. However it would be quite unrealistic to believe that pressure from perceived national interests would disappear. The lobbying organisations would bring forward their efforts to a much earlier stage. European defence manufacturing co-ordination would not be a panacea for the present difficulties—a considerable amount of painful adjustment would be necessary—but it would introduce some rational procedures into what is now a fragmented and cut-throat market. For Britain it would mean a considerable loosening of the links with the United States but that would be preferable to our past ambivalence. History and Presidential hugs on the steps of the White House count for little in hard commercial and political decisions. Britain, together with Europe, could negotiate from a position of strength and relative equality.

The difficulties with European rationalisation has already led to some British companies, particularly GEC, seeking to buy some, or parts of, US manufacturers. The clear intention is to gain privileged access to the American defence market. That would certainly reduce the pressure on the US government to buy UK exports because if a British company could acquire new orders for its factories within America, it would lessen the need to sell across the Atlantic. That would endanger even more jobs in the UK.

Konver is the arms diversification programme within the European Union. It was created in 1993 at the insistence of the European Parliament and against the wishes of the Commission. European MPs had been receiving reports from their own constituencies that military bases and manufacturing sites were being closed without restructuring assistance being given by national governments. They felt that it was a common European problem and that the EU should provide money for defence dependent regions. It was originally funded to a total of £108 million and included the provision of advisory services and new equipment.

The European Parliament stipulated that all the money should be spent on converting to purely civil applications, not dual-use or new military functions. It also allowed funds for alternative uses of closed military bases. This was particularly relevant in Germany where the departure of Soviet and some Western forces had left many bases empty and people unemployed. This over-extended the coverage of the programme and ensured that Germany, the richest country, was also the main beneficiary. It was also a weakness in that most of the civilian jobs on military bases were of a lower skill level and were more available in the local community. The higher skilled jobs of redundant defence industry workers were less easy to transfer and were a greater loss to both the local and national economies.

The EU initiated Konver 2 in 1994 and British regions took the sensible step of forming themselves into a national association of defence dependent communities. Despite, or perhaps because of, the lack of interest by the then British government, they were able to co-ordinate and lobby effectively. Germany received £182.5 million of Konver 2 funds by the end of 1995, the UK £78 million, France £58 million and Italy £38 million. The other countries received smaller amounts. Konver was an extremely helpful initiative and demonstrated that the European Parliament was a better barometer of public opinion than the Commission.

There will be a continuing loss of jobs regardless of the type of defence industrial structures that emerge within the EU. This is a problem common to most member countries and could be dealt with both on a national and a European basis. Konver could make a major contribution by providing grants specifically for re-training packages. It could also set up joint initiatives with such organisations as the UK Defence Diversification Agency. Konver is due for review in 1999 and it would be beneficial if the programme received increased funding and was re-focused specifically on the diversification needs of the defence manufacturing industries in the regions. Military base conversion and the aim of "promotion of tourism" could be eliminated.

Research and development is a key area of the defence industry. There has been a vast waste of money by national governments within the EU on competitive and often overlapping research. The cloak and dagger operation mounted by MI6 against the French in 1995 to steal submarine research was more reminiscent of Cold War spy novels than an example of how to deal with a Nato ally. The French had made a technical breakthrough that would allow them to track previously undetectable submarines. The British military had always claimed that the Polaris and Trident fleets were immune from attack as they could never be found by an enemy. The new discovery appeared to jeopardise that immunity. MI6 set up a front company and bribed a French engineer to pass details to one of its agents. The information was passed to the UK Defence Evaluation and Research Agency at Farnborough for analysis.[29]

There has been a significant change in the relationship between civil and defence research in Europe in recent years. During the 1970s and early 1980s it was accepted that defence research was ahead of that in the commercial sector. This was due to two main factors: the amount of financial and technical resources provided by governments and the large numbers of scientists and engineers who were employed on military work. That perception has now changed. Military research and its applications were found to have been over-elaborate and expensive. The competitive nature of the international markets, particularly in electronics, has forced prices down and improved performance in the civil field. The defence manufacturers are now looking to 'spin-in' technology from consumer products.

Euclid (European Co-operative Long-term Initiative for Defence) is the EU common defence research programme. It could be extended to become directed at both defence and civil initiatives. It could also provide a sound basis for genuine multinational co-operation on new forms of dual-use technology. There would be considerable scope for possible diversification projects. If Euclid is used only to research new defence technology, its potential will be increasingly limited as the market declines. There would be a consequent reluctance to provide sufficient funding. EU governments and companies supported the Esprit programme of pre-competitive civil research and there is no reason why a re-focused Euclid should not receive a similar welcome. The hesitancy of traditional competitors, within and across national borders, to discuss leading edge technology with each other would be reduced if information was genuinely shared and led to a more secure, if smaller, marketplace. Some defence research will have to be retained within national boundaries if a government believes that it is 'strategic' and so essential to the country's interests that it should not have wider circulation. Governments should be able to minimise the amount of 'strategic' research as the EU achieves greater political cohesion.

Arms exports are the cause of the most intense competition between European countries. Britain and France are particularly bitter rivals. In May 1998 Britain made proposals to the EU that provided the basis for an agreement on a code of conduct between the 15 member states. The central points agreed were:

1 If a member state rejects an arms sale on the grounds of human rights or related issues, it must notify all the other EU countries.
2 If another member country is approached by the potential buyer within 3 years, it must inform the country which originally refused.
3 National reports on arms sales would be circulated to the other countries but would not be published. Only an edited EU compilation would be available to the public.

These were generally welcomed as a small step forward by anti-arms campaigners but with severe reservations. In the interests of transparency any country that is approached by a buyer after the refusal of another government should inform *all* the other EU members not just the country that rejected the sale. This would avoid one-to-one secret reciprocal deals between the large arms producing countries. National arms sales reports should be published openly, at least in the country concerned.

The Defence Manufacturers Association said that it believed that the agreement: "would not make a substantial difference to existing government policy."

Robin Cook stated that it was: "a real achievement, a substantial step forward."
He said: "from now on, our arms industries will compete on price and quality, but
not on the standards that we will all apply on human rights." It is possible to
envisage an eventual legally-binding EU code of conduct that could include the
following stipulations:

- The recipient government should not have committed gross and systemat-
  ic abuses of internationally recognised human rights within the previous
  three years.
- Military equipment should not be exported to countries where there is
  internal or external conflict, actual or threatened, unless for purely defensive purposes and recognised as such by the United Nations.
- Respect for UN or other international sanctions.
- Arms should not be exported to countries that support acts of terrorism.
- Governments of countries that receive military equipment should provide
  official guarantees that no part of it shall be re-exported.
- Exporting countries should publish full details of proposed arms exports to
  national Parliaments and the EU.[30]

The difficulties faced by those in the British government who support an ethical
arms policy should not be underestimated. They certainly have not had the backing of all their colleagues—from the very top down—and even their limited proposals run counter to the ethics and practices of the Ministry of Defence, especially the salespeople at the Defence Export Services Organisation. Many other
countries, particularly France, do not have well organised anti-arms campaigns
and their governments are under little internal pressure.

EU countries with a common policy would be in a strong position to call for
negotiations on a wider international agreement. It would be no easy task to
achieve this but even limited agreement would be preferable to the present economic rivalry that has encouraged democratic countries to sell weapons to repressive regimes.

It would be logical to allow the European Parliament—a democratically elected body—to have an overseeing role on all large contracts that involve European
arms agencies or any official EU body. A specialist defence procurement department within the EU Industry Directorate-General (DG III) could be established.
It would make recommendations to the European Parliament and Commission. It
should not involve a large amount of bureaucracy but, in any case, the present
separate national procedures involve a tremendous amount of wrangling, lobbying and acrimony. They are also time-consuming. It often takes ten years or more
to develop and deliver new equipment. A more co-ordinated European defence
industry would produce a greater degree of collaboration between manufacturers.
Workers' representatives would also be able to meet and draw up policies to
influence their employers and governments through European Works Councils.

The European defence companies have the stark choice of whether to co-operate, slim down and merge or remain divided and decline. If member states can put aside short term advantages—such as back-stabbing deals on arms exports—the EU could provide a framework that could help the manufacturers come to terms with a reduced world market for military equipment. Over the past three decades Japan and other commercial competitors, who devote less of their national resources to defence, have seized the advantage by developing the new consumer products that have swept many European goods out of the shops and showrooms.

References

1 *Conversion Survey 1996*. Bonn International Centre for Conversion. The former Soviet Union, Czechoslovakia and Germany have been taken as single entities for the period covered.
2 *Observer* 14 December 1997.
3 *Defense News* 3 October 1994.
4 Letter of 7 May 1998 to the author from J S Neilson, Director, Aerospace and Defence Industries Policy, DTI.
5 *World Military and Social Expenditures* (WMSE) 1996. Box 25140, Washington, DC., 20007, USA.
6 *Ibid.*
7 *The Guardian* 24 February 1998.
8 *Civilian Re-use of Former Military Bases 1961-1993*. Summary of Completed Military Base Economic Adjustment Projects. US Department of Defense.
9 *Conversion Survey 1996*. Bonn International Center for Conversion.
10 *Defense News* 14 November 1994.
11 *The Guardian* 16 December 1996.
12 *Understanding American Defense Industry Mergers.* Paper by Ann Markusen, Senior Fellow, Council on Foreign Relations August 1997. Markusen argues that the mergers are not Pentagon planned but driven by Wall Street interests. The outcome, however, is the same.
13 *SIPRI Yearbook 1989*. Stockholm International Peace Research Institute.
14 *Defense News* 3 October 1994.
15 *The Guardian* 23 September 1995.
16 *Conversion Survey 1996*. Bonn International Center for Conversion.
17 WMSE 1989.
18 *Defense News* 3 October 1994.
19 *Ibid.* 17 July 1995.
20 *The Guardian* 5 April 1996.
21 *The Transformation of the Russian Defence Industry* by Antonio Sánchez-Andrés. Europe-Asia Studies Vol. 47 No. 8 1995.
22 *The New South Africa: Prospects for Security and Stability.* Centre for Defence Studies, King's College, London 1994.
23 *Sunday Times* 23 July 1995.
24 *Ibid.* 28 March 1998 *and 5 July 1998.*
25 *The challenges facing the European defence-related industry.* Commission of the European Communities 1996.
26 *UK Defence Statistics 1998.* The Stationery Office.
27 *The challenges facing the European defence-related industry.*

28 *EC/EU Fact Book* by Alex Roney. Kogan Page 1998.

29 *Sunday Times* 16 June 1996.

30 For further proposals see *Gunrunners Gold*. WDM 1995. Also *About Turn, Forward March With Europe*. Chapter by Susan Willett. Rivers Oram Press 1996.

CHAPTER TEN

LABOUR IN COMMAND

Those who cannot remember the past are condemned to repeat it.
George Santayana 1863-1952

The British general election of 1997 was a long, loud and repetitive encounter. No opportunity was missed by the party spin-doctors to depict their opponents as spendthrifts ready to tax hard-working people to pay for waste and incompetence. New Labour said that tough choices had to be made. The social security bill was too large but the vulnerable could be protected without the expenditure of more public money. Schools with books, hospitals with beds available and transport that functioned were to be funded from... well, some other source, to be revealed after the election but still within previous Conservative spending limits. A myriad of policy reviews would be conducted by young thinkers and business people. The results would be for the benefit of the many, not just the few. The generalities of the manifesto were a "contract with the people." The campaign was a winner and the Conservatives, demoralised by cash for questions scandals and splits over Europe, crashed to resounding defeat.

One major area of public spending was controversy-free. Defence hardly featured in any of the broadcasts, articles or propaganda. The expenditure of over £21 billion annually of taxpayers' money went unscrutinised and unnoticed. After the election the new Defence Secretary, George Robertson, announced a Strategic Defence Review that he hoped would be published before the end of 1997. The two largest and most expensive elements of Britain's defence, Trident and Eurofighter, would not be included.

The Strategic Defence Review

The Review was published in July 1998. The omission of Trident drastically reduced its scope and credibility. It would have provided the opportunity for debate, not just about cost, but also about whether Britain still needed nuclear weapons for its own security. It need not have been a re-run of the old arguments between the 'unilateralists' and the 'multilateralists.' Both camps had been overtaken by events. Trident was in service. The four nuclear-armed submarines could not be wished out of existence or "scrapped" as some had hoped. On the other hand there was no logical reason for their deployment. The Warsaw Pact had disappeared and nobody could identify the enemy that was needed to replace it.

The timidity of New Labour in refusing to respond to the challenge of creating a non-nuclear defence strategy was ironic. In all other areas of policy the country was told to face up to the future and forget the past. Realistically, there were to be no more jobs for life; people had to take financial responsibility for their retirement; hereditary peers were on the way out. The unthinkable had to be thought. Britain was to be given a good shaking. If some loose bits fell off, they would be swept up and thrown away. Even the monarchy was re-branded as an in-touch-with-the-people institution although the single parents within the Queen's large family were not prodded out of the door to find low-paid work.

The military establishment was the exception. The Review did not even attempt to scratch its surface. Some optimists had expected radical change but many political analysts did not find it surprising. They had already noticed the government's highly respectful attitude towards the powerful. In contrast, people who were on the outside looking in—the 'socially excluded'—were told that they would be dealt with in a way that was good for them.

The Review's uncritical acceptance that Western and democratic interests could best be protected through an enlarged Nato was not an accurate appreciation of the way the world was moving. Again, it displayed a conservative attitude towards established authority, in this case American military power.

The real political and cultural challenge to the West will come from the continuing rise of powerful Islamic movements in what has been termed 'the age of insurgency.' Armed independence movements such as Hamas in the Middle East and the Tamil Tigers in Sri Lanka cannot be contained, defeated or accommodated by massive armed blocs. Population movements from the poor to the richer countries may create unstable conditions and civil disorder within the industrialised nations of Europe.[1] There are likely to be escalating disputes over the control of water sources. These very real challenges demand understanding and the search for a *modus vivendi*, not the creation of larger military alliances. To ask Nato, with the permission of the US or the United Nations, to intervene in these areas of potential conflict would make as much sense as Nato intervention in Britain's own problem in Northern Ireland.

There was no examination of the arguments surrounding the expansion of Nato. The Review could have assessed how the government wished to see Nato cope with a changed world situation. If Britain is to cooperate effectively with its partners in the alliance, it should have a clear understanding of what it wants to achieve. Many experts feel that the organisation should be scaled down to reflect the reduction in the external threat. It should not become an uncosted, unrealistic military insurance policy for any country willing to pay the entrance fee.

The Review continued the time-honoured tradition of British military expectations exceeding the likelihood of fulfilling them. Grand plans would be made and then cut or abandoned when the money ran out. There were no proposals for opening up the Ministry of Defence to public and Parliamentary scrutiny. None of the 25 major projects—most of which have huge cost overruns or delays—were cancelled. It confirmed that the acquisition of 232 Eurofighters: "remains central to our plans." That was an assurance to the manufacturers and their employees but past experience shows that when the Treasury starts its fight-back, the numbers could well be reduced due to "a lessening of tension" or "changed circumstances in Europe."

It announced a reduction in the defence budget of £685 million or 3 per cent (after accounting for inflation), by 2001, out of a budget of nearly £23 million. That was not a slice but a sliver. It was less than one quarter of the total cost overrun of £3 billion on the 25 largest defence projects in the one year 1996/97. The defence budget was forecast to be £22.295 billion in 1999/00; £22.830 billion in 2000/01; £22.987 in 2001/2. The defence share of national income was predicted to fall from 2.7 per cent to 2.4 per cent. This was based on the uncertain assumption that the economy would expand. Only 2,500 troops would be transferred from Germany to the UK. In 1997 there were around 23,000 soldiers within the command of the British Army of the Rhine at a cost of £1.3 billion a year.[2] The UK has a greater proportion of its army stationed outside its own territory than any other major army in the world. Germany is economically strong and well defended by its own forces. Much of the Review was more a general blueprint for international intervention than a policy for national defence.

There were positive points in the Review, in particular the reduction in stocks of fissile (nuclear) materials and a new initiative to improve vocational education and training for the armed forces. However, on the main questions of cost and strategy, the defence ministers, like their predecessors, were captured by the military establishment without a struggle.

The main editorial in the *Financial Times* summed it up: "The top brass can start their victory celebrations. The UK government's Strategic Defence Review has come up with a paltry £685 million of underlying savings over three years. True, the military will have to withdraw from some fine London properties but there will be few casualties among front line troops and two big new aircraft carriers have been gained, for action in distant seas."[3] *The Times* called it: "a fair-minded and sensible extension of Tory thinking." Presumably that was intended as a compliment. General Sir Charles Guthrie, Chief of the Defence Staff said that it was "very good."

Since Labour jettisoned its policy of unilateral nuclear disarmament, its leadership has been terrified that any discussion about defence would cause splits and disagreements within the party. The consequence was, that unlike all other areas of policy, no prior analysis had been carried out to establish the main questions that should be asked and answered. The Review said that it "did not start with a blank sheet of paper" but operated within "parameters" set out in the government's general election manifesto. Those parameters said only that Trident and Eurofighter were sacrosanct.

Consequently, during the months before publication, the Review became a battleground of lobbying, Ministry of Defence leaks and ministers defending their own patch. They and their 'outside advisers' competed to win the support of the Prime Minister. The Treasury wanted £2 billion in cuts but that was a battle that Gordon Brown was never going to win. Tony Blair, in his role as the People's Wing Commander, was hardly likely to upset the military men. Britain had its uniform pressed and boots polished but continued to march in the same direction as before.

Nuclear contagion

The Review skimmed over the problem of the increasing danger of nuclear proliferation. That was hardly surprising as Britain is a prime proliferator. For many years only five countries—the US (12,070 warheads, 1,030 tests), Russia (22,500 warheads, 715 tests), China (450 warheads, 45 tests), Britain (380 warheads, 45 tests) and France (500 warheads, 210 tests)[4]—possessed nuclear weapons and the means of delivering them. India, Pakistan and Israel, known as the 'threshold' countries, had nuclear potential. Other countries such as Brazil, Argentina, South Africa, Iraq and North Korea were nearing the threshold.[5]

In May 1998 India and Pakistan virtually crossed the nuclear threshold. In a display of crowd-pleasing nationalism both countries conducted underground tests. They also possessed medium-range missiles capable of hitting each other's territory. The West rushed to condemn them and the US immediately imposed economic sanctions. Within two months these had nearly collapsed because the large American agro-industry conglomerates persuaded the Senate to allow the export of agricultural materials. France and China had both carried out tests within the previous three years but no sanctions had been imposed. China was potentially an important trading partner being wooed by President Clinton and the US persuaded France to cut short its planned programme by passing across secret data on computer-simulated underground explosions. That information helped France enhance its nuclear capability.

Many people believe that the threat of the use of these weapons of mass destruction has prevented world conflict for the past fifty years. Potential aggressors were deterred by the knowledge that massive retaliation would follow. The logical extension of that argument was that the nuclear deterrent should be acquired by other countries that feared attack. The balance of terror that had (allegedly) prevented all-out war in Europe would then apply. That view is rarely put forward seriously—certainly not by the five members of the nuclear 'club'— as the idea that more nations should possess the means of obliterating their neighbours does not inspire confidence that the world would be a more peaceful place.

The argument made by the nuclear states that ownership of the ultimate threat was safe in their hands and should not be extended elsewhere did not cut much ice with the governments of the threshold countries. The universal principle that the enemy's bomb is aggressive, your own is defensive, clearly applied. They also reasoned, with justification, that it was hypocritical for those who possessed nuclear weapons to refuse to surrender them while denying the right of ownership to others. They also argued that nuclear arsenals were being increased by those who demanded restrictions elsewhere. The Clinton administration openly said that the Comprehensive Test Ban Treaty would: "prevent other nations from acquiring nuclear weapons and will demonstrate US global leadership."[6] That comment—doubtless intended for domestic consumption—might not have been received with total joy in other parts of the world

For many years the club had publicly demonstrated its belief that nuclear weapons conferred status and authority on those who possessed them. Were they not also the five members of the United Nations Security Council whose deliberations were listened to by the rest of the world? India and Pakistan had taken them at their word.

The atom bomb was developed to gain an advantage, not to create a balance of power. The US used it to finish the war against Japan and its thermonuclear successors were deployed as strategic bargaining chips by both sides during the Cold War. Nothing has changed. If a country's scientists and engineers are capable of developing nuclear warheads and the means of delivery—however crude— it is very tempting for its leaders to seek to exert political leverage. Such tactics raise the stakes in the game of nuclear brinkmanship. The only way forward is for early, substantial, irreversible and verifiable cuts in warhead and missile numbers, linked with reductions in the means of delivery. The nuclear club, including Britain, has shown little enthusiasm for such action.

The real argument against the spread of nuclear weapons is not that the five club members are the only ones who can be trusted, but that the bomb creates instability between possessors and non-possessors. Those without it seek to achieve parity, thereby increasing the danger of its eventual use, perhaps accidentally. The arms race has its own momentum. A further risk is created when confrontational nuclear states start to consider the possibility of the first-use of the weapon through a pre-emptive strike.

Britain's nuclear capability has been increased substantially during the international non-proliferation negotiations. By the move from Polaris to Trident this country not only retained its nuclear weapons but also increased their range and possible number of warheads. This was confirmed by the House of Commons Defence Committee when it said: "Trident's accuracy and sophistication does— and was always intended to—represent a significant enhancement of the United

Kingdom's nuclear capability. We have invested a great deal of money to make it possible to attack more targets with greater effectiveness using nominally equivalent explosive power."[7]

Britain's deterrent

The Review reduced the number of warheads carried on each of the four Trident submarines from a maximum of 96 to 48. It said that as a result: "the potential explosive power deployed on a Trident submarine is one third less than a Polaris submarine armed with Chevaline." That was extremely misleading. "Explosive power" is not the sole benchmark of a country's ability to wreak nuclear destruction on an enemy. In the jargon of nukespeak, the Polaris warheads were Multiple Re-entry Vehicles (MRVs). Trident warheads are Multiple Independently Targeted Re-entry Vehicles (MIRVS). MRVs (Polaris) allow only for sending more than one warhead to the *same* target. MIRVed missiles (Trident) greatly increase target coverage since they allow each warhead to be given its own target.[8]

Trident submarines carry 16 missiles, the same as Polaris. With the reduction to 3 warheads per missile Trident has the option of 48 separate targets in comparison to the 16 available to Polaris. The total explosive power may be less but many more cities can be destroyed. Trident can obliterate 48 cities once; Polaris could destroy 16 cities several times over. The threat posed by Trident, even with a reduced number of missiles and less explosive power, is obviously greater than that of Polaris. Trident missiles are also much more accurate than Polaris and can travel a far greater distance. Their range is 12,000 miles compared with 4,600 for Polaris.

The Review said that the running costs of Trident are £280 million a year plus about £130 million in warhead and fissile material costs. This estimated £410 million, while large enough (£10.250 billion over 25 years), did not tally with the £940 million given by defence minister John Gilbert for costs during just the one year 1996/97 (See Chapter 4). As an insurance policy, the nuclear premium is extremely expensive and not one thought to be necessary by most of our allies.

The MoD and the Navy have always argued that four Trident vessels are essential if Britain's security is to be guaranteed. They originally planned that the ageing and increasingly defective Polaris would cover the period before all four Tridents were in service. The Navy then revealed that Polaris was no longer capable of doing the job and the last of these was sent to the breaker's yard in August 1996. For the two years 1996-98 only two Trident submarines were available. Did this create a window of opportunity for the unknown enemy to strike? In 1996 Field Marshal Sir Peter Inge, then Chief of Defence Staff (later employed by British Aerospace, Vickers and Racal) said that he was "perfectly satisfied" that the deterrent could be maintained during that period.[9] If only two submarines were adequate for two years, how did he and his predecessors manage to persuade the politicians that four Tridents should be built?

One of the Trident submarines is deployed for 24 hours a day, every day of the year, with the threat of the first-use of their missiles in any conflict. The Review said that: "this is to avoid misunderstanding or escalation if a Trident were to sail during a period of crisis." Whether or not the usual suspects among the potential enemies—Colonel Quadafi, Saddam Hussein, the Iranian Ayatollahs—or the rest of the world would "misunderstand" the sailing is perhaps open to question. Would it be more alarming than the knowledge that vast amounts of submerged killing power may be aimed permanently at unknown targets?

The British American Security Council said: "as Nato conventional forces in Europe are vastly superior to any conceivable threat, including a reconstituted Russian army, there is no need for Nato to continue to threaten to use nuclear weapons first in conflict."[10] Admiral Stansfield Turner, former director of the US Central Intelligence Agency, has proposed that pending multinational agreements, the nuclear states should keep their weapons to satisfy the deterrent argument. However, these should not be deployed and must be subject to inspection by international observers. This proposal has considerable merit, not least because Russian nuclear submarines—which cannot be controlled by their land bases—are roaming under the seas. They are manned by often unpaid, under-officered sailors in badly serviced vessels. The thought that nuclear war could be triggered—accidentally or otherwise—by a group of demoralised men in a rustbucket of a submarine does not inspire confidence in the security of the nuclear balance of power. It would be far safer to have all the vessels back at their bases.

Britain's security would not be damaged by taking the lead in such an initiative. It would also save a lot of money that could be better spent within the national economies of the nuclear states. The West, through the International Monetary Fund, has pumped in billions of dollars to prop up the fragmented Russian free market system. At the same time, both military groupings circle each other with hugely expensive and threat-laden nuclear weapons.

It took 15 years from the decision to acquire Trident to the time when the first submarine was launched. The life of the four Trident boats will be about 25-30 years. Research and planning for their replacements would have to start in about 2008. The government could state that it will cease to be a nuclear power *no later* than at the end of Trident's operational life. In the meantime, it would take steps to initiate multilateral negotiations that would reduce our nuclear capacity earlier, in parallel with reductions by other countries. Opponents of this policy would have to argue an extremely difficult political case by specifying what new post-Trident weapons should be developed and at what cost. France decided to revise its defence policy and an Anglo-French proposal to start disarmament talks would carry weight.

Britain produced the atom bomb, not to deter the Soviet Union, but to show the Americans that we refused to play a minor role on the world stage. That policy failed and we became economically, diplomatically and militarily dependent on the US. Britain contributed only about 1 per cent of the total of the West's nuclear capability during the Cold War. Since then, former Soviet strategists have revealed that they were not particularly concerned about our independent deterrent. It made no difference to what they said or did. They were preoccupied with the policies of the US.

If Britain's nuclear force was not considered important by the Soviets at the height of world tension, it cannot still be necessary to maintain that expensive pretence. Given the changed world circumstances, most defence analysts now agree that if we did not already possess nuclear weapons, there would be no military necessity to obtain them. In the new situation, and within a much stronger Europe, we could have taken the opportunity to put Britain in a more realistic power context and to re-start the momentum of nuclear disarmament. The Strategic Defence Review ignored that possibility.

"Projecting power"

In his introduction to the Review, George Robertson, the Defence Secretary, said: "we plan to buy two new larger aircraft carriers to project power more flexibly around the world." The carriers will have "a wide utility, including deterrence and coercion." It was a reminder of times past when Prime Ministers spoke grandly of bringing peace, justice and the Union Jack to parts of the world that did not enjoy our way of life. Then as now, the rhetoric was not matched by the wherewithal to back it up.

If the carriers are built they will be around 40,000 tonnes each, at a total cost of about £8 billion. They will replace three smaller carriers. The Harrier jets will make way for a "future carrier borne aircraft." The military will press for the purchase of a sea version of the American Joint Strike Fighter (JSF), the costly and futuristic aircraft that is not yet in production. British Aerospace has a 10 per cent share of the Lockheed project. As the lobbying intensifies, lots of British jobs will be promised if the aircraft is bought. Back in America the US manufacturers will assure the politicians and unions that no jobs will be exported. Experts will appear in the media explaining exciting virtual reality scenarios and mock battles.

If the government continues to echo the views of Washington, the new carriers will only be deployed in operations controlled by the US. Britain will play Robin to America's Batman. The effort and expense can be guaranteed to be huge; the results uncertain. Chancellors of the Exchequer will complain bitterly about the rising cost of providing expensive floating platforms for overseas excursions. According to the Review, the ships are scheduled to be launched in the year 2012. By then they may have no obvious purpose. The political situation in the Gulf and elsewhere could have changed totally. Even if it remains much the same, they will be grandiose status symbols representing a uniquely British perception of the world. Other Europeans will watch and shrug their shoulders in disbelief.

The strand of thinking that believes that Britain has a 'special' role to play in world affairs has continued from the end of the last world war to the present day. It is as if other European countries are not dependent on oil supplies, are not concerned about Iraq or biological weapons and have little interest in what goes on outside their own borders. The mentality of the past still determines the way our military planners make policy for the future.

The defence analyst Malcolm Chalmers wrote: "In contrast to the US, the UK is no longer a global power. In the two decades after Indian independence, Britain's attempt to maintain a world-wide role cost the economy dear, contributing to its failure to be 'in at the creation' of the EEC and leading to excessive levels of military spending. To allow residual links with far-flung corners of the world, bolstered by Euroscepticism, to distort Britain's current defence effort would be to risk repeating the strategic error of those years."[11] That was written just before the Strategic Defence Review. His warning was ignored.

The traditional power delusion that proposes sending aircraft carriers to "far-flung corners of the world" even motivates our (English) football hooligans. They also project power on the unsuspecting citizens of foreign places where England play. When asked why they behave as they do, they often reply: "because we're English." They also demand "respect." Lurching around Marseilles during the 1998 World Cup they told the locals: "if it wasn't for the English you'd be Krauts." This subtle analysis of the outcome of the Second World War was lost on many of the inhabitants whose origins were far from the mainland of France.

Their is no comparison between British troops and football hooligans—not even in the bars of tourist resorts in Cyprus—but the Strategic Defence Review did reflect a less crude view of the "because we're English (or British)" argument. It was a Eurosceptic document, more for what it left out than what it said. Only one sentence was devoted to the Western European Union, the defence arm of the European Union. None of the supporting essays dealt in any depth with common weapons procurement or joint action with other European countries. Emphasis was placed on links with the US through Nato.

The British government is suspicious of European defence integration, preferring to rely on the warmed-up (Clinton/Blair) 'special relationship' with the US. It understands clearly that Nato is the projection of power by the Pentagon in Europe and is happy for it to remain that way. The Review was worried that any reduction in the contribution to Britain's "leading role" in Nato would send a "dangerous message" to the US. If past British messages to the US had been stronger, Nato's structure might well have been changed to allow a more equitable distribution of power and decision-making. The US could have become a partner rather than the leader of military planning in Europe. That is certainly the view of the French.

Making and paying for the weapons

The Strategic Defence Review team acknowledged politely the rip-offs and overcharging involved in buying the nation's weapons. Previous governments had also realised this but failed to improve matters. McKinsey, the US consultants, were hired to advise the new policy-makers. The outcome was that the government said that it intended to initiate a policy of "smart procurement." That would involve: "fuller early planning of projects; partnering arrangements with industry, particularly where competition is no longer viable; exploitation of new procurement techniques; improved estimating and predicting; improved incentives for contractors, including the use of fixed prices for contracts of up to five years duration." These were good intentions but past experience gave rise to scepticism.

In 1997 the National Audit Office demonstrated a typical case of price inflation.[12] The Sea Harrier needed improvements to its radar. Modifying the aircraft would affect its airworthiness. The responsibility for this lay with British Aerospace, the manufacturer. The company was given the contract—without competition—and produced a study on the timetable and costs. The MoD tried to agree a fixed price contract with BAe. The company refused, saying that this involved "too much risk." It said it had originally thought that the existing electronic mission processor could be upgraded but now they knew that a complete replacement would be necessary. That kind of explanation is often used by a certain type of self-employed roofer or plumber. The Ministry of Defence, no doubt realising it was over a high-tech barrel, agreed that the job should go ahead. The outcome was that the work programme was delayed by 18 months and cost £21 million more than the original estimate.

Unless the government is willing to insist on fixed price contracts, possibly through the intervention of an independent cost assessor who could adjudicate in matters of dispute, better procedures will count for little.

Britain's military-industrial complex is not a single-minded conspiracy dedicated to squeezing the public purse to pay for new and bigger weapons. It is a mixture of competing companies, ministries, poor communications, misunderstanding and, above all, waste. Cock-up rather than conspiracy is the norm. Two main departments—the Ministry of Defence and the Department of Trade and

Industry (DTI)—are involved. The MoD has traditionally reigned supreme, aloof and virtually unaccountable. The DTI, which is supposed to assist British industry, has been underfunded and given an unclear role. The difference in the influence of the two ministries is reflected in their staffing. The DTI employs 9,200 people; the MoD has 104,000 UK civilians on its payroll.

The manufacturers lobby, complain about the inefficiency of the ministries, then lobby some more and fall out with each other. This overall lack of co-ordination has been recognised for a number of years and some small steps have been taken to remedy it. The MoD, which used to believe that its only role was to sustain the 'defence of the realm,' now accepts that its decisions do have an impact on industry and that this should be taken into account when orders are placed.

The DTI was emasculated by successive Conservative governments and it badly needs a new lease of life. While vast sums of money were spent annually by the MoD, affecting large sectors of industry, traditionally the DTI was content to be a quiet voice on the sidelines. It had one civil servant in charge of the overall relationship with the MoD and was only consulted on projects worth more than £75 million.[13] The MoD decided whether or not it would take notice of the DTI's comments. Lucas Industries put it bluntly in their evidence to the House of Commons joint meeting of the Defence and Trade and Industry Committees: "The way in which industrial policy considerations are currently applied to the (defence) procurement process is largely opaque to industry" and that "the wider economic issues... appear to surface publicly only when forced into the open by controversy."[14] The Defence Manufacturers Association went so far as to call the relationship between the industry and the ministry "adversarial."

The joint committee recommended that the Ministry of Defence: "endorse the view that national security depends on a strong economy as well as strong armed forces and that it has an important role in contributing to that economic strength." That was a statement of the blindingly obvious but those in charge of procurement at the MoD would have seen it as yet another attempt to curb their unilateral right to buy what they believed to be appropriate.

No British government is going to intervene directly in industry in the way in which previous administrations—Conservative and Labour—have done in the past. There is no reason, however, that it should not take practical measures, like other European governments, to support key areas of technology and skills. Many of these are in the defence industry. British defence manufacturers have long complained that they have received less help from their government, particularly in research and development, compared with their competitors in Europe. They have far less grounds for complaint than their civil counterparts who have been even more starved of government funding.

The large companies could focus on the need to change course by setting up their own innovation centres that would bridge the existing gap between their civil and defence efforts. These could incorporate best practice from both areas without any of the secrecy and 'chinese walls' that currently exist. Local universities and other higher education bodies could contribute knowledge and resources. Universities have become increasingly militarised. Government-funded military research in universities and further educational establishments rose during the four years 1993-96 from £28 million to £40 million.[15] The national emphasis on defence R&D could be shifted towards Britain's commercial sectors by a commitment from government to play an active role in diversification.

Defence employees will have to be retrained if their careers are to be protected. Some companies already have good training programmes in place for those working on *existing* military products. Few have any plans, or inclination, to broaden their horizons and create new manufacturing opportunities in the civil field. This restricts their own possibilities for growth and leaves their staff under the threat of redundancy as contracts come to an end. Having had the high defence spending cushion removed, the companies find themselves without the right management, staff, products, marketing expertise and knowledge to face the commercial world.

Switching over

The decline and drift of the defence industry without compensatory growth in the civil sector is the worst of all possible worlds. The defence companies represent one of the last bastions of successful high technology research within the whole of the country's manufacturing industry. The survival, enhancement and diversification of the industry's expertise and technologies are of crucial importance to the future of Britain as a manufacturing nation.

Many people, including economists, engineers, trade unionists and politicians, have discussed the possible structure and activities of a Defence Diversification Agency (DDA) over a number of years. The discussions were pragmatic with as much time devoted to considering the obstacles—and there are many—as the potential. There was agreement that the DDA should be a free-standing agency headed by a small executive board made up of senior people from finance, technology, marketing, the defence industry (including employee representatives) and government departments. The DDA would have close contacts with local authorities, training agencies, City institutions and the European Union. Regional offices would be established in areas with high levels of defence production.

It would research and implement agreed technical, marketing and training plans, concentrating on those areas of advanced technology with growth potential, particularly in world markets. Experts, seconded from the Defence Evaluation and Research Agency, industry and the universities, would provide knowledge and advice on new projects. The DDA's prime purpose would be to reduce Britain's defence dependency by transferring advanced military technology into the civil sector.[16]

The creation of a Defence Diversification Agency has long been Labour Party policy. In March 1998 the Defence Secretary, George Robertson, published a Green Paper submitting draft proposals for consultation. It read like a document that had been drawn up to honour perfunctorily an election pledge rather than one that opened up possibilities for real change.

It proposed that the DDA should be established within DERA. There would be a supervisory board responsible to the Secretary of State for Defence. DERA would be encouraged to provide access to its laboratories for civil companies. The development of science parks around DERA laboratories would encourage 'spin-in' from civil to defence applications.

These aims were extremely limited and had the disadvantage of being placed in the almost entirely defence-orientated world of DERA. That organisation already has the Pathfinder programme which is focused on the same principles. The exchange of information and technology between DERA and civil companies would be useful but without a broader view of potential markets, training plans and financial assistance, the DDA would find its horizons far too narrow to operate effectively. The Green Paper was also silent on the matter of funding and staffing the DDA. DERA people have many admirable technical qualifications but knowledge of the highly competitive world of, say, consumer electronics is not one of their strengths.

Understandably, the trade unions took the pragmatic view that the Green Paper was a small step forward and indicated that they wished to play a full role in the DDA's activities. Their participation and that of some enlightened civil industrial interests could, in practice, broaden and deepen its scope to create some innovative products. Given considerable effort and ingenuity it may not suffer the same fate as Michael Heseltine's Defence Technology Enterprises of 1985.

What next?

The subject of defence is not a matter of much public debate in Britain unless war seems likely. Opinion then polarises into the camps of hawks (usually the loudest) and the more cautious doves. The latter often includes many ex-military men who can foresee the practical difficulties that lie behind the gung-ho headlines. The effect of defence costs on the public purse is of real concern to people, whether or not they are fully aware of where and how the money is spent. Education, health, social services and other areas of manufacturing have all suffered as a result of successive British governments' over-indulgence in military hardware.

Most of those active in politics—whether on the left or right—have realised the impossibility of reconciling the past demands of the Ministry of Defence with improved public services. An opinion survey of Labour MPs taken just after the 1997 election showed that by a six-to-one majority they wanted defence spending to be reduced.[17]

In the United States, the President submits annual defence budget proposals for public consideration. During the following months these are examined by Congress with senior administration officials—military and civilian—being called to testify on the detailed plans. The administration is obliged to disclose information to Congress, some of it in classified form. British governments have no such obligation nor did the Strategic Defence Review make any relevant proposals.

The men (and women) in the Ministry of Defence are extremely astute in defending themselves. They are not the warmongers of far-left slogans but they have a massive and costly edifice to protect. Their careers are at stake. The fact that they always make a point of publicly deferring to their 'masters' in government is largely cosmetic. They have seen them come and go. There have been 26 Secretaries of State for Defence since 1945. The average time in post is two years, hardly long enough to get to understand the problems, let alone to take measures to resolve them. Certainly not long enough to impose real changes on reluctant officials and officers within the MoD. Few ambitious politicians volunteer for an MoD posting. A weak minister, or one who is easily impressed by high-ranking people in uniform, is soon spotted and embraced. Visits to troops overseas with opportunities to put on combat gear and give tough-sounding press conferences are part of the process.

Even given the weaknesses and omissions of the Review, the government could take some simple steps to confirm its commitment to open government in an area of high public expenditure:

- The joint House of Commons Defence and Trade and Industry Committees should scrutinise, monitor and make recommendations to Parliament on all major MoD orders, before contracts are signed.
- Expert witnesses could be called by the joint committee.
- A new Parliamentary sub-committee should vet arms export orders. This could be drawn from the Select Committees on Defence; Trade and Industry; Foreign Affairs, the three ministries directly involved.
- Freedom of Information legislation should include the implementation of Ministry of Defence policies.
- Government defence statistics should list all orders above a certain value, contractors, dates and amounts of deliveries, payments and the amount of risk borne by the taxpayer through the Export Credits Guarantee Department (ECGD).

- The ECGD should disclose details in its annual report of the sales that it has underwritten—country by country—of both civil and military exports.
- Companies should publish in their annual report and accounts the defence contracts, their value and the manufacturing sites involved.
- The activities of the Defence Export Services Organisation (DESO) should be investigated to see if they are compatible with an ethical foreign and defence policy.
- Senior staff (above a specified grade) of the Ministry of Defence should not be allowed to enter employment with defence suppliers within three years of leaving the ministry.

Merging the ministries

There is also an important organisational step that could be undertaken. The previous Conservative government integrated the Department of Employment into the Department for Education. In the early 1980s the two Departments, Industry and Trade, were merged to form the Department of Trade and Industry (DTI). They were logical moves as they acknowledged the fact that the activities of the ministries were inextricably linked. The same principle applies to the Ministry of Defence and the Foreign and Commonwealth Office. They should be brought together. In his book *Whitehall*, a standard work on the structure and operations of British government, Professor Peter Hennessey listed the duties of the two departments:

- **Foreign and Commonwealth Office.** Responsible for communications and negotiations with overseas states and international organisations; policy-making in relation to these; the promotion of British interests abroad and the protection of her citizens; the administration of Britain's remaining colonies and dependencies; the supervision of the Secret Intelligence Service.
- **Ministry of Defence.** Responsible for the formulation and implementation of UK defence policy, the command and administration of the Armed Forces and the procurement of their equipment.[18]

It is clear that the FCO has the primary role in establishing and determining relations with other countries. Its policies should guide those of the MoD. The formulation and implementation of defence policy by the MoD depends (or should depend) on the outcome of policy-making conducted by the FCO. Both Secretaries of State are members of the cabinet sub-committee on Overseas Policy and Defence. That body also includes the Prime Minister and has overall control of UK defence policy.

To say that the integration of the Ministry of Defence with the Foreign and Commonwealth Office might present some problems would be a considerable understatement. Powerful vested interests could be relied on to provide well-organised opposition. However, the creation of a new 'Department for Overseas Policy and Defence,' under one Secretary of State, that could combine and rationalise the activities of both ministries, would be a positive challenge to a government pledged to transform Britain. The savings would be considerable. The sight of the Ministry of Defence climbing out of its bunker would provide a real millennium experience for the taxpayer.

Conclusion

The defence of Britain is not just a military matter. It also involves the protection of the national frontiers of education, health, industry, employment and welfare. In 1945 Clement Attlee and a Labour government were elected on a wave of popular support similar to that enjoyed by Tony Blair and his colleagues in the general election of 1997. Both campaigned on political platforms that focused on social transformation but both also felt it necessary to divert scarce resources to defence. The main difference was that while the Attlee administration had the legacy of Empire and the beginnings of the Cold War to deal with, Tony Blair's Labour government has a relatively free hand.

The years between the two governments were characterised by the over-ambitious, bipartisan foreign and defence policies of Labour and Conservative administrations. The UK civil economy suffered as a result. While those governments were keen to project Britain as a leading military power, they also accepted that the cost was high. Unfortunately, little was done to come to terms with the problem.

The Strategic Defence Review was largely a wasted opportunity. It could have led to a genuine change of policy that would have set Britain in a European context and away from its mixture of faded world power ambitions and deference to the United States. While it acknowledged the new types of threat to international security, it did little to take them into account in its conclusions and proposals. The traditional military logic that drove it was accepted by the government under pressure from the Ministry of Defence. Often military logic is to logic what military music is to music.

The provisions of the Strategic Defence Review may well be changed. The Treasury always wants cuts; the military inevitably asks for more money for unforeseen developments. The real challenge for the Labour government will be to implement democratic procedures to ensure that all defence proposals are properly analysed outside of the Ministry of Defence. Decision-making processes that are now kept behind its closed doors must be brought out into a wider arena.

The Labour government was elected to introduce a wide range of reforms that would improve Britain's poor performance. Its chances of success will be put at risk if costly illusions are allowed to prejudice thinking for the future. Defence expenditure and military planning are essential but they must be based on an accurate appraisal of this country's real position in the world, not on the practices and structures of the past. Making the right choices should not be too tough for a government committed to modernising a small but potentially prosperous European island.

References

1 The points were made and expanded upon by Dr. Paul Rogers of the Bradford School of Peace Studies at a seminar on 22 October 1997 organised by the Oxford Research Group

2 *UK Defence Statistics 1997.* HMSO.

3 *Financial Times* 9 July 1998.

4 *Sunday Times* 31 May 1998.

5 *SIPRI Yearbook 1994.* Chapter on Nuclear Non-Proliferation Regime. Oxford University Press.

6 *The Guardian* 7 April 1998.

7 Second Report. House of Commons Defence Committee 1993-94. Quoted in *About Turn, Forward March with Europe 1996.* Chapter by Michael Clarke. Rivers Oram 1996.

8 *The UK Trident Programme.* The British American Security Information Council 1993.

9 *The Times* 2 May 1996.

10 *Nuclear Futures: Western European Options for Nuclear Risk Reduction,* BASIC.

11 *Defence for the 21st Century: towards a post-Cold War force structure.* The Fabian Society 1997.

12 *Major Projects Report 1997.* National Audit Office.

13 *Aspects of Defence Procurement and Industrial Policy.* House of Commons Select Committee 23 November 1995.

14 *Ibid.*

15 *UK Defence Statistics 1997.* HMSO.

16 For more details see *Defence Employment Briefing* March 1992. MSF, IPMS, TGWU.

17 *The Observer* 11 May 1997.

18 *Whitehall.* Peter Hennessey. Fontana Press 1990.

Index

A

B

D

N

O

P

Y

Z